Hate Crime:
International Perspectives
on Causes and Control

Edited by Mark S. Hamm
Indiana State University

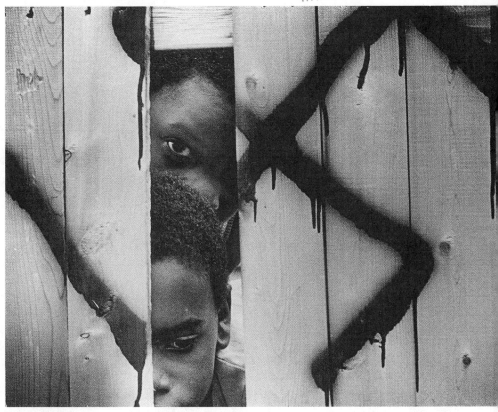

ACJS Series Editor, Ralph A. Weisheit

Academy of Criminal Justice Sciences
Northern Kentucky University
402 Nunn Hall
Highland Heights, KY 41076

Anderson Publishing Co.
Criminal Justice Division
P.O. Box 1576
Cincinnati, OH 45201-1576

Hate Crime:
International Perspectives on Causes and Control

ISBN 0-87084-350-8

Library of Congress Catalog Number 93-79364

Gail Eccleston *Project Editor*   *Managing Editor* Kelly Humble

Cover photo credit:
Gary Porter, The Milwaukee Journal/Milwaukee Sentinel

To Elie Wiesel and William Chambliss
who continue to teach us that a head without a heart
is not humanity

Foreword

WHAT IS A HATE CRIME?

There is no definition of hate crimes about which any consensus exists. Nevertheless, all definitions would seem to have at their core the symbolic status of the hate crime victim. An illegal act is perpetrated because of what a victim represents. A partial list of symbolic statuses includes racial or ethnic groups (e.g., African-Americans), nationalities (e.g., Israeli), political organizations (e.g., the Communist Party of America), religions (e.g., Hindu), sexual orientation (e.g., Gay), and even all women. As soon as one appreciates the enormous variety of individual and social characteristics that may serve as symbolic statuses, several implications follow immediately.

To begin, there is enormous heterogeneity in hate crimes. Gang violence in urban America is one example. Gang rape in Bosnia is another example. Religious riots in India, still another. And gay bashing in Germany is still another. Consistent with such heterogeneity, hate crimes are essentially part of the human condition. They have been a fact of life throughout recorded history around the world. In just the past year, there have been fatal hate crimes not just in Western Europe and North America, but in (at least) India, South Africa, Cambodia, Armenia, Guatemala, and Iraq.

It should not be surprising then, that the motives in part responsible for hate crimes are not found uniquely among hate crime perpetrators. People routinely make invidious distinctions between groups based on individual and social characteristics. For whatever reason, the need to distinguish between "us" and "them" is standard equipment for the human psyche. It should also come as no surprise that the definition of a hate "crime," is very much a function of local norms and local politics. One country's act of ethnic cleansing is another country's effort to secure defensible borders.

In short, calling attention to the key role of a victim's symbolic status is but a first step in conceptualizing and understanding hate crimes. Other characteristics of hate crimes need to be articulated that help make useful distinctions between hate crime types. Without such distinctions, the phenomenon in question is far too heterogeneous; I fear it will be impossible to develop conceptions and collect data that will be widely applicable.

I suggest that hate crimes may be usefully distinguished along at least three dimensions. First, it would seem important to determine the role of local authorities in hate crimes. In particular, it may be terribly important to distinguish between hate crimes that are expressly criminalized by local governments and hate crimes that are expressly an instrument of governmental policy. In the first case, perpetrators are acting outside the law and in the second, they are acting on behalf of the law. It follows, for instance, that comparisons between the skinheads of modern Germany with the SS of the Third Reich are probably misleading.

Second, another important distinction may be between the perpetrators and victims who are members of self-conscious and disciplined groups, and the perpetrators and victims who are not. In other words, instructive differences exist between collective behavior and organizational behavior. For example, when both perpetrators and victims are members of self-conscious and disciplined groups, there is perhaps a greater possibility of a negotiated and stable resolution. One of the great difficulties in reducing gang violence in the United States is that gangs often cannot enforce a truce among their own members.

Third, it may be important to distinguish between the role of three different audiences: the individual perpetrator himself/herself, members of the perpetrator's reference groups, and the group represented by the victim's symbolic status. For example, gay bashing may be little more than an expressive act requiring no other audience whatsoever. Or, the act may be an effort to gain approval (or avoid sanctions) from peers. Or the act may be an attempt to frighten and demoralize Gays as a group. And of course, all three may be present at various levels of importance. But, the overall message is that motives for hate crimes will vary with the intended audience.

My goal in suggesting these three dimensions on which hate crime may be distinguished is to emphasize that conceptions of hate crimes need to be subdivided. I suspect that little scientific progress will be made until important distinctions between different kinds of hate crimes are routinely and systematically made.

INFERRING MOTIVE

Whatever the distinctions that are made between different types of hate crimes, the defining characteristic of a hate crime is the motive. But, motives are often very difficult to infer from the known facts about a crime. In the United States, at least, most interracial crimes are not hate crimes. The fact that the perpetrator and the victim may be of different races has nothing directly to do with the motive. In an interracial society, some crimes will involve people of different races by the luck of the draw alone. For example, a small group of male teenagers may be in a rowdy frame of mind and ready to confront any convenient target. That target may be a homeless person, a teenager from another neighborhood, rivals from the same high school, an attractive woman, or a local shopkeeper. Which target is selected may be determined by nothing more than which target they come upon first. The symbolic status of the victim is irrelevant; one target is as good as any other target.

In addition, insofar as race is associated with wealth, economic motives may be incorrectly interpreted as racial. The fact that people of one race may steal from people of another race may simply be a function of differences in wealth that happen to be associated with race. Indeed, the race of the victim may be unknown to the perpetrator even after the crime is committed (e.g., in a burglary).

Finally, one must distinguish between hate crimes and actuarial crimes (Berk, Boyd & Hamner, 1992). For actuarial crimes, a person's individual and social attributes do not directly motivate the crime. Rather, they serve as markers revealing some *other* attribute making that person a desirable crime target. For example, an effeminate man may be robbed not because he is thought to be gay, but because he is thought to be unable to defend himself.

In short, it is sometimes difficult to determine whether a hate crime has really been committed. At the very least, this makes any interpretations for official hate crime statistics very difficult.

But, even if hate crime motives can be established, they may not be the only motives. All of the usual crime motives may also play a role: economic gain, revenge, hostility, and so on. And, it is sometimes important to consider these other motives before an incident is labeled a hate crime.

Perhaps the most important complication is whether the hate motivation is an initial cause or a proximate cause. For example, a drug deal gone sour may take on hate crime motives if the buyer and seller are from different ethnic groups. What began as an aborted economic transaction may acquire racial animus. Or, an assault on a gay male may begin as a hate crime and evolve into a robbery. The motivation for the *robbery* is economic and has nothing to do with the symbolic status of the victim. In both illustrations, the conceptual issue is whether a hate crime has been committed; it matters *when* in the sequences of events that hate motivation enters.

Another complication is premeditation. It is probably useful to distinguish between a well-planned assassination attempt, for example, and a serious, but spontaneous, assault. In the first case, the victim is selected weeks in advance and a plan of action is carefully developed. In the second case, violence may have been triggered in a matter of moments from the immediate features of the situation.

To summarize, if the definition of a hate crime depends on the motives of the offender, those motives need to be empirically established. Even seemingly simple clues can be misleading. Consider, for example (based on a real incident) a case in which an elderly Jewish man found swastikas spray painted on his garage door. While this might seem like an obvious hate crime, in fact, the spray painting was done by a Jewish neighbor. The two men had a long-standing dispute about their property line and the spray painting, done in secret by the neighbor, was an act of vandalism. Swastikas were chosen because they were especially offensive, but it was not the victim's Jewishness that motivated the acts.

HATE CRIME STATISTICS

Given the complexity of hate crimes, statistics on incidence, prevalence, and changes over time must be treated skeptically. The problem is not just underreporting, in which case inferences from time trends about increases and decreases would be sound. More serious is variation in reporting over time and from place to place. Apparent trends may easily result from changes in public awareness that, in turn, affect what is reported to the authorities. Differences across political jurisdictions may be substantially determined by local reporting practices. There is also variation over time and from place to place in the ways hate crime statistics are assembled and disseminated.

For example, police departments in the United States differ in how patrol officers record hate crimes. It is increasingly common to have a box in an offense report that is to be checked if a hate crime is suspected. But, there is almost always some uncertainty about whether a hate crime has actually been committed. A key policy issue, therefore, is how to place the burden of proof. Should a hint that a hate crime has occurred be sufficient or should the police officer be nearly certain? Differences over time or across jurisdictions in how the burden of proof is placed can have a dramatic impact on reports of hate crimes. But this is just the first step. Police departments vary from one another and over time in the kind of follow-up investigations that are undertaken. Some departments have detectives whose only investigative job is hate crimes. Others have detectives who investigate hate crimes along with other felonies. And this kind of organizational variability can make a considerable difference in the number of confirmed hate crimes. In short, hate crime statistics have at least as many problems as other crime statistics.

A critical implication is that in order to study variation in hate crime figures, either over time or over jurisdictions, one must first understand the social processes that generate the statistics (Duncan, 1984). One must understand what leads people to report hate crimes, what factors determine whether their reports are recorded, how those records are stored and manipulated, and how the final figures are disseminated. In the absence of that knowledge, summary data on trends and patterns are almost impossible to interpret.

In practice, the study of hate crime statistics requires following a set of hate crime reports from the time they are officially recognized to the time they are released in aggregate form. A "life history" of the hate crime reports in a particular jurisdiction must be written. One might learn, for example, that when hate crimes are committed along with other felonies, the hate crime designation gets lost. One implication is that the official statistics overrepresent "pure" hate crimes. While such research is not glamorous, it is absolutely essential, for at least macro studies of hate crime.

ASKING THE COMPLEMENTARY QUESTION

Finally, I wonder if too much attention is being directed at the wrong question. Virtually all of the writings I have seen on the prevalance of hate crimes ask why hate crimes occur. But a complementary question is, Why don't they occur more often? The roots of hate crimes lie within all people (Herek, 1992; Hamner, 1992). There may be no more common social construction than between groups to which we belong and groups to which we do not belong. And it is in the comparison between the two that our self-esteem in part is maintained. In other words, invidious distinctions are a regular part of social living. We compare families, neighborhoods, schools, professions, nationalities, races, religions, political parties, and age groups. We compare homosexuals to heterosexuals. We compare men to women. The list of individual characteristics and social entities is almost endless. In short, the necessary conditions for committing a hate crime are within all of us.

It follows that a critical question is why invidious distinctions are not more routinely translated into hate crimes. Why is the rivalry between some high schools expressed through competitive sports while the rivalry between other high schools is expressed as gang violence? Why does some racism stop at offensive jokes while other racism produces police brutality? Why in some cities does xenophobia generate residential segregation while in other cities xenophobia leads to arson? In each of these instances, a key question is why the application of invidious distinctions commonly stops short of violence.

Similar issues arise at the level of the individual. At least as interesting as why some skinheads attack Asians is why other young men in similar circumstances do not. At least as interesting as why some members of a college fraternity commit a gang rape is why other members do not. And at least as interesting as why some inner city teenagers participate in driveby shootings is why others do not.

CONCLUSIONS

I do not dispute that hate crimes commonly occur or that of late, ghastly hate crimes have been routinely captured by the evening news. But I am very uneasy with statements about the nature of hate crimes or why they occur. I am also skeptical when spatial patterns or time trends in hate crimes are reported. The basic science is just not there. We need lots of data-rich empirical research, conducted by scientists who can approach the data with open minds. I hope that this volume will be seen as a useful step along that path.

Richard A. Berk
University of California, Los Angeles

REFERENCES

Berk, R.A., E.A. Boyd & K.M. Hamner (1992). "Thinking More Clearly About Hate-Motivated Crimes." In G.M. Herek & K.T. Berrill (eds.) *Hate Crimes: Confronting Violence Against Lesbians and Gay Men.* Newbury Park, CA: Sage Publications.

Duncan, O.D. (1984). *Notes on Social Measurement: Historical and Critical.* New York, NY: Russell Sage Foundation.

Hamner, K.M. (1992). "Gay Bashing: A Social Identity Analysis of Violence Against Lesbians and Gay Men." In G.M. Herek & K.T. Berrill (eds.) *Hate Crimes: Confronting Violence Against Lesbians and Gay Men.* Newbury Park, CA: Sage Publications.

Herek, G.M. (1992) "Psychological Heterosexism and Anti-Gay Violence: The Social Psychology of Bigotry and Bashing." In G.M. Herek & K.T. Berrill (eds.) *Hate Crimes: Confronting Violence Against Lesbians and Gay Men.* Newbury Park, CA: Sage Publications.

Preface

There is nothing new about the subject of this book. Wild hatred has driven people throughout history to extremes of violence against others because of their race, ethnicity, religion, or lifestyle. From the European Vikings of the Middle Ages, to the Ku Klux Klan of the American Civil War era, to Hitler's dreadful stormtroopers of the German twentieth century, social and political fanatics have been responsible for atrocities that defy the imagination. Unfortunately, they continue to this day in the ravages of "ethnic cleansing" in Bosnia-Herzegovina; and in skinhead attacks against foreigners in unified Germany.

This book does contribute something very new, however, toward our understanding of this ancient crime. Rather than relying strictly on the historical record, official documents, or journalistic accounts—as most reports on the subject do—*Hate Crime* is a modern compendium of international studies grounded in the principles of social science research, social and political theory, and public policy analysis. In the pages to follow, the authors document such diverse findings as the rate and severity of intimidation and violence against immigrants in the ghettos of East London; in the refugee hostels of Germany, Denmark, and the Netherlands; against Jews in the suburbs of Dallas, Texas; and against African Americans on the streets of Milwaukee, Detroit, San Francisco, and New York City. The authors also describe and analyze state responses to hate crimes rendered by public officials from Amsterdam to Paris; from Bonn to Ottawa; and from Stockholm to London and Washington. Hence, not only do the authors unpack the phenomenological foreground and structural background of committing hate crime—or acts of "paki-bashing," "nigger bashing," and "beserking"—but they also provide a code for translating these findings into criminal justice reforms.

At its simplest level, then, this anthology attempts to solemnly describe the criminology of hate crime and present effective ways to control it. Along the way, the authors raise two compelling and important questions.

The first question relates to the incidence and prevalence of hate crime in the various nation-states analyzed at the time of this research (1989-1992); or, more importantly, since the collapse of the Soviet Empire and the destruction of the Berlin Wall: *How widespread is the problem of hate crime in the world today?* The answer is, of course, dependent on the quality of hate crime statistics, which are dependent upon the quality of data gathered in the various countries examined.

Today, nowhere is the answer to this question more urgent than in Germany; and nowhere, because of Germany's past, is the question more appropriately contemplated. But for the most part, we have already been given the answer by powerful ruling elites who control the international media.

On November 23, 1992, banner headlines across the front page of *USA Today* proclaimed,"Violent Hatred: Refugees, Jews Targets of Neo-Nazis." Along with a large and colorful photograph of angry skinheads *Sieg Heiling* in Berlin Square, the accompanying story documented 1,800 officially recorded acts of right-wing violence during 1992. "The right-wing trail of death," warned an official from the German Ministry of Justice, "has just begun." Indeed, it had. A month later, *The New York Times, The Times* of London and *der Spiegel* all reported that at year's end the tally of right-wing violence included 17 homicides and 2,220 attacks against foreigners. The international media then simply exploded with information about German skinheads and other young extremists; ranging from stories about their violence and their social backgrounds, to stories about their beer drinking, political beliefs, and romances. Even *The Economist,* London's staid and highly respected publication in international affairs, carried a dramatic front-page picture of a skinhead with an SS insignia shaved on the back of his head.

Then, just as quickly, the international media lost interest in Germany's neo-Nazi movement. Following an aggressive law-enforcement campaign against the far-right in December of 1992, hate crime began to wane. By the Spring of 1993, media sources still interested in the problem, such as *The Nation,* reported that "Strong, if extremely belated, judicial and police measures against [right-wing] violence have reduced the number of attacks against foreigners since the beginning of the year. There has been a decline of nearly 50 percent from the comparable period last year" (April 5, 1993:441).

This book offers a more sobering picture of the German problem. The media's portrait is derived from official statistics published by the German Ministry of Justice. Media officials base their stories on the uncritical assumption that these statistics are an accurate reflection of the incidence and prevalence of right-wing violence in Germany today. They are not.

The frequency of attacks against foreigners on German soil is counted at the local level by police officials who file reports to federal authorities in Bonn. About half of these police officials (those from the former East) have only recently implemented crime reporting procedures. Furthermore, these attacks are reported in various ways across the 16 German states. Therefore, official statistics are based solely on cases of right-wing violence brought to the attention of local police officers, many of whom are inexperienced in criminal justice record-keeping procedures and many of whom have disparate opinions about what constitutes an act of right-wing violence. Obviously, these official statistics tell us nothing about the frequency of unreported cases.

In Chapter 1, Benjamin Bowling presents results from a well-controlled victimization study conducted among immigrants in the East End of London. He shows that hate crime victims vastly underreport their victimizations. Consistent with previous British studies, Bowling found that fewer than five percent of the attacks against immigrants were reported to police. In other words, roughly 95 out of every 100 attacks went unreported.

In Chapter 2, Alexis Aronowitz reviews the German social scientific literature on right-wing violence. Among other provocative discoveries, she concludes that there has never been a social scientific victimization study conducted on German immigrants in the post-communist era. (Professor Aronowitz's finding speaks volumes about the German research community's resolve to understand hate crime.) Bowling's study does, however, provide a baseline for making an informed estimate of the problem.

To repeat, in 1992 the German Ministry of Justice reported 2,220 acts of right-wing violence against foreigners. This official figure was reduced by "nearly 50 percent" in the first three months of 1993. If current rates of violence remain constant, then, the German Ministry of Justice can predict a 1993 year-end total of approximately 1,110 attacks. Assuming that German immigrant cultures share with British immigrants: (a) the same inability to identify their attackers, and (b) the same tendency to avoid contact with police on matters related to racial harassment and assault, then this figure (1,110 attacks) represents roughly five percent of the total problem, presuming that the immigrant-inhabited urban areas of Germany have social and ethnic mixes similar to those found in London's East End. Under these explicit conditions, we may predict that the number of attacks on foreigners in Germany during 1993 will exceed 22,000.

But this is a conservative estimate. A study released by the German Department of Labor in 1991 indicated that one in every five foreigners in the federal states was the victim of a violent attack during 1990 (there have been no Department of Labor studies on the subject since). Applying this official figure to the 9 million foreigners now living in Germany, and then reducing it by 50 percent, we may estimate that the total number of victimizations in 1993 may approach nearly 900,000.

This means that each day *at least* 60 immigrants—or some three immigrants every hour—are harassed, beaten, or firebombed by groupings of young white males who often revere the memory of Adolf Hitler and Nazism. Seen in this context, then, Germany's problem is exceedingly more widespread than reported by the international media. But more important, it compels us to see that the demons of Germany's past have not yet lost their grip on the world.

Such an alarming finding is unlikely to find its way onto the Op-Ed pages of the world's newspapers, let alone mainstream television and radio shows—especially after Germany's widely heralded 1992 law-enforcement campaign against the far-right. In advanced totalitarian societies, the state routinely uses its power to keep the public in line. In modern democracies, gentler means are used. The public must be persuaded to leave power in the hands of the ruling elite—large multinational corporations who now control the world's economy; and, hence, its politics and culture. By necessity, mass media projects a world view congenial to these big corporations; a view that inevitably determines what we may think about world affairs. So, instead of groveling before the totalitarian's jackboot, citizens in a free democracy lounge in front of TV sets or read newspapers. In any event, the posture is passive, compliant, and ever-beholding to the powers that be.

By contrast, social science research and theory prods us into a standing position. And as we leave the narrow strictures of what the international media tells us about hate crime, we are introduced to a more elegant empiricism that takes us into speculative territory. And it is here that the authors of this anthology raise their second crucial question: *How serious, in fact, is the threat of hate crime to the safety and security of the world today?*

The answer to this question rests on the quality of definitions used to describe the individual and social nature of the criminal events described in this book. According to chapters by Aronowitz, Rob Witte, Tore Björgo, Jeffrey Ian Ross, and myself, definitions matter because they make the criminal phenomenon comprehensible to social control agents and thereby implicate the appropriate state mechanisms to deal with the problem. More than simply reflecting the nature of crimes of hatred, then, appropriate definitions also attract attention to its potential control.

*   *   *

It is with these issues in mind that I proudly present *Hate Crime: International Perspectives on Causes and Control.* This is not a book about the past. It is, rather, an exposé on the historical present that is being played out at this very moment in neighborhoods around the world. At one end of the block stands the velvet glove of law enforcement, at the other, the iron fist of hatred, and in the middle, a frightened immigrant. The case of hate crime clearly demonstrates that we cannot understand the nature of criminality without understanding both its immediate construction out of social interaction, and its larger construction through processes of political and economic authority. Developed from the canons of social scientific inquiry, this book provides a scholastic street map for understanding the politics of hate crime and possibilities for teaching, research, public policy, and community activism.

Mark S. Hamm
Indiana State University

Acknowledgments

The authors have many to thank for their assistance, encouragement, and inspiration. Benjamin Bowling extends his gratitude to Alec Ross for help in transcribing responses to the survey's open-ended questions, Harris Research for conducting the survey, and the respondents who gave their time to be interviewed. He is also grateful to all those connected with the North Plaistow Racial Harassment Project, in the British Home Office and elsewhere who commented on earlier drafts of the chapter, and in particular, to Bill Saulsbury, Jim Sheptycki, and Martin FitzGerald.

Alexis Aronowitz offers a special thanks to the Anne Frank Foundation in Amsterdam for their assistance in providing and tracking down materials for her chapter. Jeffrey Ian Ross extends special thanks to Paul Bond and Michael Dyck for research assistance, Edwin Webking for making files available, and Natasha J. Cabrera for comments. Mark Hamm owes a debt of gratitude to Milton Firestone for maintaining computer files, and Valerie Jenness for critical comments.

Finally, this anthology would not possible without the tenacity, patience, and hard work of Ralph Weisheit, Series Editor of the Academy of Criminal Justice Sciences/Anderson Monograph Series on Crime and Criminal Justice.

Contents

[It is] one of the most striking paradoxes of modern European history—namely, the coincidence of a general softening of social life with an eruption of ever more lethal forms of mass violence.

—James Miller
The Passion of Michel Foucault

Actual American life as experienced by most people is so boring, uniform and devoid of significant soul, so isolated from resonances of European culture, that it demands to be "raised" and misrepresented as something wonderful.

—Paul Fussell
Bad or, The Dumbing of America

You tell me what it means. You tell me what it means.

—Willie Nelson and Bob Dylan
Across the Borderline

1

Racial Harassment in East London

Benjamin Bowling
Home Office Research and Planning Unit—London, England

INTRODUCTION

This chapter arises out of an action research project to develop new strategies to combat racial attacks and harassment[1] in one locality in East London (see Saulsbury & Bowling, 1991; Bowling & Saulsbury, 1992). The first stage of the project entailed collection of information on the nature and extent of the problem from a range of sources, one of which was a victimization survey.[2] Since the project ended in July 1991, there has been time for reflection on the survey results, their value and limitations.

One key limitation of the survey is attempting to understand a complex social problem like racial violence using a methodology that reifies experience into static, decontextualized incidents (Genn, 1988; Farrell, 1982; Bowling, 1993). This stems from the dominant approach to the study of crime and victimization which tends to conceptualize crime as a collection of criminal incidents or events of norm violation (Skogan, 1986; MacLean, 1986; Genn, 1988). This approach, in turn, reflects the orientation of modern criminal justice systems which are built to process discrete criminal incidents. An alternative would be to conceptualize victimization and offending not as events, but as *processes* (MacLean, 1986; Genn, 1988). This would draw attention to the fact that victimization does not occur in an instant, but is more complex, dynamic, and dislocating for the victim than the notion of an incident can capture (Pearson et al., 1987; Stanko, 1987; Bowling, 1993; Sheptycki, 1992). Much can be learned from studying criminal incidents (we often have no choice), but more important are the social processes that are their author (Goldstein, 1990).

Thinking processually draws attention to the dynamic of social relationships among victim, perpetrator, communities, the police, and the criminal justice system; the continuity between physical violence, threat, intimidation, and perceptions of safety and danger (Kelly, 1987; Stanko, 1990); the relevance of repeated or systematic victimization (Farrell, 1992; Sampson & Phillips, 1992); the broader context of the crime and the social relationships that inform definitions of appropriate and inappropriate behavior (Bowling, 1993).

This chapter explores some of the issues that emerge when trying to reconcile a processual conceptualization of racial violence with victim survey data. First, it briefly reviews earlier surveys of racial violence in Britain. Second, the chapter provides some context for the survey in the form of geographic, demographic, and social characteristics of the locality. Third, it presents the findings from the survey. Finally, the chapter reflects on the value and shortcomings of the survey and suggests future research directions.

RESEARCH ON RACIAL ATTACKS AND HARASSMENT

The Extent and Nature of the Problem

A number of crime surveys have attempted to estimate the extent of racial violence in Britain. A Home Office study estimated that approximately 7,000 racial attacks would be reported to the police annually (Home Office, 1981:14). A Policy Studies Institute study, Black and White Britain, estimated that the frequency of racial attacks might be closer to 70,000 (Brown, 1984:256). The first Islington Crime Survey estimated that 17 percent of assaults aimed at the residents of the London Borough of Islington were racist in nature. The authors estimated that approximately 870 cases occurred in Islington in the previous year, of which 4.5 percent were recorded by the police (Jones, MacLean & Young, 1986). The Newham Crime Survey found that one in four of Newham's ethnic minority residents was a victim of some form of racial harassment annually, two-thirds of whom had been victimized more than once. The 116 victims of racial harassment interviewed in the Newham survey gave details of a total of 1,550 incidents that they had experienced in the previous year, of which just over five percent were said to have been reported to the police (London Borough of Newham, 1986:34-50).

Surveys suggest that ethnic minorities[3] are overwhelmingly the victims of racial violence. The 1981 Home Office report found that white people were 50 times less likely than Asians[4] and 36 times less likely than Afro-Caribbeans to be victims of a racial attack (Home Office, 1981). A replication of this study conducted in 1987 found the differential victimization rate to be even more pronounced, with that for Asians being 141 times that for whites, and for black people 43 times that for whites (Seagrave, 1989:20). This pattern is now accepted wisdom on the subject (see FitzGerald & Ellis, 1990; Gordon, 1990; Hesse et al., 1992). The 1988 British Crime Survey found that ethnic minorities were more at risk than whites for many types of crime[5] and that many offenses against them were seen as racially motivated. Forty-four percent of assaults directed against Asians and one-third of those directed against Afro-Caribbeans were thought by respondents to be racially motivated, as were about one-half of the incidents involving threats (Mayhew, Elliott & Dowds, 1989:50).

Surveys have also been used to investigate the nature of the problem, though qualitative research has often produced richer data. A qualitative component of the 1981 Home Office study suggested that racial violence against ethnic minorities consisted of "assaults, jostling in the street, abusive remarks, broken windows, slogans daubed on walls...sometimes on repeated occasions." That instances of this nature were "interleaved with far more serious racially motivated offences (murders, serious assaults, systematic attacks by gangs on people's homes at night)," the report noted, increased the feeling of fear experienced by ethnic minorities. Recent research confirms that racial violence often takes the form of repeated attacks and harassment and that this can have a very serious effect on its victims. A report by Sampson and Phillips (1992), for example, found that 23 families of Bengali and Somali origin on one estate in East London suffered 136 incidents in a six-month period. The situation in some areas of Britain echoes the 1981 Home Office report which concluded that:

> It was clear to us that the Asian community widely believes that it is the object of a campaign of unremitting racial harassment which it fears will grow worse in the future. In many places we were told that Asian families were too frightened to leave their homes at night or to visit the main shopping centre in town at weekends when gangs of young skinheads regularly congregate (Home Office, 1981:16).

The problem has been generating increasing concern within central and local government agencies and the police in Britain since the early 1980s. In 1986, a government Home Affairs Committee report described racial attacks and harassment as "the most shameful and dispiriting aspect of race relations in the United Kingdom" (House of Commons, 1986). This view was endorsed by the then Home Secretary Kenneth Baker in 1991 who described the problem as "unquestionably the most obnoxious and destructive aspect of the racial discrimination that still festers in our country" (Home Office, 1991:1). But despite this level of governmental concern and changes in ethos, policy, and practice in a range of statutory agencies, there is little evidence that policies directed at tackling perpetrators, assisting victims, or preventing racial violence have been effective. In 1989, the central government interdepartmental racial attacks group found "few examples of effective multi-agency liaison ... [and]... relatively few examples of effective unilateral action by individual agencies" (Home Office, 1989: par. 34). There is little evidence that racial violence has decreased in incidence, prevalence, or in its effect on minority communities in Britain; if anything the reverse may be said to be the case (FitzGerald, 1989; Ginsburg, 1989; Dunhill, 1989; Cutler & Murji 1990; Gordon 1990; Hesse et al., 1992). The development of a coordinated or "multi-agency" approach may hold the key to the problem, but it is evident that some serious obstacles have to be overcome if it is to fulfill its promise of an effective strategy (Home Office, 1989; 1991; Saulsbury & Bowling, 1991; Bowling & Saulsbury, 1992; 1993; Neyroud, 1992; Hesse et al., 1992)

THE NORTH PLAISTOW AREA

Before describing patterns of racial harassment in North Plaistow, something should be said about the geographic, social, economic, historical, and demographical characteristics of East London in general and the study site in specific.

Geography

The London Borough of Newham, one of 33 boroughs in Greater London, lies to the east of the City of London beyond the "old" or "inner-East End" neighbourhoods of Tower Hamlets. North Plaistow is one of the London Borough of Newham's 12 housing districts that is coterminous with the electoral wards of West Ham and Plashet (See Figure 1.1). The boundaries of North Plaistow do not reflect those of a "natural community" or "natural area" in that it has no individual identity, no commercial or neighborhood center of its own, and has a heterogeneous population. Rather, three of its boundaries are marked by physical barriers. A London Underground line (which actually runs *over-ground* at this point) marks its southern edge and forms a boundary that divides Newham north-south; a British Rail line bounds the area to the West; West Ham Park cuts the area off to the North; and it narrows to a wedge to the East. Despite its physical distance from the heart of the East End, North Plaistow forms part of the "outer" or "extended" East End (Hobbs, 1988; Husbands, 1983). Dick Hobbs (1988) argues that to define the physical boundaries of the East End or East London more generally without attempting to define its culture is "a mere exercise in cartography":

> Not a street, borough or town, East London is a disparate community bonded by a culture rather than by any single institution or governmental agency. This one-class society locates its own boundaries in terms of subjective class definition, and east of the City of London you are either an East-Ender, a middle-class interloper, or you can afford to move sufficiently far east to join the middle classes of suburban Essex[6] (Hobbs, 1988:87).

This may be an oversimplified characterization of a large geographical area with a population of diverse class and ethnic backgrounds. But Hobbs' view reflects a specific understanding of East End culture as exclusively working-class and white

Figure 1.1
Geographical Map of North Plaistow

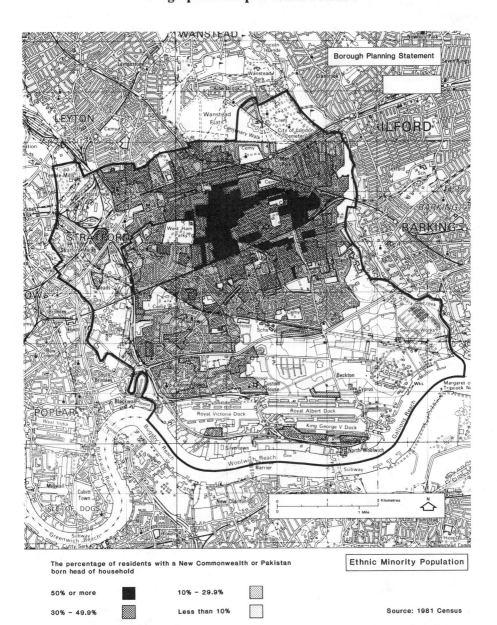

The percentage of residents with a New Commonwealth or Pakistan
born head of household

50% or more	10% – 29.9%	
30% – 49.9%	Less than 10%	

Source: 1981 Census

At the 1981 Census 26.6% of the Borough's population lived in households where the head of household was born
in the New Commonwealth or Pakistan

and which identifies other class and ethnic groups as infiltrators or interlopers—by definition not "one of us" (1988:86-90).

Social and Economic Characteristics

Although North Plaistow is part of an outer London borough, it displays many of the characteristics of an "inner city" area. It has a high degree of relative and primary deprivation in terms of its local economy, housing, physical environment, and social facilities. A Government survey based on 1981 census data identified the London Borough of Newham as the second most deprived local authority district out of 365 in England, after Hackney and only just ahead of Tower Hamlets, two of its neighboring boroughs (Department of the Environment, 1983). Of Newham's 24 wards, the two that make up the study site—Plashet and West Ham—are the third and twelfth most deprived, respectively. Large sections of the project area were identified as "extremely deprived" according to government criteria; that is among the worst off (2.5%) in England. The project area has a high level of unemployment; 14 percent and 13 percent of economically active residents of Plashet and West Ham, respectively, were unemployed at the time of the 1981 census.

Housing

The random sample of the survey indicated that 45 percent of the area's residents rented from the council, 40 percent were owner occupiers, 3 percent rented from Housing Associations and 12 percent rented privately or lived in some other type of housing.[7] Thirteen of Newham's 114 tower blocks (8 stories or more) stand in the project area. The narrower, eastern end of the project area is comprised mainly of terraced houses most of which are owner occupied, though some are privately rented. This eastern portion of the study site borders one of the centers of one of Newham's several Asian communities. Green Street and Plashet Road are both busy shopping streets with many Asian-run food stores, supermarkets, candy stores and restaurants as well as "traditional" East-End shops. Moving westward through the area there are more streets of terraced houses punctuated by several high- and low-rise housing estates.[8] Most of these estates were built between 1963 and 1967. On the southern edge and towards the middle of North Plaistow is the Chadd Green estate which is dominated by five 15-story tower blocks.[9] Towards the south western corner of the study site stand a pair of 22-story tower blocks built in 1966.

Population

Newham has one of the most ethnically diverse populations in the country. Recently published data from the 1991 Census indicate that 42.3 percent of Newham's population is comprised of ethnic minorities, compared with 20.2 percent for Greater London and 5.9 percent for the whole of England and Wales. It is important to be aware of the extent to which ethnic minorities are concentrated in specific regions and cities around the country, in particular localities within those regions, and in "pockets" within those localities (Smith, 1989). Within the London Borough of Newham the ethnic minority communities are concentrated in pockets towards the north of the borough. Asian communities are concentrated mainly in East Ham, Upton Park and Plashet, while Afro-Caribbeans live mainly in Forest gate or in small pockets of Upton Park and Plashet (Newham Monitoring Project, 1991:1; London Borough of Newham, 1986). South of the borough there are far fewer ethnic minority residents as a result of a combination of factors including former council housing allocations practices and a both perceived and actual local tradition of racial exclusionism, violence, and support for racist politics (Husbands, 1983:18-20, Newham Monitoring Project, 1991).

The eastern end of Plashet ward forms part of Newham's Asian community while the south western edge of West Ham ward borders Plaistow and is *en route* to Canning Town. The total population of the study site is 19,492 (1981 census estimate) and has an ethnically mixed population. Of the random sample of 751 residents of the study area generated by the survey, 65 percent were white, 11 percent Afro-Caribbean, 10 percent Indian, four percent African, three percent Pakistani, and one percent each Bangladeshi, Chinese, Filipino, "other Asian," and "other." These figures compare with 1981 Census data that suggest that 36 percent of West Ham and 18 percent of Plashet residents lived in households where the household head was born in the countries of the New Commonwealth and Pakistan.

Racism and Racial Violence in East London[10]

In East London, racial antipathy and exclusionism, and territorial defensiveness among the white community appear to be deep seated and reflected in support for racist politics and racially motivated violence (Husbands, 1982; 1983; Hobbs, 1988). Hobbs describes racism as "part of East London's ideological inheritance... manifested in various ways including a long history of racist attacks on a variety of ethnic groups" (1988:11). Husbands (1982) charts geographical continuities in racial vigilantism and extreme right-wing politics in the East End from 1900 to 1980. The British Brothers' League emerged in the inner-East End at the turn of the twentieth century and, in the pre-war years agitated against "aliens"—Jewish immigrants fleeing Eastern Europe (Husbands, 1982:7-10). The anti-black and anti-Chinese rioting of 1919 in London focused on seafarers and others in Limehouse, West India Dock Road, Poplar and Cable Street, all in the East End (Fryer, 1984:310).[11] In the inter-war years the inner-East End saw the rise of political parties such as the British Union of Fascists (BUF) and anti-Semitic agitation (Husbands, 1982:14-15). The post-war Union Movement, built on the remains of the BUF, was also involved in anti-Semitic and anti-black agitation and there is evidence of "racial vigilantism" from the beginning of the 1950s (Husbands, 1982:15). Anti-black rioting in 1958 affected parts of East London such as Hackney and Stepney, although this was not as widely reported as that occurring elsewhere in the country, such as Nottingham and London's Notting Hill (Fryer, 1984:380).

East London is cited as the geographical origin of the skinheads in 1969[12] (Mungham & Pearson, 1976:7). This development in the politics and style of British youth culture coincides with the coining of the term "Paki-bashing" to refer to systematic attacks on ethnic minority individuals and communities in various localities in the East End and elsewhere (Mungham & Pearson, 1976; Husbands, 1982:18). In a three-month period in 1970, 150 people from ethnic minorities were seriously assaulted and one was stabbed to death in East London (Gordon 1986:2).

Politically organized racism also found a home in both the inner and extended East End during the 1970s with the emergence of the National Front (NF). In the mid-1970s, the NF set up an "advice center" in Canning Town, in the south of Newham. In 1974, during the period in which the NF were campaigning for forced repatriation of people from the New Commonwealth[13] and Pakistan, they polled 29 percent of the vote in Hudsons ward and 25 percent in Canning Town, both in the south of the borough (Husbands, 1983:9-10, Newham Monitoring Project, 1992:28). In the 1977 Greater London Council election the East End provided nearly one-third of the NF's total vote with the party gaining more than 20 percent of the vote in some constituencies (Miles & Phizacklea, 1984; Husbands, 1983). During the late 1970s and early 1980s, East London continued to be the focus for both politically organised racism and racial violence (Husbands, 1982:15-19; Layton-Henry, 1984:108-121; Miles & Phizacklea, 1984:118-135; Hiro, 1991). Clashes between the National Front and anti-racist demonstrators occurred regularly from 1978 until the collapse of the NF in the 1979 general election and local government elections in 1981 (Miles & Phizacklea, 1984:104).

In the late 1970s, there appeared to be an increase in "street-level" activity by organized and semi-organized racists (Husbands, 1982:18; Layton-Henry, 1984). Of these, the most blatant was a "rampage" down Brick Lane in the inner-East End by 150 skinheads during which windows were smashed and people assaulted (Bethnal Green and Stepney Trades Council, 1978; Commission for Racial Equality, 1979). From 1978 until the end of the decade racial violence appeared to escalate in East London. Nine apparently racially motivated murders occurred in East London between 1978-1981 (Bethnal Green and Stepney Trades Council, 1978:57; Gordon, 1984:8; Newham Monitoring Project, 1991:38; Hesse et al., 1992). These included the murder of a 10-year-old boy in 1978 and of an Asian women and her three children in Walthamstow in 1981 after gasoline was sprayed through their letter box and ignited (Hesse et al., 1992).

In 1985, a year that Hesse et al. describe as the year of "the burning of the houses," there were numerous arson attacks on the homes of Asian families in East London (Hesse et al., 1992:22-38). The most tragic incident was the gasoline-fire attack that resulted in the death of an Asian woman and her three sons at their home in Ilford just to the east of Newham. This was the third arson attack on the family's home in three years and came only three weeks after a very similar arson attempt.[14] 1985 also saw an increase in violence directed against the Jewish community.[15] Clearly, there are parallels with the recent events in Germany, though these should not be over-drawn. Nonetheless, the extent of concern about racial violence directed specifically against the Asian community is evident from newspaper reports over the period.[16]

During the remainder of the 1980s and into the 1990s racial violence has continued to be directed against ethnic minorities in East London and elsewhere (Hesse et al., 1992:38-45; Home Office, 1989, 1991; Gordon, 1990). Whether the problem has abated is debatable. However, there appear to have been no fatalities in East London until December 1991 when a Tamil refugee was allegedly "beaten to death" by a "racist gang" in Manor Park, Newham.[17]

This history of sporadic attacks against ethnic minority individuals and persistent campaigns of harassment against families forms the backdrop for the survey data presented below (see also London Borough of Newham, 1987, 1988; Tompson, 1988). This context applies to East London in general, rather than North Plaistow specifically, though this locality has been the scene of some serious and well-known outbreaks of violence and campaigns of harassment (Tompson, 1988; Newham Monitoring Project, 1991). If a micro-sociogeographical approach were adopted, however, North Plaistow might not be considered the most problematic area in East London in general or in Newham in specific. Other areas, such as neighborhoods in the inner-East End and in the south of Newham were considered areas where racist sentiment was deepest and violence was more common (e.g., Husbands, 1982, 1983). Nonetheless, in 1987, when the North Plaistow Racial Harassment Project was initiated, police statistics indicated that Newham had the highest rate of reported racial incidents in Greater London, just ahead of neighboring Tower Hamlets.[18] At the time, North Plaistow Housing District had the highest number of recorded cases in Newham.[19]

RACIAL HARASSMENT IN NORTH PLAISTOW

Problems in North Plaistow

At the start of the survey, respondents were asked a few questions concerning how they felt about the area in which they lived and about the problems they faced living there. Despite the poor economic and social conditions in North Plaistow, many more respondents thought it a good area (60%) rather than a bad one (28%). Most people thought the big problems in the area were rubbish and litter (51%), crime (44%) and unemployment (32%). Table 1.1 illustrates the proportion of respondents who considered racial attacks on Afro-Caribbeans and Asians to be a problem.

As expected, a large proportion of Afro-Caribbean and Asian respondents considered this a problem; more surprising was the sizeable proportion of white respondents who thought it so. Sixty-four percent of Asian women, 62 percent of Asian men, 50 percent of African and Afro-Caribbean women, 45 percent of African and Afro-Caribbean men, 24 percent of white women and 35 percent of white men said that racial attacks on Afro-Caribbeans and Asians was either a big problem, or was a bit of a problem in the area.

Table 1.1
Respondents Believing Racial Attacks on Afro-Caribbean and Asian People to be a Problem in the Area (%, N=1,174)

	White male	White female	Afro-Caribbean male	Afro-Caribbean female	Asian male	Asian female
Big problem	11%	9%	13%	19%	22%	32%
Bit of a problem	24	20	32	31	40	32
Not really a problem	42	49	43	30	35	28
Don't know, not stated	23	22	13	19	3	8
Total %	100	100	100	100	100	100
N of cases	211	271	63	67	294	233

Source: North Plaistow Racial Harassment Project.

As can be seen from Table 1.2, when asked whether they themselves had experienced racial harassment within the previous 18 months, the majority of survey respondents said they had not.[20] However, about one in five ethnic minority respondents did mention at least one instance. Unexpectedly, considering the local history of violence directed specifically against ethnic minorities, a small proportion of white people also said that they had experienced a racial incident. A more detailed description of the experiences of different ethnic and gender groups will be presented later in this section.

Table 1.2
Types of Racial Incidents Mentioned (%, N=1,174)

	All	White male	White female	Afro-Caribbean male	Afro-Caribbean female	Asian male	Asian female
insulting behavior/verbal abuse	7%	3%	4%	13%	18%	13%	12%
threatened damage or violence	2	2	1	3	4	4	3
attempted physical assault	2	3	1	3	3	3	3
actual physical assault	3	3	1	5	4	5	2
attempted damage to property	1	1	*	2	3	3	3
actual damage to property	3	2	1	5	6	4	4
attempted theft	1	–	1	2	3	3	2
actual theft	3	3	3	2	4	3	3
arson or fire attack	*	–	–	2	1	*	–
attempted arson or fire attack	*	–	–	2	1	1	–
any of the above	11	7	8	17	21	19	18
none/don't know/not stated	89	93	92	83	79	81	82
Total %	100	100	100	100	100	100	100

Source: North Plaistow Racial Harassment Project.

In all, 163 of the 1,174 survey respondents mentioned an incident of racial harassment in the 18 months between January 1988 and June 1989. Broken down by ethnic and gender groups, these included 11 out of 63 Afro-Caribbean males, 14 out of 67 Afro-Caribbean females, 57 out of 294 Asian males and 43 out of 233 Asian females, 14 out of 211 white males, 21 out of 271 white females (unweighted figures).[21]

Between them, these 163 victims mentioned approximately 831 incidents.[22] This figure assumes that respondents' descriptions of the number of times they were victimized was accurate.[23] They may not be able to recall the number and nature of incidents accurately over a period of 18 months—some may be forgotten, others may have occurred longer ago and "telescoped" forward into the reporting period; others may have occurred during the reporting period, but "telescoped" backward and thus not mentioned by the respondent. Because there is no clear common definition of racial harassment and attack, some respondents may have defined incidents as *racial* when the motivation was arguable, or when they could not even be certain that a person from another racial group was responsible for the incident. Others may have ignored incidents they regarded as minor or unimportant.[24] The figures are clearly subject to a wide margin of doubt, but nevertheless, given that roughly 10 percent of the adult population of the area was interviewed, as many as 7,000 instances of insulting behaviour, threat of or actual violence, theft, damage to property (or attempts to do any of these things) where the victim believed that the incident was directed at them because of their race may have occurred in the 18-month period in question.

DETAILED DESCRIPTION OF INCIDENTS

The preceding results are based on information supplied by our whole sample of 1,174 residents of North Plaistow. Of the 163 respondents who said that they had experienced one or more incidents, 114 agreed to provide us details of their experience. These 114 respondents provided details of 158 incidents.[25] These respondents comprised between two-thirds and three-quarters of all those who stated that they had been experienced a racial incident in the previous 18 months. The information in the following section is based on their testimony. The victims who told us about the incident were slightly more likely to be male than female, were much more likely to be under 45 than over, and were little different from the occupational class structure of the sample as a whole. Of the 158 incidents described in detail, the race-gender breakdown is as follows: 58 Asian males, 45 Asian females, 13 Afro-Caribbean males, 13 Afro-Caribbean females, 14 white males, 12 white females and 3 people of "other" ethnic origin.

Types, Locations, and Times of Incidents

As can be seen in Table 1.3, by far the most common form of harassment consisted of insulting behavior or verbal abuse, which the majority of victims suffered. The next most common forms of harassment were actual damage to property, actual physical assault, and actual theft.

The most frequently mentioned location for the incident was the victim's home (23%) which would include attempted break-ins, damage to property, incidents on the doorstep and offensive material through the letter box. Nearly 6 out of 10 incidents occurred in the immediate vicinity of the victim's home, including incidents that occurred directly at or on their home, those that occurred in the street outside the victims home (16%), outside or inside the building in which their home was located (12% and 4%, respectively) and near their garage (4%).

Table 1.3
Types and Numbers of Incidents Suffered by Respondents
Over an 18-Month Period (weighted figures)

Form of Harassment	Incidents	%
Insulting behavior/verbal abuse	303	41.8
Actual and attempted damage to property	114	15.7
Threatened damage or violence	98	13.5
Attempted assault	81	11.2
Actual assault	72	9.9
Actual and attempted theft	53	7.3
Actual and attempted arson	3	0.4
unweighted n = 163	724	99.8*
*Column does not equal 100 because of rounding		

Source: North Plaistow Racial Harassment Project.

Incidents ocurred at all times of the day and night. Thirteen percent occurred in the morning, 29 percent during the daytime, 30 percent between 6 p.m. and midnight, 11 percent between midnight and 6 a.m., and 4 percent sometime during the hours of darkness.

There were a very large number of "less serious" incidents and many "very serious" ones. Some appeared to be unique events while others were said to be part of a pattern of repeated attacks and harassment. Some of the victims identified in the survey said that the experience had little impact on them, while for others, the experience, threat, and fear of racial harassment had a considerable effect on their lives. Because the patterns for each of these variables differ considerably when comparisons are made between ethnic and gender groups, a *general* description becomes meaningless. A fuller presentation of the results will be provided for each group below.

Perpetrators[26]

The survey indicated that the people involved in carrying out the harassment or attack were predominantly male, white, between the ages of 16 to 25, and were most often in a group. Only 15 percent of those victims interviewed in the survey said that the perpetrator was of school age, 57 percent said they were between 16 and 25 years old while 27 percent said their assailants were older. Two-thirds of the Asian victims said that their assailants were white, one-fifth that they were Afro-Caribbean and one-tenth, a "mixed" group. All the incidents mentioned by Afro-Caribbean respondents involved white perpetrators. Of the incidents mentioned by white respondents half involved Afro-Caribbeans, 12 percent involved other white people (41% of those mentioned by white women), 11 percent were a mixed group and seven percent involved Asians. The perpetrators tended not to be known to the victim and in the cases when they were known, they were not well known.

PATTERNS OF VICTIMIZATION FOR EACH ETHNIC AND GENDER GROUP

It is evident from the survey that a wide range of different experiences has been defined by respondents as racial incidents. The data suggest that there are very different experiences among the various ethnic and gender groups. Thus, it becomes impossible to speak of the typical case of racial harassment, attack, or insult. The experiences are varied to the extent that it is necessary to hesitate before considering every instance reported in the survey to be in the same class of events, behaviors, or experiences. In addition to between-group differences, there are differences *within* groups. The incidents mentioned in the survey by one ethnic-gender group appear to cover a wide range of activities, some of which appears to depend upon other characteristics of the victim and perpetrator, and the context of the incident. What follows is an analysis of the quantitative data from the survey broken down by ethnic and gender group, incorporating *selected* quotes from the survey's open-ended questions to illustrate of the types of incidents mentioned.[27]

Asian People

Eighteen percent of the Asian women interviewed in the survey said that they had suffered a racial incident in the preceding 18-month period (n=45). The attacks and harassment they mentioned mainly took place close to their homes. One in three incidents mentioned in the survey were directed against them in, or very near, their homes; another one in three occurred in the immediate vicinity of where they lived. In most cases, the aggressors were young white men and boys not known to the victims. In just over one incident in 10 did the victim know any of the people involved, and when they were known, they were not known well—most often just by sight.

The survey indicated that Asian women were the group upon whom racial harassment had the greatest impact. Although their victimization rate was not the highest of all ethnic-gender groups (rates for Asian men and Afro-Caribbean women were higher), the effect of victimization seemed particularly severe and to have serious long-term and cumulative effects. Of the women who were victimized, 60 percent became fearful as a result of their experience, and one in three said that the worst effects were still continuing. Nearly 7 in 10 Asian women (both victims and non-victims), said they worried either "a great deal" or a "fair amount" about themselves or a member of their family being victimized. Only one in 10 Asian women interviewed in North Plaistow did not worry at all about being racially attacked or harassed.

Nineteen percent of the Asian men interviewed in the survey had experienced a racial incident in the preceding 18 months. Again, the majority of the harassment mentioned by Asian men occurred near their homes, though a proportion occurred at or traveling to work. Most commonly, the perception that the incident was racially motivated was based on the perpetrator's reference to their race. This perception was also based on the feeling that they were being singled out for harassment; one in five felt that these attacks would not happen to them if they were white and another seven percent said that the incident formed part of a pattern of methodical harassment. One in 10 said they were told to "go back to your own country."

One interesting point is that, of the 103 incidents mentioned by Asian respondents, no fewer that 39 (38%) were directed at Asian council tenants. Only 14 percent of the Asians sampled were council tenants, suggesting that those living in council accommodations are almost three times as likely to tell us in detail about an incident than are Asians as a whole. The majority of council estates in North Plaistow are away from the eastern portion of the study site which has a high proportion of Asian residents (more than 50%). Council-owned housing lies mainly in the center of the area (e.g., the Chadd Green estate) and on the western edge of the area where there is a low proportion of Asian residents (less than 10%).

The types of incidents described in full in the survey range from verbal abuse and insults to serious assaults and arson, and reflect the type of harassment and attacks reported in other surveys:

Most recent incident:
I was watching TV at home, and a gang of kids came, shouted abuse, and started throwing stones, hitting and breaking windows in my house, and of my car. *What was it about the incident that makes you believe the attack was racially motivated?* They called me a black f____ Paki, and they said I shouldn't be here, to go home.

Second most recent incident:
It was some kids I chased off earlier in the day. They came and threw stones at my windows, breaking them, shouting "Go away Paki." *What was it about the incident that makes you believe the attack was racially motivated?* The fact that they hate anyone who is a "Paki" as they call us. They tell me to go away.

Third most recent incident:
We were at the back of our garden, and we heard a noise. We came out to find the windows of our car broken. *What was it about the incident that makes you believe the attack was racially motivated?* Because I'd had trouble with racial harassment before.

Most recent incident: Came in and called me Paki and started throwing bricks at me. They didn't hurt me because I had thick coat on. They called me Paki before they started throwing the bricks at me.

Second most recent incident: A gang of teenagers started shouting at me "Paki" go home and abuse. Nothing else.

Third most recent incident: It's happened so many times—they come up in groups and call me names—they call me rude names and call me Paki. I want to move away from here because I'm frightened to live here now because it happens so often.

Most recent incident: Someone put container of liquid through letter box. Failed to make a fire. Could have been serious. *What was it about the incident that makes you believe the attack was racially motivated?* Because of the sort of attack—putting fire through letter box. Neighbors had one similar incident. (Pakistani)

Africans and Afro-Caribbeans

Twenty-one percent of the African and Afro-Caribbean women interviewed in the survey had experienced a racial incident in the preceding 18-month period (n=13). Although it was higher proportionately, the harassment experienced by most African and Afro-Caribbean women was similar to that experienced by Asian women—that is, occurring close to home and carried out by groups of young white men. Most often the victim's race was mentioned or racist abuse was used by the perpetrator. Fifteen percent of the incidents were said to have been part of a process of methodical harassment.

About one in three of the incidents mentioned by African and Afro-Caribbean women were said to have occurred in their place of work. In most instances this involved white male co-workers, which might suggest some correspondence with black women's experiences of sexual harassment in the workplace. The remainder involved clients and customers at work; one woman described an instance of abuse that had occurred at the local housing office:

An elderly white person came into the office shouting "Bloody Blacks. Go home. You're not wanted here." Then he went out of the office. *What was it about the incident that makes you think that it was racially motivated?* The actual words he comes out with. He doesn't want to be seen by any black or Asian members of staff.

Seventeen percent of African and Afro-Caribbean men interviewed in the survey suffered a racial incident in an 18-month period (n=13). In common with other groups, Afro-Caribbean men were most likely to be harassed in the vicinity of their homes. However, they were the most likely of all groups to mention threatened or actual property damage, this being the case in nearly one-half the incidents mentioned. When explaining their belief that the incident was racially motivated, Afro-Caribbean men said that the perpetrators had referred to their race. Others mentioned that they were told to "go back to your own country" or that they were the only black people in their neighborhood and were being singled out for harassment. Several commented that the damage to their property was done with no apparent motive other than racism:

> [I] came home from college and found damage on my door and it has been set on fire, with graffiti on the wall calling me names... the next time I met these people... it resulted in violence." *What was it about the incident that makes you think it was racially motivated?* "Because there was no other reason I [can] think of for them to attack me and try to burn my place down.

> *Most recent incident:*
> A white guy came out of a pub and started abusing me. He called me a "wog" and a "nigger." He first called me a wog and when I challenged him he called me nigger. It nearly turned [in]to a fight but a police car drove by and we broke it up. It ended in just words between us. *What was it about the incident that makes you believe the attack was racially motivated?* Well his words. Wog and nigger. If that isn't racial, what is?

> *Second most recent incident:*
> I was walking down this road... I had a suit on as I was going for an interview when a blue van drove past and a white guy threw an egg at me. It was a fresh egg. Well the egg broke and stained my suit. I...had to go back home to change. I was late for the interview and didn't get the job. *What was it about the incident that makes you believe the attack was racially motivated?* Eggs don't just drop from the sky. I was wearing a suit and these white guys threw an egg at me to mess me up.

> Petrol was poured through the letter box and set alight. That's all.

Someone smashed my car windscreen. Nothing was taken. It happened in the evening or night. *What was it about the incident that makes you believe the attack was racially motivated?* All over the car was written "Out, out Paki."

White People

Eight percent of the white women interviewed in the survey had experienced a racial incident in the 18-month period in question (n=12). In many ways the incidents mentioned by white women were similar to the incidents mentioned by women from other ethnic groups. A large proportion occurred near their homes and involved abusive language and insulting behavior. One important difference between the incidents mentioned by white women and other groups was the likelihood that theft was involved. Those mentioned by white women were twice as likely to involve theft as those mentioned by Asian women and four times as likely as those mentioned by Afro-Caribbean women.

Seven percent of the white men interviewed in the survey had experienced a racial incident in the preceding 18 months (n=14). The incidents mentioned by white men show some divergence from the incidents mentioned by other ethnic-gender groups. Just under one-half the incidents mentioned by this group (43%) involved the theft of property. People of all ethnic-gender groups mentioned incidents of "racially motivated" theft, but the rate for white men is between two and five times that of the other groups. In the majority of incidents mentioned by white men the perpetrators were said to be Afro-Caribbean (78%), mixed but mainly Afro-Caribbean (11%), or Asian (11%). The most frequent reason for believing that the incident was racially motivated (in one-half of the incidents mentioned) was a perception that the incident arose from "racial vengeance, getting back at white people."

It appears that some quite different experiences are subsumed within white people's experiences of racial incidents, and this creates problems for analysis. There are those who have been the victims of crime committed by or thought to have been committed by Afro-Caribbeans, and to a lesser extent Asians. This experience is then interpreted to have been directed against them because they are white.

Most recent incident:
Car window was smashed. Cassette was stolen. Car smashed. *What was it about the incident that makes you believe the attack was racially motivated?* Car was parked in front of this block... people know my car. I think it was done purposely.

Second most recent incident:
Somebody try to break in. An attempt to break in through front door. When I came home the front door lock was [broken]. Nothing stolen. *What was it about the incident that makes you believe the attack was racially motivated?* That I can't say. Not sure. But I think it may be racially motivated.

About three of them. One of them pulled on my [chain]. [I didn't] have much money on me...they took my money, jewels, watch, beat me up. *What was it about the incident that makes you believe the attack was racially motivated?* The group was all blacks. Nothing else.

It is evident that some of the white respondents do believe that black people harbor hostility towards them:

I'd had words with a black man earlier for trying to steal my geraniums. At 3 o'clock in the morning I had a brick put through my window. *What was it about the incident that makes you believe the attack was racially motivated?* A lot of the young blacks in the area always hate whites. They whisper as you go by and I feel their hatred.

Others complained of unprovoked attacks:

Eight people jumped out of a car and started hitting me and my mates. One of them had a bar. They just started hitting. With a bar. On my head and that. *What was it about the incident that makes you believe the attack was racially motivated?* They had no other reason. I was just in the street and they started, with my mates, hitting you know, with a bar.

In one case the respondent appeared to have come into conflict with their black neighbors after being accused of attacking them or their property:

Most recent incident:
She just used to shout up the stairs. Things like you f____ white trash. All this type of thing, I can't remember everything she call[ed] us. *What was it about the incident that makes you believe the attack was racially motivated?* Because of the names she called us, white b_____ and white trash. She said we did things to her home because we did not like colored people.

Second most recent incident:
Downstairs this time smashed the place up, tore light fittings wrote NF on her wall...said we done it because we didn't like black [people]. *What was it about the incident that makes you believe the attack was racially motivated?* She blamed us because she said we were against her because she was black.

A significant group of white women also appeared to have been victimized because of their association with black people, the subject of the next section.

Interracial Relationships

A striking feature of the victimization described by white women was the proportion of incidents carried out by other white people. White perpetrators were involved in more than four out of 10 incidents directed against white women; in three out of 10 incidents the perpetrators were *all* white and in a another 12 percent the people involved were a mainly white group. The most plausible explanations for this are that these white women were victimized because they were members of interracial families, had interracial children or because they associated with Asian or Afro-Caribbean people. Four white respondents commented that the reason they believed that the incident was racially motivated was because the perpetrators expressed "disapproval of racial mixing." One Afro-Caribbean man also commented that he had been "given hassle" by a "white gang" because he was "with a white girl:"

as I was walking down the street a big posse of white kids said to me; eh! nigger shouldn't be walking with a white girl.

That such a large proportion of the experience of white women should be at the hands of other white people indicates the importance of recognizing the complexity of the problem of racial harassment (FitzGerald & Ellis 1990:54). Moreover, given dominant attitudes of the white community towards "racial-mixing," this finding should be hardly surprising (see Hall et al., 1978:240; Hiro, 1991:308-313; Small, 1991:517-8; Root, 1992).

EXPERIENTIAL CONTEXT

There are considerable conceptual problems involved in analyzing and interpreting race and gender differences in the experiences of "racial" victimization. Objectively, there are clear differences between groups and these have been pointed out above. There are, however, other *subjective* experiential differences that have not been captured by the survey.

It is evident from the discussion of the local context that the experience of living in Newham is different for different ethnic groups. White East Enders think of East London as their natural home, one over which they are able to exert a territorial imperative and which they act to defend (Husbands, 1982, 1983; Smith, 1989; Hesse et al., 1992). The literature reviewed above bears witness to the sense of territoriality, racial exclusivity, and hostility to "interlopers" felt among the white community in the area. This provides white East Enders with a sense of place, identity, and security that does not extend to North Plaistow's ethnic minorities. The opposite side of this coin for ethnic minority communities is the experience of being defined as "out of place" in the neighborhood in which they live and, quite possibly, in which they were born. The language described by the ethnic minority victims in the survey—being told that they are "not wanted here," to "go home" or "back to where you came from"—illustrates that point. Sadly, even at a time when the majority of the ethnic minority community in Newham will be *indigenous*, the very notion of a "real East Ender" carries racially exclusive connotations.

The literature on racial violence contains no reference to a historical pattern of attacks, abuse, or violations of white communities, or of specific localities within Newham where harassment of people *because they are white* has ever taken place. Moreover, it is necessary to take account of unequal relationships of economic, political, and social power between ethnic minorities and the white majority communities. These factors are central to understanding the different experiential context for white and ethnic minority communities. As Pearson et al. suggest:

> For white people, for example, racial harassment and racial attacks are undoubtedly merely incidental, [unique] events which are rarely, if ever, encountered. For black and minority groups, on the other hand, these are areas of experiences which are part and parcel of everyday life. A black person need never have been the actual victim of a racist attack, but will remain acutely aware that he or she belongs to a group that is threatened in this manner (Pearson et al., 1989:135)

Some account must also be taken of the relationship between popular and politically organized racism and the manifestation of racial violence in East London. In particular, it is evident that the pattern of violence directed against ethnic minorities reflects and reinforces racist ideologies, while this is not the case for the victimization of white people. As many authors have demonstrated, the presence of ethnic minorities in Britain in general and in specific localities has been constructed as a problem both politically and in the popular consciousness (Gilroy, 1987; Solomos, 1988, 1989; Smith, 1989). While racial attacks and harassment are activities participated in by a few, there are connections to be made with the attitudes and behavior of larger sections of the population. Susan Smith argues that forms of political and "common sense" racism have permeated all levels of British society (Smith, 1989:146; see also Barker, 1981; Fielding, 1981; Gilroy, 1987:11; Solomos, 1989). This, some have suggested, influences public opinion in the form of "low-level racism" (Husbands, 1983), "a sentiment that infuses daily life and is widely but abstractly expressed by a broad cross-section (perhaps a majority) of the population" (Smith, 1989:148). In a similar vein, Solomos argues that terms of debate about migration, civil unrest, crime, and the "inner city" have become subtly infused with racial stereotypes and symbols (Solomos, 1989; see also Miles & Phizacklea, 1984; Solomos & Racket, 1991; Keith, 1991). Others have argued that there is also "bottom-up" or "experiential racism"—"a reaction by white Britons to those broad patterns of local socioeconomic change that are outside their control and that coincide with (but of course have no necessary causal relationship to) the presence of black people" (Smith, 1989:149). It would be too simplistic to say that widespread racial antipathy determines the expression of racial violence, but, as Smith argues, racist sentiments "provide a reservoir of procedural norms than not only tacitly inform routine activity, but are also able to legitimatize more purposive explicitly racist practices" (Smith, 1989:150). It is evident that such a reservoir exists in East London.

These comments are not intended to dismiss as unimportant or invalid white people's experiences of crime, nor their perceptions of them as being "racially motivated." On the contrary, these findings present a challenge to orthodox definitions of racial violence. On one hand they suggest that white people may be exposed to anti-black sentiment and violence because of their association with people from ethnic minorities. On the other hand, they suggest that white people do perceive themselves as vulnerable to offenses committed against them by ethnic minorities and that a "racial" motive is frequently ascribed to them (see also McConville & Shepherd, 1992:110-111).

PATTERNS OF REPORTING

Levels of reporting racial incidents can be estimated by comparing survey estimates of the prevalence of the problem with official records. Over the same period, the police recorded 152 racial incidents.[28] The local Housing department had approximately 85 "active" cases over this period that accounted for approximately 350 incidents.[29] Indeed the types of incidents found in official records and the survey are broadly similar: 59 percent of the incidents recorded by the police consisted of insulting behavior, 20 percent involved attempted or actual damage to property, 9 percent were attempted or threatened assault and 6 percent were actual assaults[30] (n=152). It would be fair to say that, in terms of patterns of incidents and their "seriousness," official records signify a fairly representative, if small, sample of the "incidents" of harassment and attack occurring in North Plaistow. Police records and the survey do differ in terms of the characteristics of victims and offenders, however. Three-quarters of the victims recorded by the police were Asian, one-fifth Afro-Caribbean, while only three percent were white and one percent "Mediterranean." Police records, therefore, suggest that Asians are much more likely to be victimized and whites much less likely to be victimized than the survey statistics. As a consequence of there being far fewer white victims in the sample of police records, there are far fewer ethnic minority perpetrators. Police records showed that 94 percent of suspects were male and 95 percent were white, the remaining five percent being Afro-Caribbeans. This may reflect the need for evidence of racial motivation before the police will record an incident as racially motivated. Nearly three-quarters of the victims recorded by the police were female and just under one-quarter were male. This is a somewhat different picture from the survey, in which victimization rates are about the same between sexes with the exception of Afro-Caribbean women, who were more likely to be victimized than their male counterparts.

Assuming that the incidence of the problem estimated in the survey is valid and that like is being compared with like, a comparison between police records and the survey would suggest an overall reporting rate of just over two percent to the police and around five percent to the Housing Department. Although many instances of verbal abuse and insulting behavior were reported to the police and to the Housing Department, the very large number of incidents occurring alone makes this low reporting rate unsurprising. Moreover, in many cases the victims did not know who their assailant was (particularly in cases of damage to property) or did not feel that they would be able to identify them after the incident.

When survey respondents who detailed their experience in full were asked why they had not reported the incident they had experienced to the local authority or the police, two-thirds stated that reporting would be pointless and that these agencies would not do, or would not be able to do, anything. Another 10 percent said it had happened before and nothing had been done about it. The following comments were made: "they wouldn't have been interested. It wasn't important enough to report it to the police;" "they don't care about us. They say they are busy, and there's too many cases like mine for them to cope;" "police know this type of problem. They don't do anything. You cannot report each incident. The are not doing anything;" "because it happens so often there doesn't always seem to be any point to reporting it;" "it happens all the time to black people and nothing would be done;" "it's useless. They'll do nothing. It has happened before and nothing was done about it;" "well the boys drove away so what use would it have done to report to the police. They'd probably just laugh in your face."

People appear to make an assessment about the willingness or capacity of the police and other agencies to make a practical intervention in these less serious incidents and make their decision about whether to report on that basis. However, it is also important to recognize that simply because an incident was not reported to the police it does not mean it had no effect on the victim, particularly those incidents which form a pattern of harassment. On the contrary, particularly in the case of Asian women, the survey suggests that even threats can have an unsettling and lasting impact.

AGENCY RESPONSES

Having looked at the extent of racial harassment and attack, its nature and patterns of reporting, attention will now turn to the response of local statutory agencies to reported incidents. Of the incidents described in full in the surveys that were reported, 90 percent were reported to the police, 45 percent to the Housing Department and a small percentage to other statutory and voluntary agencies.

The survey found that in eight of 10 incidents reported to the police, an officer visited the scene. This figure is rather higher than in the British Crime Survey (BCS) which found that 65 percent of reported crimes nationally were attended by a police officer (Mayhew et al., 1989). Of those interviewees who knew which type of officer attended, two-thirds said it was a home-beat officer. This would indicate that the police policy of conducting follow-up visits in racial harassment cases was being put into effect.[31] In common with the BCS findings, the North Plaistow survey found that beyond this initial visit most victims did not get feedback about the progress of their case. However, in nearly one-half of the incidents mentioned by Asian people, at least a second contact was made. Nonetheless, two-thirds of the survey respondents felt they were not kept properly informed about the progress of their case.

Less than one in 10 respondents said that they were very satisfied with the way the police handled their case. This is less than one-half the proportion of crime victims saying they were very satisfied in the BCS (Mayhew et al., 1988). Most often dissatisfaction was felt because victims believed that the police did not do enough, because they failed to keep the respondents informed or because they seemed uninterested. Despite this low level of satisfaction with the police response, two-thirds of respondents felt the police were generally sympathetic towards the victims of racial harassment.

In 90 percent of cases the police did not refer the victim to any other agency. In six percent they were referred to Victim Support Newham and in three percent, to another community group.

The Housing Department

In just over one-half (55%) of the incidents mentioned in the survey that were reported to the Housing Department, a Housing officer visited the victim's home. Victims were visited at home by Housing officers in a smaller proportion of cases than did police officers probably because people tend to report their experiences directly to the Housing office (for reasons such as getting repairs done), rather than telephoning for immediate assistance. In those cases where a Housing officer did visit, they tended to make more follow-up calls with 40 percent of victims receiving a second contact and 26 percent further contacts. Even so, only 13 percent of victims were very satisfied with the way they had been informed about the progress of their case and 73 percent felt they should have been kept better informed.

The level of satisfaction with the Housing Department's response was similar to that with the police. In only eight percent of incidents were the victims very satisfied with the way in which the Housing Department had handled their case. Respondents were diassatified most often because it was felt that the Housing Department did not do enough, that they appeared uninterested, and that they failed to keep the victim informed about the progress of their case. As with the police, despite low satisfaction, two-thirds of respondents felt the Housing Department was sympathetic towards the needs of victims of racial harassment and attacks.

Other Agencies

The instances of racial harassment and attacks mentioned in the survey were reported to a range of agencies other than the police, Housing and Education Departments, though these amounted to very few cases. Eight percent were reported to Newham Council for Racial Equality, four percent to Social Services, three percent to Victim Support and six percent to other agencies (including their employers, the London Fire Brigade, and local bus depots). It seems that agencies other than the police and Housing were not considered by victims in most instances, with around one-third of respondents unable to give a reason for not reporting. When they did offer a reason for not reporting, it was most often that there was "no point," that they had never thought about it, or that it was nothing to do with the agency in question. One-quarter of those not reporting to the Council for Racial Equality and Victim Support said they had never heard of them.

The Overall Response

In general terms, less than five percent of respondents who expressed an opinion in the survey said they were very satisfied with the way racial harassment was dealt with in the project area (N=98). One-half expressed some degree of dissatisfaction, with one in five saying that they were very dissatisfied. There was the perception that racial harassment had not declined over the preceding five years despite the fact that over this period local statutory agencies took the problem increasingly seriously, committed themselves publicly to tackling it and developed polices to combat it. For those who have the most experience of racial harassment either as individuals (i.e., victims and multiple victims) or as a social group (i.e., Asian women), far more thought that it had gotten worse rather than better. Just over one-half of the Asian women who expressed an opinion said that racial harassment had stayed the same, more than one in three thought that it had gotten worse, while only one in 10 thought it had gotten better.

LIMITATIONS OF THE SURVEY AND FUTURE RESEARCH DIRECTIONS

The survey aimed to describe the nature and extent of the problem in North Plaistow; to identify where and when it occurred, and to describe the victims and offenders. It sought to uncover the degree to which attacks and harassment were reported and to examine how statutory and voluntary agencies responded. The survey demonstrated that racial violence was widespread in the project area and that it was having a severe impact on specific members of the local community. It showed that Afro-Caribbean and Asian people were most likely to be victimized, that groups of white young men were most often the aggressors, and that incidents occurred most frequently in the vicinity of the victim's home. The survey also suggested that very few people reported their victimization, and when they did, they were rarely very satisfied with the outcome.

However, as we argued in the final report on the project, many of these facts were already well known to local statutory agencies, as were the concerns expressed by many of those surveyed (Saulsbury & Bowling, 1991:20-29). The survey left no doubt that action to tackle racial violence was needed. But the answers to the descriptive questions did not really stimulate ideas about how to tackle the problem. We were missing what seemed to be vital explanatory information—*how* and *why* racial attacks and harassment were occurring in the locality, and *why* statutory agencies seemed not to be responding appropriately to reported incidents.

We still knew little about the process of victimization other than the short time-slice that comes to be defined as the criminal event. In particular, we knew little about what happened after the incident or after reporting to the police. We had no information about how criminal and civil justice action (or inaction) affected victim and offender or the wider community. And we knew next to nothing about alternative responses to victimization such as self-defense, retaliation, forgiveness, restitution, or conciliation. Still obscure was the nature of the *relationships* between victims and perpetrators or minority and majority communities and how racism and violence influenced the behavior patterns of each. While racial victimization seemed dynamic, the survey had reduced the process to a static and de-contextualized snapshot.

As I have argued in this paper and elsewhere, the problems encountered in this survey seem to reflect a more general problem with victimization surveys (Bowling, 1993). In particular, important factors appear to be precluded by the survey's inherent emphasis on the criminal event. If this is the case, then those in other localities and contexts wishing to gather information on which to base policy initiatives or practical action must think very carefully about the conceptual basis of their research and the methods used to it carry out.

This survey, like most of the others described at the start of this paper, produced only a partial and limited account of racial violence. It focused mainly on the experience of crime victims and of their experiences of reporting to the police. Information on perpetrators—which is surely essential for an understanding of racial victimization—

comes only from the victim's perspective. While the most basic of descriptions of the perpetrators have been formulated, we still have no empirically grounded explanations of their actions. A means to overcome this might be to conduct surveys of perpetrators and their associates in parallel with surveys of victims (though this could be a sensitive and difficult exercise). It might be possible to conduct surveys of offending by using the "self-report method" in localities with high rates of racial victimization. Another approach would be to extend surveys of racist attitudes (e.g., Husbands, 1983) to cover racially motivated violence and attitudes towards it.

Some of the problems mentioned above may be addressed by the next generation of crime, victimization, and offending surveys. Alternatively, as has been argued by many authors, qualitative as well as quantitative research methods may be used to develop a holistic analysis (Bell & Newby, 1977; Walklate, 1989, 1990; 1992). One approach involving a combination of qualitative and quantitative methods that has been useful in criminology is the case study. Yin (1989:23) describes a case study as "an empirical inquiry that: investigates a contemporary phenomenon within its real-life context; when the boundaries of the context are not clearly evident; and in which multiple sources of evidence are used." These features lend themselves to an empirical, holistic, and processual account of crime. Surveys alone can try to deal with phenomenon and context, but by dint of the need to limit the number of variables to be analyzed, their ability to investigate context is extremely limited (Yin, 1989:23). Context, history, and process can best be captured using evidence from sources such as historiographical material, in-depth interviews and observation, as well as official records and surveys. Case studies provide the opportunity for explaining specific types of crime because asking how and why requires that processes be traced over time as well as describing frequencies and incidence. Ethnographic or life- history accounts of people identified in a survey seem to have tremendous potential in this regard in that they offer the opportunity for the research subjects to describe their experiences in their own terms.

To understand offending, victimization, and state intervention, the actions and experiences of the social actors involved and the points at which they intersect must be charted. To achieve this, interviews with survey respondents could be expanded to follow the whole process of offending and victimization. Starting with the historical context of any given instance, data could be collected on the events involved in the commission of the offense, its immediate aftermath and long-term consequences for those involved. Qualitative accounts of the subjective reality of each actor in particular instances will help give substance to the skeletal descriptions provided by surveys.

In providing a multifaceted account of the expression and experience of violence, a case study can identify multiple sites for intervention. It offers the potential for evaluating the effectiveness of policing and the criminal justice system. By charting the moments at which criminal justice agents intervene in the process of victimization and survival, the impact of their actions can be assessed. At present, the police and criminal justice system appear only fleetingly in survey descriptions. And yet both victim and offender may have to interact with them over an extended period (totaling hours, if not days and weeks) after the event. Surveys could ask respondents what happened *after* the initial response, but would soon become cumbersome in the attempt. The case study, with its historical element, is suited to exploring some of these connections and could retain quantitative verification if it incorporates a survey.

A recent "local inquiry" into racial violence conducted by the London Borough of Waltham Forest (Hesse et al., 1992) illustrates the potential of the case study method for researching this particular problem. The report of this inquiry draws primarily on evidence presented to a panel of inquiry—testimony from victims and their advocates, vitriolic counterblasts from local racists, and records from the police and local authority housing department. This contemporary material is then set in the context of the local history and geographical spread of racial violence. Incorporating a survey into a case study might enable researchers with a quantitative bent to have their cake and eat it too. Such a study would have the validity and reliability that stems from representative sampling while incorporating an investigation of the context necessary to comprehend racial violence as a process.

CONCLUSION

It seems evident from research and other sources of information emerging in numerous localities that racial violence is a global phenomenon.[32] How it is expressed or experienced in specific localities is, of course, influenced by specific local histories of violence, ethnic or racial identities, and broader social, political, and economic contexts. The ubiquity of racial attacks and harassment is also reflected in a common perception that they are potentially or actually one of the most dangerous forms of crime. The expression of racism in violence in various forms has the effect of terrorizing ethnic minority communities and has the potential to escalate into major conflagration and disorder. Finding ways to combat not only racial violence, but also the racism in which it is rooted, must surely be one of the most pressing concerns for police, central and local government agencies, community and anti-racist activists, and private citizens concerned with the safety of ethnic minorities in particular and the maintenance of civilized society in general. Discovering and understanding the nature and extent of violent, aggressive or threatening racism, the form it takes, the effect it has on minority (and majority) communities, and finding some explanation for its manifestation in specific localities is inevitably part of this process. The North Plaistow Racial Harassment Survey aimed to contribute to such an understanding; although it can by no means claim to be a blueprint, if others can learn from both the progress and mistakes made it will have provided a modest contribution to this goal.

NOTES

1   There are a range of terms used to describe the expression of racism in violence. For the purposes of this paper "racial violence" will be used as a generic term to refer to violence motivated partly or wholly by racism. The more precise terms of "racial harassment" and "racial attack" will be used where appropriate. The definition of racial harassment used by the project and for the purposes of this paper is based on the definition adopted by the Commission for Racial Equality (CRE), which is as follows: "Racial harassment is violence which may be verbal or physical and which includes attacks on property as well as on the person, suffered by individuals or groups because of their colour, race, nationality or ethnic or national origin, when the victim believes that the perpetrator was acting on racial grounds and/or there is evidence of racism. Racist behavior (which can cause racial harassment) can be defined as any hostile or offensive act or expression by a person of one racial group against a person of another racial group or any incitement to commit such an act, where there is an indication that motivation is racial dislike or hatred." Despite the use of the term "racial" rather than "racist" violence, it should be made clear that the violence that forms the subject matter for this chapter pertains to racism, rather than "race" *per se*. Thus, the problem is not simply one of neutral conflict between races but, rather, one of *racism*—the "ideologies and social processes which discriminate against others on the basis of their putatively different racial membership" (Solomos, 1989: xiii).

2   The survey was based on a random sample of 751 residents of the study area and a "booster sample" of Asian residents giving a total sample size of 1,174. These interviewees completed a short *General Questionnaire* that, after covering several general issues relating to crime and racial harassment, ascertained whether the respondent had suffered a racial incident. This sample forms the basis for the analysis of the prevalence and incidence of the problem. Of the 163 respondents who mentioned a racial incident, 114 (70%) completed a *Victim Questionnaire*. It was intended that up to three incidents would be recorded in detail for each victim. In the event, not all subsequent incidents were recorded. The total number of incidents recorded in detail was 158. These form the basis for the analysis of patterns of incidents, the effects suffered, etc. The fieldwork was carried out by *Harris Research* using "ethnically matched" interviewers during May and June 1989.

3   In the British context the language of "race" and racism is used to identify the subordination of black people (i.e., people from the Caribbean, Africa and the Indian subcontinent) and to articulate strategies of resistance to such subordination (e.g. Smith, 1989). It has been said that the language of "ethnicity" has been useful neither theoretically nor politically. However, in a broader geographical context, the term "black" does not resonate with the identity of many victimized minorities. Additionally, in a global political context the terms of "ethnicity" have recently gained renewed impetus. Simple black/white divisions cannot explain, for example, the violence directed against "ethnic" Romanians living in Poland, or the targeting of all "foreigners" by the German neo-Nazis. It may be that the language of culture, identity, and politics needs to be rethought (eg., Hall, 1992). For the purposes of this essay, the term "ethnic minority" will be used to refer to people subject to violence or other forms of oppression because of

their skin pigmentation, language, cultural, or geographical background. The use of this terminology acknowledges that in some circumstances *nonblack* ethnic minorities may be the subject of violence expressed by majority communities. Despite the use of the terms of ethnicity, a critical perspective would retain its focus on racism as a term to investigate the structures that place people from ethnic minorities in a subordinate position; and to analyze the racial ideologies that serve to justify such subordination (see Smith, 1989).

4   In Britain the term "Asian" usually refers to people whose origins lie in countries of the Indian subcontinent, including India, Pakistan, and Bangladesh and is used as such in this paper. The term "Afro-Caribbean" is used in this paper to refer to people whose origins lie in Africa or the Caribbean.

5   After taking account of social and demographic factors.

6   This "subjective class-definition" is also a racially exclusive one. Hobbs informs us that many of the respondents in his study were racist; "all Asians were "Pakis" and Afro-Caribbeans, "coons," "niggers," "macaroons," etc. Once, someone described their prospective next-door neighbors as "Pakis with turbans." Another explained how he had "clumped a lippy Paki." Another had moved out of an area because it was "overrun with niggers" (Hobbs, 1988:12)

7   This compares with 1981 census data which found that 59 percent of West Ham residents and 41 percent of Plashet residents, respectively, rented from the council.

8   For the term "housing estate" (which sounds rather grand to North Americans) read "housing project."

9   The Chadd Green estate was built in 1967 and each block contains 56 flats. A recent proposal for environmental improvements listed the estate's problems as: "crime, fear of crime, vandalism, racial harassment, squatting, noisy parties, rent arrears, and the alienation of the tenants from their environment." This proposal also noted that 20 percent of the estate's residents were unemployed and 44 percent of all tenants were claiming housing benefit. Sixty-one percent of the tenants have current applications to transfer out of the estate.

10 The focus of this chapter is specifically on East London. However, it should not be thought that racial violence occurs only in this locality. On the contrary, there is evidence of similar violence occurring in numerous places across the country this century and in particular since the 1950s. See, for example: Pearson, 1976; Hall et al., 1978; Commission for Racial Equality, 1979, 1981, 1987a, 1987b, 1988; Institute of Race Relations, 1979, 1987; Home Office, 1981, 1989, 1991; House of Commons, 1982, 1986, 1989; Klug, 1982; Gordon, 1984; Fryer, 1984:376-383; Layton Henry, 1984; Reeves, 1989:44, 125-152; Seagrave, 1989; Gordon, 1990; FitzGerald & Ellis, 1990; Bowling, 1993.

11 Similar "riots" occurred in South Shields, Liverpool, Glasgow and South Wales (Fryer, 1984).

12 The skins adopted a uniform with half-mast trousers, braces, "bovver boots" and close-cropped hair, now familiar the world over. The skinhead style with its "severe and

puritanical self-image [and] formalized and very 'hard' masculinity" (Clark & Jefferson, 1976:156) lent itself to an overtly violent stance towards "Pakis" and "queers." The skinheads had a strong sense of class and geographical location: "The importance of one's own patch, one's own football team, and the defence of working-class territory and neighbourhood loomed large in the skinhead's lifestyle" (Mungham & Pearson, 1976:7). This territorial defensiveness is closely linked to Paki-bashing as a ritual and aggressive defence of the social and cultural homogeneity of the community against its most obviously scapegoated outsiders" (Clarke, 1975:102).

13 Former colonies, primarily in Africa, the Caribbean, the Indian subcontinent and South East Asia most of which gained their independence in the post-war period. Distinct from the "Old Commonwealth" countries of Canada, Australia, and New Zealand.

14 *The Guardian,* July 16, 1985.

15 *Searchlight,* October 1985.

16 See, for example: *The Guardian,* July 16; *The Sun,* 14 August; *The Economist,* 17 August; editorial comment, *Asian Times, New Society* 23 August.

17 *The Independent,* October 20 1992; *Anti-Racist Alliance Bulletin* December, 1992.

18 In 1986 208 racial incidents were recorded in Newham and 189 in Tower Hamlets (House of Commons, written answers no 92 and 93 4th December 1986); in 1987, these figures had risen to 364 for Newham and 242 for Tower Hamlets (Metropolitan Police, 1989c, cited in Saulsbury & Bowling, 1992:51).

19 Racial Attacks in Newham: Police Statistics for Jan/Jun 1987. Report to London Borough of Newham Council Police Subcommittee 17th September 1987.

20 Respondents were asked whether they had experienced "any form of insult, threat, violence, damage to or theft of property, or any attempt to do any of these things which was racially motivated. By racially motivated I mean an act directed at you because of your race." They were then read a list of some types of offence and were asked to say whether any of them had happened to them personally within the previous 18 months (July 1, 1987 to December 31, 1988).

21 Three of the 163 respondents who mentioned an incident of racial harassment were of "other" ethnic origin. Thirty-five of the 1,174 respondents were of "other" or unknown ethnic origin.

22 Because Asian people—the group believed, *a priori,* to be those most likely to be victimized—were deliberately oversampled, the number of incidences in the sample reduced to 724 when weighted to correct for the oversampling.

23 An arbitrary value of 10 was assigned when respondents simply said that they had been victimized "many times."

24 An attempt was made to offset this problem by explaining to respondents that: "I don't just want to know about serious incidents, I want to know about small things too. It is often difficult to remember exactly when the small things happened so please try to think

carefully." Nonetheless, the well-documented underreporting of incidents to the police may also apply to reporting incidents to survey interviewers. The authors of the Islington Crime Survey, for example, concluded from one interview that: "...some segments of the population are so overexposed to [racist assaults] that it becomes part of their everyday reality and escapes their memory in the interview situation" (Jones et al., 1986).

25   One-hundred eighteen when weighted to compensate for oversampling Asians.

26   In one-fifth of the incidents detailed in full in the survey the victim had no idea who the perpetrator was (33 out of 158 unweighted). The following analyses are made on the basis of those where it was known.

27   Most of the survey items were precoded leaving open-ended only questions such as what actually occurred in the incident, why the respondent believed the incident to have been racially motivated, why the incident was not reported to the police and other local agencies (in cases where it was not) and what happened as a result of a police detection (in cases where perpetrators were detected). The responses to these questions as recorded by the interviewer were transcribed in full. Because details were not recorded in every instance and because of the poor quality of some of what was recorded, these transcripts were not analyzed fully. It is stressed, therefore, that the quotes selected for inclusion in the text are intended only as *illustration* of the quantitative survey findings.

28   The Metropolitan Police have a system for recording and monitoring racial incidents. All those incidents "in which it appears to the reporting or investigating officer that the complaint involves an element of racial motivation; OR any incident which includes an allegation of racial motivation made by any person" are recorded on a special racial incident form. These forms are often completed after the event by home beat officers and are collated by the community contact office.

29   A Housing Department "case" is an address, individual, or family. Instances of racial harassment and attack reported to Housing are recorded on a case file. Any given case might involve only one instance of harassment or attack, though most involve several incidents and some involve many instances of repeated harassment. Cases are defined as "active" for one year after an incident has been reported to the Housing Department.

30   When offenses were against the person, 12 percent of the cases (n=11) resulted in physical injury; three involved medical attention, and another two in hospital treatment.

31   The Metropolitan Police first used Home Beat (community) Officers to conduct follow-up visits to victims of racial attacks in several selected localities in 1982. This policy was generalized to the Metropolitan Police District as a whole in 1986 (see Commissioner of Police for the Metropolis, 1986).

32   See, for example: in the USA and Canada in this volume; in Germany, Norway, Sweden, France and elsewhere in Western Europe in T. Björgo & R. Witte (eds.) (1993); in a range of Western and Eastern European countries in *CJ Europe*, Nov.-Dec. 1991.

REFERENCES

Barker, M. (1981). *The New Racism*. London: Junction.

Bell, C. & H. Newby (eds.) (1977). *Doing Sociological Research*. London: Allen and Unwin.

Bethnal Green and Stepney Trades Council (1978). *Blood on the Streets*. London: Bethnal Green and Stepney Trades Council.

Björgo T. & R. Witte (eds.) (1993). *Racist Violence in Europe*. London: Macmillan.

Bowling, B. (1993). "Racial Harassment and the Process of Victimization: Conceptual and Methodological Implications for the Local Crime Survey." *British Journal of Criminology,* Vol. 33 No.1 Spring.

Bowling, B. & W.E. Saulsbury (1992). "A Multi-Agency Approach to Racial Harassment." *Home Office Research Bulletin,* No. 32.

_____ (1993) "A Local Response to Racial Harassment." In T. Björgo & R. Witte, *Racist Violence in Europe*. London: Macmillan.

Brown, C. (1984). *Black and White Britain: The Third PSI Survey.* London: Heinemann.

Clarke, J. (1975). "The Skinheads and the Magical Recovery of Working Class Community." *Cultural Studies*, Vols. 7 and 8 pp. 99-102; also in S. Hall & T. Jefferson (eds.) *Resistance Through Rituals*. London: Hutchinson.

Clarke, J. & T. Jefferson (1976). "Working Class Youth Cultures." In J. Mungham & G. Pearson *Working Class Youth Culture*. London: Routledge.

Commission for Racial Equality (1979). *Brick Lane and Beyond: An Inquiry into Racial Strife and Violence in Tower Hamlets.* London: CRE.

_____ (1981). *Racial Harassment on Local Authority Housing Estates.* London: CRE.

_____ (1987a). *Living in Terror: A Report on Racial Violence and Harassment in Housing.* London: CRE.

_____ (1987b). *Racial Attacks: A Survey in Eight Areas of Britain.* London: Commission for Racial Equality.

_____ (1988). *Learning in Terror: A Survey of Racial Harassment in Schools and Colleges in England, Scotland and Wales, 1985-87.* London: Commission for Racial Equality.

Cutler, D. & K. Murji (1990). "From a Force into a Service?: Racial Attacks, Policing and Service Delivery." *Critical Social Policy*, March/April.

Department of the Environment Inner Cities Directorate (1983). *Information Note No. 2 1981 Census, Urban Deprivation*. London: DoE.

Dunhill, C. (1989). "Women, Racist Attacks and the Response from Anti-Racist Groups." In C. Dunhill (ed.) *The Boys in Blue: Women's Challenge to the Police.* London: Virago.

Ekblom, P. & F. Simon (with S. Birdi) (1988). *Crime and Racial Harassment in Asian-run Small Shops: The Scope for Prevention.* Crime Prevention Unit Paper 15, London: Home Office.

Farrell, G. (1982). "Multiple Victimization: Its Extent and Significance." *International Review of Victimology*, Vol. 2 pp 85-102.

Fielding, N. (1981). *The National Front.* London: Routledge.

FitzGerald, M. (1989). "Legal Approaches to Racial Harassment in Council Housing: The Case for Reassessment." *New Community,* Vol. 16 (1) pp. 93-106.

FitzGerald, M. & T. Ellis (1990). "Racial Harassment: The Evidence." In C. Kemp (ed.) *Current Issues in Criminological Research.* British Criminology Conference Vol. 2. Bristol: Bristol Centre for Criminal Justice.

Fryer, P. (1984). *Staying Power: The History of Black People in Britain.* London: Pluto.

Genn, H. (1988). "Multiple Victimization." In M. Maguire & J. Pointing (eds.) *Victims of Crime: A New Deal?*, pp. 90-100. Milton Keynes: Open University Press.

Gilroy, P. (1987). *There Ain't No Black in the Union Jack: The Cultural Politics of Race and Nation.* London: Hutchinson.

Ginsburg, N. (1989). "Racial Harassment Policy and Practice: The Denial of Citizenship." *Critical Social Policy* No. 26. pp. 66-81.

Goldstein, H. (1990). *Problem-Oriented Policing.* New York, NY: McGraw-Hill.

Gordon, P. (1984). *White Law.* London: Pluto.

_____ (1990). *Racial Violence and Harassment.* Runnymede Research Report (Second Edition) London: Runnymede Trust.

Grimshaw, R. & T. Jefferson (1987). *Interpreting Policework.* London: Allen and Unwin.

Hall, S. (1992). "New Ethnicities." In J. Donald & A. Rattansi, *Race, Culture and Difference.* London: Sage.

Hall, S. C. Critcher, T. Jefferson, J. Clarke & B. Roberts (1978). *Policing the Crisis: Mugging the State and Law and Order.* London: Macmillan.

Hesse, B., D.K. Rai, C. Bennett & P. McGilchrist (1992). *Beneath the Surface: Racial Harassment.* Aldershot: Avebury.

Hiro, D. (1991). *Black British White British: A History of Race Relations in Britain.* London: Grafton.

Hobbs, D. (1988). *Doing the Business.* Oxford: OUP.

Home Office (1981). *Racial Attacks: Report of a Home Office Study.* London: Home Office.

_____ (1986). *Home Office Good Practice Guide for the Police: The Response to Racial Attacks.* London: Home Office.

_____ (1989) *The Response to Racial Attacks and Harassment: Guidance for the Statutory Agencies.* Report of the Inter-Departmental Racial Attacks Group, London: Home Office.

_____ (1991). *The Response to Racial Attacks and Harassment: Sustaining the Momentum: 2nd Report of the Inter-Departmental Racial Attacks Group.* London: Home Office.

House of Commons Home Affairs Committee (1982). 2nd Report *Racial Attacks.* London: HMSO.

_____ (1986) 3rd Report *Racial Attacks and Harassment.* London: HMSO.

_____ (1989). 1st Report *Racial Attacks and Harassment.* London: HMSO.

Husbands, C. (1982). "East End Racism 1900-1980: Geographical Continuities in Vigilantist and Extreme Right-Wing Political Behavior." *London Journal,* Vol. 8 No.1.

_____ (1983). *Racial Exclusionism and the City: The Urban Support for the National Front.* London: Allen and Unwin.

Institute of Race Relations (1978). *Police Against Black People.* London: IRR.

_____ (1987) *Policing Against Black People.* London: IRR.

Jones, T., B.D. MacLean & J. Young (1986). *The Islington Crime Survey: Crime, Victimisation and Policing in Inner-City London.* Aldershot: Gower.

Keith, M. (1991). "Policing a Perplexed Society?: No-Go Areas and the Mystification of Police-Black Conflict." In E. Cashmore & E. McLaughlin (eds.) *Out of Order?: Policing Black People.* London: Routledge.

Kelly, L. (1987). "The Continuum of Sexual Violence." In J. Hanmer & M. Maynard (eds.) *Women, Violence and Social Control,* pp. 46-60. London: Macmillan.

Klug, F. (1982). *Racist Attacks.* London: Runnymede Trust.

Layton-Henry, Z. (1984). *The Politics of Race in Britain.* London: Allen and Unwin.

London Borough of Newham (1986). *Planning Newham: Handbook and Atlas of Development and Planning Proposals in the Borough.* London: London Borough of Newham.

_____ (1987). *The Newham Crime Survey.* London: London Borough of Newham.

_____ (1988). *Written Evidence Presented to the Inter-Departmental Racial Attacks Group (RAG).* London: London Borough of Newham.

McConville, M. & D. Shepherd (1992). *Watching Police, Watching Communities.* London: Routledge.

MacLean, B.D. (1986). "Critical Criminology and Some Limitations of Traditional Inquiry." In B.D. MacLean (ed.) *The Political Economy of Crime: Readings for a Critical Criminology.* Scarborough, Ontario: Prentice-Hall.

Mayhew, P., D. Elliott & L. Dowds (1989). *The British Crime Survey.* Home Office Research Study No. 111 London: HMSO.

Metropolitan Police (1986). *Report of the Commissioner of Police of the Metropolis for the Year 1985.* London: HMSO.

_____ (1989). *Racial Incidents 1988: 2 Area (East).* London: Metropolitan Police.

Miles, R. & A. Phizacklea (1984). *White Man's Country: Racism in British Politics.* London: Pluto.

Mungham, G. & G. Pearson (1976). "Troubled Youth, Troubling World." Introduction to G. Mungham & G. Pearson. Working *Class Youth Culture.* London: Routledge.

Newham Monitoring Project (1991). *Forging a Black Community: Asian and Afro-Caribbean Struggles in Newham.* London: Newham Monitoring Project/Campaign Against Racism and Fascism.

Neyroud, P. (1992). "Multi-Agency Approaches to Racial Harassment: The Lessons of Implementing the Racial Attacks Group Report." *New Community,* Vol.18 No. 4 July.

Pearson, G. (1976). "'Paki-Bashing' in a North Eastern Lancashire Cotton Town: A Case Study and Its History." In J. Mungham & G. Pearson (eds.) *Working Class Youth Culture.* London: Routledge.

Pearson, G., A. Sampson, H. Blagg, P. Stubbs & D.J. Smith (1989). "Policing Racism." In R. Morgan & D.J. Smith (eds.) *Coming to Terms with Policing: Perspectives on Policy,* London: Routledge.

Reeves, F. (1989). *Race and Borough Politics.* Aldershot: Avebury.

Root, M.P.P. (ed.) (1992). *Racially Mixed People in America.* London: Sage.

Saulsbury, W.E. & B. Bowling (1991). *The Multi-Agency Approach in Practice: The North Plaistow Racial Harassment Project.* Home Office Research Study No. 64. London: Home Office.

Sampson, A. & C. Phillips (1992). *Multiple Victimization: Racial Attacks on an East London Estate.* Police Research Group Crime Prevention Unit Series Paper 36. London: Home Office Police Department.

Seagrave, J. (1989). *Racially Motivated Incidents Reported to the Police.* Home Office Research and Planning Unit Paper 54. London: Home Office.

Sheptycki, J.W.E. (1992). "The Limitations of the Concept of the 'Domestic Violence' Incident in Policing and Social Scientific Discourse." In D. Farrington & S. Walklate (eds.) *Offenders and Victims: Theory and Policy.* British Criminology Conference 1991. Vol.1. London: British Society of Criminology/Institute for the Study and Treatment of Delinquency.

_____ (1993). *Innovations in the Policing of Domestic Violence: Evidence from Metropolitan London.* London: Ashgate.

Skogan, W.G. (1986). "Methodological Issues in the Study of Victimization," pp. 80-116. In Fattah (ed.) *From Crime Policy to Victim Policy.* London: Macmillan.

Small, S. (1991). "Racialised Relations in Liverpool: A Contemporary Anomaly." *New Community,* Vol.17 No.4 July.

Smith, S. J. (1989). *The Politics of 'Race' and Residence: Citizenship, Segregation and White Supremacy in Britain.* Cambridge: Polity.

Solomos, J. (1988). *Black Youth, Racism and the State: The Politics of Ideology and Policy,* London: Cambridge University Press.

_____ (1989). *Race and Racism in Contemporary Britain.* London: Macmillan.

Solomos, J. & T. Racket (1991). Policing Urban Unrest: Problem Constitution and Policy Response. In E. Cashmore & E. McLaughlin *Out of Order?: Policing Black People.* London: Routledge.

Stanko, E.A. (1987). "Typical Violence, Normal Precautions: Men, Women and Interpersonal Violence in England, Wales, Scotland and the USA." In J. Hanmer & M. Maynard (eds.) *Women, Violence and Social Control.* London: Macmillan.

_____ (1990). *Everyday Violence.* London: Pandora.

Tompson, K. (1988). *Under Siege: Racial Violence in Britain Today.* Harmonsworth: Penguin.

Walklate, S. (1989). *Victimology: The Victim and the Criminal Justice Process.* London: Unwin Hyman.

_____ (1990). "Researching Victims of Crime: Critical Victimology." *Social Justice,* Vol. 17 (3) 41 Fall, 1990.

_____ (1992). "Appreciating the Victim: Conventional, Realist or Critical Victimology?" In R. Mathews & J. Young (eds.) *Issues in Realist Criminology.* London: Sage.

Walsh, D. (1987). *Racial Harassment in Glasgow.* Glasgow: Scottish Ethnic Minorities Research Unit.

Yin, R.K. (1989). *Case Study Research.* London: Sage.

2

Germany's Xenophobic Violence: Criminal Justice and Social Responses

Alexis A. Aronowitz
Central Texas College—European Division

In the city of Saarbrücken during a 1991 demonstration against racist attacks on foreigners a banner was displayed that read: "Yesterday the synagogues burned, today it's the refugee centers." Within the past two years Germany has witnessed an increase in violent attacks against foreigners in both the old and the new federal states.[1] A study released by the Federal Department of Labor in 1991 indicated that every fifth foreigner in the new federal states was the victim of a violent attack during the previous year (Schibli, 1991). The media frequently portray the attackers as neo-Nazis. State and federal law enforcement agencies are at odds on classifications and measurement of the phenomenon. Politicians, police, and social workers are in disagreement as to possible solutions to the problem. This paper will discuss the extent of the current problem in Germany and look at the victims as well as those responsible for committing acts of terror against them. The development of the neo-Nazi and skinhead movement in Germany, assessments of causes for the increase in "hate crimes," as well as criminal justice responses and innovative projects introduced to fight the increasing problem will all be addressed.

BACKGROUND: FOREIGNERS IN GERMANY

It is difficult to discuss foreigners in Germany without further examining their various countries of origin and reasons for being in Germany. It is important to understand the relationship between Germans and foreigners and its differential development in the eastern and western parts of the country. Right-wing extremists have differentiated their victims and not all foreigners in Germany are subject to attack.

Furthermore, the government's response to attacks on foreigners also differs depending upon the target group. This will be discussed here at greater length.

Germany is currently dealing with four different foreign populations. The first group is the allied forces stationed within its borders since the end of the war. While in the "West" allied forces and their families have long enjoyed friendly relations with the Germans, Soviet soldiers stationed in former East Germany have recently become the victims of violent attacks.

The second group is "ethnic Germans," a broad definition that extends citizenship to millions of eastern Europeans and citizens of the Commonwealth of Independent States who can claim distant German ancestry. While these individuals are not legally classified as asylum-seekers, they too have been the victims of right-wing assaults.

The third group is comprised of foreign guest workers. In the 1950s and 1960s what was then known as West Germany began importing foreign "guest workers," predominantly from Turkey and Italy to help rebuild the economy. Within 10 years the families of many of these foreigners came to Germany to join them. By the 1990s "West" Germany had become a multicultural society. Government offices were established at the federal and state level (Ausländerbeauftragte) and programs were designed to promote integration, ethnic understanding, and exchanges between Germans and foreigners. "East" Germany, also, imported foreign "guest workers" — mostly from Vietnam and Mozambique (Schibli, 1991). Currently, foreigners make up eight percent of the population in the old federal states; in the new federal states foreigners comprise only one percent (*der Spiegel*, 36/1992; *Neues Deutschland*, 6/7 October, 1990). Foreign workers in the eastern part of Germany were kept geographically isolated from Germans in high-rise buildings or containers set up to accommodate them (Schmidt, 1992). In contrast to "West" Germany's attempt to integrate its foreign population, contact between East Germans and foreign workers was strongly discouraged if not outwardly prohibited (Benedict, 1991a). Another situation added to the strain between "East" Germans and their foreign population. While "West" Germans always enjoyed the right of unrestricted travel, their eastern counterparts were limited to socialist countries. "East" Germans simply lacked exposure to and understanding of foreigners (Schmidt, 1992). Forty years of isolation has now manifested itself in a "diffused fear" of anything that differs from the familiar (Huth, 1991). In "West" Germany very few of the "guest worker" population have been the target of neo-Nazi or right-wing attacks as opposed to the situation in the new federal states where attacks on African and Vietnamese guest workers are documentated daily in news reports. This situation changed, however, on November 23, 1992 with the death of three Turkish citizens. The impact on governmental responses has been far-reaching.

Germany's fourth foreign population embodies the refugees or asylum seekers. Since the relaxation of travel restrictions on Eastern Europeans and the mass migration of refugees to western Europe, Germany's liberal asylum laws have made it a favorite destination. Almost two-thirds of those who apply for asylum in

Europe do so in Germany as compared to 20 percent in France and 3.5 percent in Britain (*Independent*, 10/5/91). Foreigners seeking to remain in the country continue to enter Germany at a rate of about 20,000 a month. By the end of July 1992 approximately 234,000 people had applied for asylum in the Federal Republic of Germany. The Federal Office for the Recognition of Refugees (Bundesamt für die Anerkennung ausländischer Flüchtlinge) estimates that the number will reach one-half million a year by year's end.[2] This is in part due to Germany's economic prosperity as well as to its geographic location and liberal asylum laws. These laws grant new arrivals automatic entry at the border, a provisional residence and a meager income until all paperwork can be processed, a matter that oftentimes takes up to two years. While the asylum-seekers are awaiting a decision by the Department of the Interior (Innen-senat), they are assigned to various cities and housed in buildings, homes, or make-shift containers. They are prohibited from seeking legal employment; some are able to obtain work illegally. Asylum-seekers have borne the brunt of attacks in both the old and the new federal states.

THE POLITICAL UPHEAVAL AND
ITS SUBSEQUENT IMPACT

The Germans refer to it as the "Wende," or turning point. On November 9, 1989 the Berlin Wall opened ushering in a new era of political freedom for the once socially repressed east. These abrupt changes which began as massive demonstrations in Leipzig (September) and East Berlin (October) of that same year and ended less than two months later, toppled a 40-year, hard-line communist rule. By July of the following year the powerful West German Deutsch Mark (DM) became the common currency. Economic reform was on its way and by reunification on October 3, 1990 "East" Germany was promised that within a few years it would enjoy the same economic prosperity as the west (*der Spiegel,* 36/1992a). Factories producing substandard products were closed down; unemployment became rampant in many small cities and towns. In the "East" German city of Rostock[3] the unemployment rate is officially listed at 13 percent; in Lichtenhagen, at 17 percent. *der Spiegel* (36/1992a) reports that this number could actually be doubled if one includes those underemployed. A society ruled for 40 years by an oppressive totalitarian government, yet one which was ordered, regulated, and provided housing, employment and social security, suddenly collapsed leaving many unprepared to cope with the abrupt, newfound freedom, unemployment, uncertainty, and general disorientation and demoralization.

The impact of the political upheaval on youths was dramatic. The dissolution of a political orientation followed by the restructuring of the work market let its impact be known on social relations as well. "East" German youths were raised in a society in which educational and job security was the norm, where it was unnecessary and unknown to fear unemployment. In a society that previously provided training, education, and work to all its members, competition between classmates for the same position now prevailed (Schubarth, 1992). Money once available for youth clubs, meeting places, or sports organizations for young people was suddenly nonexistent. Youths were forced to fend for themselves. Schubarth (1992) argues that in situations where youths are left on their own with no structure or guidance, they become susceptible to such dangers as drug addiction, occultism, or gambling.

Youths were faced with another problem. The former German Democratic Republic, with its secret security forces and propaganda mechanism intact, suppressed political opposition. Disagreement with the system resulted in punishment ranging from loss of one's job to harsh prison sentences and possibly death (if one tried to escape to the west). Suddenly, in their newfound freedom, "East" youths were expected not only to have, but also to defend their beliefs when challenged by others—something with which these youths were inexperienced. This made them particularly susceptible to "new, subtler forms of manipulation" (Schubarth, 1992).

Numerous opinion polls conducted with former "East" German youths within a two-year period after the "Wende" indicated the following: (in December 1990) approximately two-thirds of the "East" German youths were concerned about the uncertain developments in the areas of rent and income; one-third were afraid of the future. In Heitmeyer's (1989) study of rightist orientations among youths 16-17 years old, he found fear of competition, fear of not finding a job, and fear of loss of status and success to be influencing factors. In another study four-fifths of the "East" German citizens surveyed believed that the social security was previously better in the East than in the West; every second person believed the Reunification process was progressing worse than expected; four-fifths polled judged the economic situation in the East after introduction of the DM to be very bad. The percentage of those in the "East" viewing themselves to be second-class citizens rose since Reunification from 75 percent to 84 percent.[4] The collapse of a political ideology after 40 years left youth without a system of values (Winkler, 1992). Attitudes concerning the changes in Germany range from disinterest to mistrust, disappointment, and frustration.

Couple this situation, the political and economic uncertainty in the new federal states, with a massive influx of foreigners. Many sociologists, politicians, and pedagogs believe these are the breeding grounds for a rise in right-wing ideology and an increase in the level of violence against Germany's foreign population.

ATTACKS ON FOREIGNERS: THE SITUATION WORSENS

Attacks on foreigners in Germany are not a new phenomenon. Such attacks have been sporadically documented over the past 11 years.[5] A number of cases have received particular attention due to either the brutality of the attack[6] or the large number of attackers or victims. Three such incidents stand out and serve as turning points in the recent developments. Attacks on hostels for foreigners have occurred in both the old and the new federal states. While attacks in the "East" have traditionally been given more media coverage, Runge (1992) reports that of the 60 fires that occurred in foreign hostels in an eight-month period prior to Hoyerswerda, 3/4 occurred in the "West." But Hoyerswerda became a turning point. Five nights of attacks on foreigners ended on the night of September 23, 1991 when the authorities could no longer guarantee the safety of the 230 foreigners residing in the city. Amidst bottle- and Molotov-cocktail tossing youths stood the local residents who shocked the world with their unconditional support for those attacking the foreigners in their town. Media coverage showed town citizens surrounding the shelter and clapping as youths attacked the residents with stones and bottles. City officials were ashamed at the international disappointment and shock expressed over the incident, yet did not regret the forced evacuation of the foreigners (Matussek, 1991).

But Hoyerswerda was only the beginning. Less than one year later the scene in Rostock-Lichtenhagen not only repeated itself, it became more horrifying. A frightening new trend began to emerge. Violent attacks were no longer committed only by gangs of youths but were supported by citizens in the towns weary of large numbers of foreigners being deposited in their backyards. Nightly television coverage showed middle-aged citizens not only verbally supporting the attackers, as was experienced in Hoyerswerda, but themselves tossing stones at foreigners and police.

Violent attacks on the hostels for asylum-seekers in the "East" German city of Rostock on August 22, 1992 triggered a wave of angry attacks against foreigners that have since become a daily occurence. Within a five-week period foreigners' dwellings throughout the country were attacked daily with rocks, stones, and Molotov cocktails. These latest attacks have been described by politicians and those sympathetic to foreigners as the latest in a series of pogroms. In the eastern German town of Quedlinburg a refugee home was the target of rightist violence for three nights (mid-September, 1992). As individuals sympathetic to foreigners staged a demonstration to show their support, local residents pelted pro-foreigner demonstrators with beer bottles and fireworks. A frightening new trend is developing: violence is no longer the exclusive tool of the young, radical, extremist. The spread of violence toward foreigners is being witnessed by mainstream citizens.

The third turning point came on November 23, 1992 in the "West" German town of Mölln. Two arsons were set in buildings housing Turkish families. Forty-five persons were left homeless, nine were injured in the fire and three family members—a 51-year-old grandmother and two young girls (10 and 14) were killed. These were not asylum-seekers. They were Turks who had lived and worked for many years in Germany. The youngest victim was born here. The German government could not move them to another city to protect them, as had been done on numerous occasions with refugees. An attack on Turkish citizens, on people who were well integrated, working, and contributing to the German economy, left foreigners wondering if any of them were safe anywhere in Germany.

Extent of the Problem: How Do We Measure It?

The extent of the problem is difficult to measure. Not only are we left with a diffused picture concerning who is orchestrating and carrying out these attacks, but the task of obtaining reliable statistics on the number of attacks provides some difficulties. Statistics released by the Federal Office for Internal Security (Staatsschutz) portray the following diffuse picture: of the 334 suspects arrested by the police for suspicion of violence against foreigners, only four were members of right-wing extremist organizations. Forty-four were skinheads, and 286 could not be delegated to any particular "scene" or organization. The only common element between these offenders was their hatred of foreigners (*TAZ*, 10/25/91). The sensational media reports portray only the tip of the iceberg.

The Bundeskriminalamt (BKA)—Federal Criminal Office—in its attempt to track the extent of crimes against foreigners has categorized these attacks into three areas: physical attacks on persons (Angriffe gegen Personen), arson (Brandanschl ge), and other offenses (sonstige Straftaten). The 1991 statistics reflect an increase in the number of attacks on foreigners by eight-fold over the 1990 statistics (*TAZ*, 2/1/92). In October 1991 alone the BKA registered 904 racist offenses—four times as many as in the entire previous year. The following provides a breakdown of offenses between January and the beginning of December 1991:

Table 2.1
Number and Types of Attacks on Foreigners in Germany
as Reported by the Federal Criminal Office[7]

325   arsons
188   offenses against persons (physical assaults)
1561 other offenses (vandalism/destruction of property and propaganda offenses)
2074 total offenses against foreigners
During the same time frame the BKA registered 776 suspects in these attacks against foreigners and their dwellings. Of these, only 12 are women.
47% of the male suspects are between the ages of 18 and 21
31% were below the age of 18
suspects were taken into custody in only one-half of these cases
only 57 suspects were placed in pretrial detention

As of the end of 1991 Germany had no reliable data system to track offenses against foreigners. As each of the 16 federal states may report or record offenses differently, these statistics are only a weak reflection of the actual conditions in Germany. A critical article in Berlin's *TAZ* (1/2/91) draws attention to the inaccuracy of the BKA's statistics citing specific instances (in which foreigners were injured or killed) that fail to appear in the national statistics. Additionally, the BKA's statistics do not reflect the same statistics reported by the Bundesamt für Verfassungsschutz (Office for the Protection of the Constitution). While the Verfassungsschutz in Cologne reports "600 offenses with right-wing motivations," the Bundeskriminalamt reports 1,800 offenses against foreigners and their habitats" (Gast, 1991). At the same time that the BKA reports 2,074 attacks for the year 1991, the Verfassungsschutz reports 1,483 such offenses and breaks them down in the following fashion:

Table 2.2
**Number and Types of Attacks on Foreigners in Germany as Reported
by the Office for the Protection of the Constitution[8]**

	(East)	(West)	GERMANY 1991	GERMANY 1990
Killings	1	2	3	2
Arson and attacks with explosive devices	123	260	383	47
Destruction of property with excessive violence	171	477	648	119
Physical assaults resulting in injury	198	251	449	102
TOTAL	493	990	1,483	270

A further statistical discrepancy lies in the fact that many foreigners do not report their victimizations to the police (they may be illegal aliens, fear of police cohesion with right-wing offenders) or that offenses, such as fires in the refugee hostels cannot be directly linked to arson (*der Spiegel*, 36/1992a).

Who Are These Young Radicals?

All too often the press reports acts of violence by neo-Nazi groups. Germany is in fear of an increase of neo-fascist activities. To assess the depth of the current problem it is necessary to understand the driving forces behind the violence.

When fires are set at asylum-seeker hostels, when foreigners are attacked, it is difficult to determine whether the acts are politically motivated and the result of an organized right-wing extremist group or whether these are the acts of young violent delinquents.

The difficulty in classifying such anti-foreign actions is further examplified by the following: A high-ranking police officer in the Section State Security[9] (Polizeilicher Staatsschutz) works in the office responsible for the investigation of crimes involving right-wing extremist or terrorist activities. Crimes investigated by this office are characterized into one of seven categories: threats or insults to political opponents, threats or insults with anti-Semitic overtones, neo-Nazi vandalism, antisemitic vandalism, the dissemination of fliers with illegal contents, damage to graveyards, and other offenses (nonpersonal). According to the officer, unless while a youth is attacking a foreigner he simultaneously yells "Sieg Heil," the crime will not be investigated by this office but instead will end up in the office dealing with violence among youths (Arbeitsgruppe Jugendgruppengewalt). In order for a crime to be investigated by this office it must clearly show right-wing extremist overtones.

Another frightening phenomenon, and one that further complicates the issue of just who these young people are and what they stand for, involves misrepresentation by the press in their desire to sell a story. The *Bild am Sonntag* (9/14/92) tells the following story: a reporter from the Cologne television crew from the studio RTL-plus filmed five skinheads standing in front of a war memorial, their arms raised in a Nazi salute, crying "Sieg Heil." Shortly after the show aired, one of the skinheads was arrested for violation of Paragraph 86a, "using a sign of a forbidden organization and use of the Nazi greeting." The story told to the police at the station: the young men were given two cases of beer and promised a DM 1,000 for their cooperation. They never did receive their promised DM 1,000 and the prosecutor in Dresden is currently seeking criminal charges against the RTL-plus camera team. The *TAZ* (12/17/91) reports of three further incidents in which RIAS TV (November 14) and RTL-plus (October 19) paid skinheads in a Berlin district either money or alcohol to vandalize apartment buildings in which foreigners lived. On December 14 the Tokio Broadcasting System is alleged to have paid skinheads in Berlin to yell "Sieg Heil" before the camera.

In what appear to be clear-cut cases of neo-Nazi activities, the borders are still diluted. The Nazi greeting is often used by youths as a form of provocation and is no solid indicator of association with right-wing groups or support of their ideology. More typical of these young individuals is the picture portrayed by the office for State Security: alcohol, boredom, contact with the right-wing scene without being ideologically or permanently attached to it, an accute predisposition or pension towards violence (*TAZ*, 10/25/91). Through violence one gains social recognition and is taken seriously (Heitmeyer, 1990:65). Farin and Seidel-Pielen (1991:75) identify another unifying factor—a weak group identity built not on its own goals or future dreams, but on the fear generated in others when they are confronted by a group of skinheads.

The Verfassungsschutz (the Office for the Protection of the Constitution—Germany's domestic intelligence agency) which closely follows the activities of right-wing organizations and their activities reported that in 1991, 1,088 persons were seized as suspects involved in "acts with proven or suspected rightist extremist motivations" (1992). Of the total, 19 percent were already known to the office. The following information concerning their activities could be discerned:

- 150 persons, at least 126 of them skinheads, had already committed one or two other violent acts with rightist extremist motivations

- 28 persons (only 2.6% of the total), almost all of them skinheads, were members or followers of right-wing organizations

- 12 of these (1.1% of the total), among them, 10 skinheads, were known to have membership in numerous neo-Nazi organizations

The Senate for Internal Affairs in the state of Hessen attributes 5 percent to 10 percent of the acts of violence against foreigners to organized right-wing groups (*der Spiegel*, 50/1992b).

THE SKINHEAD SCENE

Tattoos, a shaved head, Doc Marten boots, bomber jackets = neo-Nazi. This is the portrait fed to the public by the press. A closer look at the skinhead scene portrays a different picture.

The skinhead movement grew out of the working class among youths in London in the 1960s. What brought them together was a desire to set themselves apart from society—a show of pride in their working-class roots, and a common interest in Reggae and Oi! music. While violence was always a part of the skinhead scene—there was never a tendency to direct this against foreigners. Skinheads were better known for attacks on Punks or those in the left-wing scene (Autonomen).

It was not until the middle of the 1970s that the skinhead movement began to splinter and become allied with the right-wing ideology (the British Movement and the National Front). This phenomenon entered the German scene by the mid 1980s with Michael Kühnen and his "Aktionsfront National Sozialisten" (Socialist Action Front).

The press' negative image of skinheads had much to do with their polarization and isolation from the rest of society. While left-oriented youths found political shelter within the school or "alternative" political groups, right-wing youths were further isolated. Particularly for youths from the "East," is that everything "negative, corrupt and oppressive" came from a socialist, left-oriented government (thus driving the youths further to the right). No other youth [sub]culture has been so isolated by its own age-group (Farin & Seidel-Pielen, 1991:74). This exclusion from all sides of society gave fascist organizations an upper hand in infiltrating the skinhead movement and winning youths by providing them with that which the state would not: access to bars, meeting places and someone to listen to them.

Violence in "East" Germany began escalating in the early 1980s in football stadiums. It was at this same time that Germany began witnessing its first skinheads. The majority were members of the youth subculture although small numbers began drifting to the right. These youths, unlike skinheads from the "West" had qualified apprenticeships or advanced training and came from well-respected and integrated families. Their parents were diplomats, functionaries of the ruling party, the SED, teachers, military officers. (Benedict, 1991a).

The "right" draws membership from mainly five sources: (1) the militant and violent soccer scene (hooligans); (2) a relatively small circle of Nazi-Skins or Faschos; (3) young men released after their mandatory military service or those who have attended officer training school; (4) those released from prison; (5) those relatively "normal" youths who join seeking friendship, camaraderie, excitement (Benedict, 1991a; Brück, 1992).

Not all skinheads adhere to a right-wing ideology. The first skinheads drifted out of the Punk scene which many found to be too politically oriented. When skinheads began drawing into their ranks "nazi-punks" and "nationalistic soccer fans" they then became attractive to members of fascist organizations such as Free

Workers Party (Freie Arbeiter Partei) and the Nationalistic Front (Nationalistische Front). Many nonpolitical skinheads left the movement at this time. These neo-Nazi skinheads became known within "right" and "left" circles as the "Boneheads." They are characterized as "storm troops" for fascist groups such as the Nationalistic Front, the Free Workers Party or White Power. These groups are predominantly male; their main activities center around drinking; watching porno and horror videos; and attacking foreigners, homosexuals, and "left wingers" (Anarchistische Gruppe/ Rätekommunistinnen, 1991). An equally violent and dangerous group of skinheads are those who also include among their main activities attacks on foreigners, but who are nonpolitically aligned.

There are other offshoot skinhead groups with diverse orientations. The Oi-skins associate with punks and soccer fans, rarely with Nazi-skins. Another splinter group is the Trojanskins. Their orientation is apolitical and they oppose racism. Further to the left are the Redskins whose political orientation leans towards socialism. There are also small numbers of Anarchoskins (anarchist skinheads) whose main purpose is political work. It was out of these three factions: the Oi-skins, the Trojanskins and the Redskins that the organization SHARP was born (Anarchistische Gruppe/Rätekommunistinnen, 1991).

SHARP—Skinheads Against Racial Prejudice—an organization born in the United States and adopted in Germany. Within their ranks various political orientations exist (everything from apoliticism to traditional, more center-to-left party membership). While they are strictly against any form of racism, their main objective is to stage parties, concerts, or discos. There is an unusually larger number of females within their ranks (up to 40%) who in most cases are seen as equals (Anarchistische Gruppe/Rätekommunistinnen, 1991). In Berlin, SHARP members work together with Turkish youths in anti-fascist groups (*TAZ*, 12/14/92).

The skinhead scene is not a new phenomenon to the West. Between the years 1983 and 1987, 25 individuals (in "West" Germany) died as a result of attacks by skinheads. In 1991 attacks with right-wing motives (in both the old and the new federal states) claimed the lives of three victims. By August of 1992, 10 lives had been claimed as a result of right-wing or skinhead activities. This number climbed to 17 by the end of 1992. These are the most deaths attributed to right-wing activitity (excluding the Munich Oktoberfest attack 1980) since 1945. While the raw number of attacks on foreigners is highest in the (West) German state of Nordrhein-Westfalen, the reader must keep in mind the distribution of foreigners differs in the old and the new federal states. Table 2.3 indicates the distribution of violent attacks on foreigners (Farin & Seidel-Pielen, 1992).

The likelihood of becoming the victim of an attack in the eastern state of Sachsen-Anhalt was 20 times greater than that in the western state of Nordrhein-Westfalen.

Table 2.3
Serious Attacks Involving Fires or Personal Violence

State	Population in millions	Number of Attacks	Foreigners in millions	Attack per Foreigner
Nordrhein-Westfalen	17	153	1.4	1:9,150
"West" Germany				
Sachsen-Anhalt	3	44	.02	1:454
"East" Germany				
New Federal States	16.9	168	.15	1:892
Old Federal States	62	389	4.8	1:12,340

Source: Farin & Seidel-Pielen, 1992.

While experts in the field made earlier claims of disorganized youths acting spontaneously, this notion is now being challenged. Wagner, former chief of the Landeskriminalamt (State Police) for the five new federal states agrees that these violent youths are predominantly "disorganized" youths in the sense that they maintain no formal political ties to right-wing groups. Their actions, however, are not spontaneous (Wagner, 1991). Police are finding skinheads more organized. They appear at their destination fully outfitted with weapons (baseball bats, billyclubs, boards, gas pistols, star-pointed metal pieces, knives and guns, cb radios, and video cameras with which to film their attacks). Often their victims have been chosen in advance. In Magdeburg (May 1992) 60 skinheads stormed a birthday celebration at which 20 youths from the punk scene were in attendance. A telephone call just minutes before sent the police (including the special command) on a false alarm in a section of the city far away from the actual scene of attack, giving young skinheads enough time to storm the party and beat to death a 23-year-old (Löblich, 1992). Police searches of apartments throughout Germany are turning up large caches of sophisticated weapons as well as what government officials suspected might be "hit lists" (*Stars and Stripes*, 11/27/92; *der Tagespiegel*, 11/29/92, 12/6/92).

The Bundesamt für Verfassungsschutz, which closely follows the activities of right-wing organizations and their activities, reports that the number of young, violent, skinheads approximates 6,500. Of the 3,500 skinheads in the new federal states, approximately 1,200 are aligned with the neo-National Socialist movement; almost all of the approximately 3,000 skinheads in the eastern part of the country are politically oriented (*Verfassungsschutz Bericht,* 1992). The Verfassungsschutz reports that these skinhead activities are taking on a more (right-wing) politically oriented direction. (*Freitag*, 10/15/91).

The police and experts in the field of rightist activities and youth violence argue that differences between "East" and "West" rightists exist not only in their historical development but also in their willingness to display violence. (Madloch, 1991; Farin & Seidel-Pielin, 1992, *Verfassungsschutz Bericht,* 1992). While the skinhead movement in the "West" grew out of a youth subculture and not all skinhead groups have become politicized, the skinhead movement in the "East" grew out of a national-socialist opposition to the communist regime. Furthermore, skinheads in the "East" are more closely aligned with neo-Nazi ideology than their western counterparts (*Verfassungsschutz Bericht*, 1992). Heitmeyer (1992) argues that "antiforeign violence" in the East is closely linked with neo-Nazi groups who use violence to impose their ideological beliefs upon their society. Madloch (1991), however, argues that right-wing extremists in the former "East" are more radical and militant than their western counterparts, yet trail them in political, ideological, and organizational structure. In opposition to these groups in the East, there exist in the West more uncoordinated youth groups (e.g., skinheads) who employ violence to accomplish their (apolitical) goals. Experts do agree on one thing, though. Youth groups in the "East" are quicker to resort to violence, and they are more violent when they act. Furthermore, it is argued that the "East" is more receptive to the use of violence against "undesirables." "Overworked police in Dresden cooperate with Nazi youths against asylum-seekers from Eastern Europe. Citizens from Leipzig applauded when right-wing youths used iron bars to beat up (foreign) gamblers to drive them away from Sachsenplatz (a square in the city). Business owners employ "Faschotroops" to "maintain order..." (Farin & Seidel-Pielen, 1992).

The similarity that these two groups share is the age and gender structure. Sixty-nine percent of the 1,088 persons involved in acts of violence (*Verfassungsschutz Bericht*, 1992) were under the age of 21. Almost all (97.3%) are under the age of 30. Only three percent are females.

POSSIBLE CAUSES OF RIGHT-WING EXTREMISM

Emile Durkheim, in *Suicide* (1951) observed that a disturbance or change in societal norms and the subsequently-linked danger of disorientation can lead to such behaviors as suicide, psychosomatic illness, apathy, and irrational aggressive or violent behavior (Funke, 1991; Heitmeyer, 1992).

Heitmeyer argues that growing right-wing extremism is not an accidental occurrence, but can be explained as the result of dramatic societal disintegration leading to individualization. In the former German Democratic Republic emphasis was placed on mutual participation in the community; individualism was scorned and punished. In the "East" youths grew up in a highly structured, relatively authoritarian state. When that structure crumbled it left a high degree of uncertainty concerning the future. Heitmeyer attempts to explain the appearance of radical, violent behavior by youth in "East" Germany as a result of political changes.

Heitmeyer (1992) identifies and differentiates between individuals who can be placed into one of three groups based upon the following two criteria: adherence to an ideology of inequality (the superior vs. the inferior race) and the acceptance of and predisposition to use violence.

The first group identified by Heitmeyer is comprised of youths who may support an ideology of inequality that takes the form of racism (dislike of foreigners, superiority of Germans) but neither advocates nor uses violence. These are relatively normal youths who do not come to the attention of the authorities.

The main characteristic of the second group is its willingness to use violence. While the main focus is violence, the ideology is employed only to legitimize the violence. Skinheads fall into this second category.

The third category is dominated by an ideological belief in the superiority of the German race and violence is employed to support or sustain the ideology. Organized, institutionalized neo-Nazi groups belong to this third category.

Adolescence in the former "East" was rigidly controlled, emphasis was placed on conformity, and adolescence was seen as nothing more than a transitional phase to adulthood and its consumate responsibilities. Youths who exhibited autonomous or independent tendencies were punished by the state. Decisions concerning studies, apprenticeships, jobs, or apartments were dictated by the government. Little room was left for independent thinking.

The "Wende" introduced changes in the developmental processes of these youths. No longer was adolescence an easy transitional period but one that was now characterized by individualism, competition, and the freedom to make one's own decisions. However, the familiar social and governmental safety nets were no longer there to "catch" youths who made wrong decisions.

Korfes argues that the "Volksgemeinschaft," this sense of community or belonging that once existed, could again be created. Through their aggressive and discriminatory behavior against foreigners, youths could create a sense of belonging, of oneness as Germans. "The feeling of one's own superiority gives one strength, and hate of anything foreign helps suppress the feeling of uncertainty and one's own powerlessness" (1992).

In contrast to Heitmeyer's psychosocial approach to explaining the growth of right-wing tendencies among youths in the "East," historians and sociologists point to another phenomenon to explain the differential development right-wing activities between "East" and "West."

If one examines history books in the former German Democratic Republic one will find an amazing avoidance of Germany's role in the Holocaust. In the "East," the year 1945 was designated the "Stunde Null" (hour zero), the time at which the German Democratic Republic's history began (Schubarth & Schmidt, 1992). The "East" adopted a Stalinistic political model and strengthened its ties to the former Soviet Union. The polarization of the two Germanys allowed each to place the blame of the Holocaust upon the other.[10] Acceptance of the fascist ideology became synonomous with a rejection of the communist or socialist ideology. Therefore, in history books and in political science or history instruction in the schools, a strong anti-fascist ideology prevailed. Students were taught that the masses (Germans) were lied to and seduced into their participation in the war. History books in the "East" portrayed Germans, next to the Soviets and Poles, as World War II's greatest victims (Schubarth & Schmidt, 1992). "East" Germany's role in World War II was strongly associated with the anti-fascist resistance movement and with new editions of history books the percentage of Germans involved in the resistance movement increased from 14 percent in 1951 to 23 percent in 1957 to 30 percent by 1970 (Schubarth & Schmidt, 1992). Youth collectives and organizations were in large part given the names of resistance fighters. "East" Germany's approach to dealing with its involvement in one of the most heinous periods in history was to view itself as the victim, overemphasize its involvement in the resistance movement (strong emphasis was placed on the KPD—Kommunistische Partei Deutschland—the German Communist Party) and to refuse to deal with its responsibility or guilt in the systematic annihilation of millions of people in extermination camps (Heitmeyer, 1992).

Two issues must be reemphasized here. First, "East" Germany refused to recognize its responsibility in the war, thus minimizing possible feelings of responsibility or guilt. Second, an anti-fascist ideology was not only emphasized in schools, but was literally forced upon "East" German youths in their day-to-day lives during their free-time activities. This highly structured, involuntary ideological and political system, as well as "East" Germany's refusal to deal with and confront its own responsibility in the war are factors that Heitmeyer and others (Schubarth, 1992; Schubarth & Schmidt, 1992) believe may have been responsible for the predisposition to Nazi ideology in the East when the political system crumbled in 1989.

Schubarth (1992) identifies two approaches to explaining a possible disposition to right-wing extremism in the former "East."

The first is a sociological approach to the problem. A socioeconomic development forced upon the "East" by the "West" did not take into account a shifting or reorientation of values and norms that left a cultural vacuum, one which, according to Schubarth (1992) allows "inhumane political ideologies to surface. Individuals who view themselves as helpless in the process of social changes and see themselves as victims of a modernization process, can find plausible explanations (and solutions) in right-wing extremist arguments" (Schubarth, 1992).

A second theoretical foundation takes a psychological or psychoanalytic approach to the explanation of the development of right-wing extremism in "East" Germany. It looks to the personality traits in the individual and how this individual deals with conflict or dissonance in his surroundings. The "scapegoat" hypothesis proposes that individuals faced with conflict solve this conflict by placing the blame on a weaker or socially isolated individual or group. Beck (1986) sees in "East" Germany the tendency for a "scapegoat" society in a twofold fashion. As was previously mentioned, "East" German history precluded responsibility for the atrocities of World War II viewing itself as the victim and placing the blame elsewhere. Secondly, that which affects the present situation, "East" Germans have made foreigners the scapegoat for current problems: high unemployment, lack of sufficient housing, the economic woes of the current government.

The "Hoyerswerda Syndrome:" law-abiding citizens, spectator, cheering on violent hooligans attacking a refugee center. In an attempt to explain the "Hoyerswerda

Syndrome," Heitmeyer (1992) utilizes the following sources:

The historical source lies in Germany's refusal to recognize its role as aggressor in the war. By counting itself among the victims, it was not necessary to critically assess its role in the war.

The second and main source is one specific to "East" Germany. Those living under a repressive and authoritarian regime suffered extreme uncertainty during the political changes and exhibited a collective inferiority complex in comparison to their "brothers" in the "West" (which in part was the image that "West" Germans liked to portray in dealing with their poorer eastern neighbors the "Ossies"). To reestablish a balance, a sense of stability and control over their own lives, the weak seek out those who are weaker, on whom the blame can be placed. Right-wing ideologies and groups can easily find a foothold in such periods of uncertainty with their promise to reestablish order and "cleanse" the neighborhood of impurities (foreigners). After all, the violent attacks on foreign hostels were able to accomplish in a few short days, that which politicians had been unable to accomplish in months, namely, the immediate removal of asylum-seekers and closure of their hostels. When a political rationalization and public acceptance exist for such behavior, the possibility exists not only to act, but to desensitize guilt feelings.

Another factor exacerbates the problem and propogates the existence of neo-Nazi violent groups. "Normal" citizens, unable to take part in violent altercations with undesirable foreigners, support such extreme action on the part of others. These "others," be they neo-Nazis, skinheads, or violent youths, are strengthened in their own convictions by public support. In Essen (West) in August 1990 the police reported a case of people in a neighborhood paying DM 5,000 to skinheads to attack a hostel for asylum-seekers located at the end of their block. They feared property values would decrease (Heitmeyer, 1992). Failure of the police to react or inconsistencies on the part of the criminal justice system further reinforces this conviction and behavior.

RIGHT-WING IDEOLOGY AND PRACTICE IN THE OLD AND THE NEW FEDERAL STATES

To properly analyze the current situation in Germany and to understand the underlying motivations behind the attacks on foreigners it is necessary to examine the historical development of right-wing political parties and incidences in both the old and the new federal states. "West" Germany's democratic constitution has long allowed the existence of "rightist" political parties, providing they do not "endanger the democratic state" (Strafgesetzbuch, Paragraph [Statute] 84, 85). The existence of right-wing political parties in "West" Germany has witnessed two distinct phases (Wippermann, 1990). The first phase in "West" Germany's history was the existence of right-wing parties, youth organizations, publishers, and press releases between 1948/1949 until 1969. To this era belong the following fascist parties: German Right Party (Deutsche Rechts Partei or DRP) the Socialistic Reichs Party (in 1952 outlawed by the German Supreme Court), the German National Democratic Party (Nationaldemokratische Partei Deutschlands or NPD) and the the youth organizations Viking Youth (Wikingjugend) and the Alliance of Youth True to the Homeland (Bund Heimattreuer Jugend), organizations that either exist today or can point to off-shoots that draw youth into its membership. Between 1966 and 1969 the NPD won seats in regional elections, but when it failed in 1969 to gain seats in Germany's parliament this ushered in the second phase which witnessed a decline in organized and open right-wing political parties.

At the same time, however, fascism was undergoing a reorientation in the form of a division between the rightists whose aim was to gain power politically and those whose goal was to gain power through terroristic means: "Aktion Widerstand" (Action Resistance), "Wehrsportgruppe Hoffmann" (Hoffman's Paramilitary Training Group), "Deutsche Bürgerinitiative" (German People's Initiative), "Kampfbund Deutsche Soldaten" (Fighting Alliance of German Soldiers), "Aktionsfront Nationaler Sozialisten" (National Socialistic Actionfront), "Freiheitliche Deutsche Arbeiterpartei" (Independent German Workers Party), to name a few (Wippermann, 1990).[11] Extremist parties began networking with fascist groups outside of Germany. The strength of right-wing political parties was evidenced with the birth of the Republicans (REP's). One year before the 1989 elections in Berlin the party was formed. With no previous history and only 1,000 members after the elections, the party won 90,000 votes. Beginning in 1989 the REP's and other fascist parties were winning parliamentary seats in local elections throughout Germany.

The development of fascism took on a different form in "East" Germany. Under the ruling socialist political party, fascism was strictly prohibited. Organized right-wing political parties did not enter onto the scene until the Berlin Wall fell and political parties began pouring in from the West. Eisenhammer (1991) noted that:

> the potential for neo-Nazi violence is both quantitatively and qualitatively more dangerous in the east than the west of the country. With the collapse of Communist repression, a considerable potential for aggression has been released, which, in conjunction with the many right-wing extremists who have come in from the west, is now being allowed relatively free rein, due to the insufficiency of the local security forces.

The lack of organized right-wing political parties in the former German Democratic Republic before the fall of the Wall did not, however, preclude the birth and existence of skinheads (Farin & Seidel-Pielen, 1992). Historians report that the "right-wing potential" existed on a subcultural level (Nazi-punks, hooligans, skinheads) until around 1984/1985. Beginning in 1986 the scene began to take on political structure. In 1986 foreigners began falling prey to organized groups of skinheads. The extent, however, to which these individual cases are documented is suspect. Research in "East" German archives[12] led to a report of a refugee being burned by right-wing extremists in the city of Erfurt in 1988. This fact went publicly unknown due to the political ramifications it could have had on countries sending foreign workers to the "East" Germany (Schmitz, 1991). The director of the Berlin Division for State Security reports of earlier right-wing activities in the greater Berlin area in 1988. Police failed to register reports of young victims seriously injured by skinheads who were identified to the police. There are even countless reports of police standing idly by while "fascist skinheads attacked foreign workers, punks or other oppositional youths" (Farin & Seidel-Pielen, 1991). These attacks too, went unreported as such right-wing activities simply "did not exist" in an antifascist state like the German Democratic Republic (Gast, 1991; Schibli, 1991; Farin & Seidel-Pielen, 1991).

CRIMINAL JUSTICE RESPONSE

By December of 1992, 17 people, eight of them foreigners,[13] were killed by rightist individuals, skinheads or violent hooligans. The Verfassungsschutz reports over 2,000 criminal acts against foreign asylum-seekers, foreigners, and residents, as well as Jewish Holocaust memorials and cemeteries (the Jewish barracks housing a museum at the Sachsenhausen concentration camp mysteriously burned down) this year (*IHT,* 12/12-13/92). The Bundeskriminalamt has reported the number of attacks on foreigners has doubled since 1991 (*Berliner Morgenpost*, 12/10/92). The tendency is a sharp increase over the 1991 statistics. While the government debated the asylum issue, attacks against foreigners continued on an almost daily basis. No branch of government has been spared criticism. German politicians now ask themselves why they waited so long to respond.[14] During the 1960s and 1970s the government attacked left-wing radicals with a vengeance. Why was it incapable of responding when the terror came from the right? (*Letzebureger Journal*, 11/26/92; *der Spiegel*, 49/1992).

The German penal code contains statutes prohibiting offenses that could be classified as hate crimes: Paragraph (statute) 130 prohibits "Volksverhetzung" (incitement against a racial or ethnic group to include encouraging violence against these people or racial or ethnic slurs). Smearing swastikas on Jewish cemeteries is not simply an act of vandalism, but one of psychological violence. Furthermore, unlike American First Amendment protections to possess and display Nazi paraphernalia, this is prohibited under paragraph 86a (prohibited are displays of the flag, pieces of a uniform, sayings and greetings of organizations prohibited by law). Despite the fact that this violation is punishable by up to three years in prison, countless news reports and newspaper clippings showed large gatherings of youths and adults carrying Nazi flags, their arms outstretched in the Nazi greeting shouting anti-foreign slurs, marching through the streets of various cities throughout Germany (*TAZ*, 10/6/92). It could be argued that police were outnumbered and unable to take a firm stand against such actions. However, these demonstrations were not a spontaneous gathering that caught the police offguard, but were planned well in advance.

Applications had been made and issued in numerous cities and towns for marching permits. (*TAZ*, 6/28/91). Police continually ignored the activities; no arrests were made.

As acts of violence against foreigners increased, so too did criminal justice responses. After Hoyerswerda, Hünxe, Rostock, and Mölln, the government responded with more oppressive tactics, the sharpest occurring after the Mölln attacks. While attacks against foreigners have increased dramatically since 1990, police, court and government actions against violent hooligans slowly became more aggressive and punitive. As attacks on foreigners increased after the fall of 1991 (Hoyerswerda), it was not until Rostock that the police really began to crack down. And it was the Mölln deaths that drew international criticism of Germany and its inability to control anti-foreign violence within its borders. Mölln became a turning point.

Prior to Mölln, the police response to the activities of skinhead attacks on foreigners, particularly in the "East," had been described as ambivalent. Police had often been accused of sympathizing with right-wing attackers.[15] At best their actions had been described as "slow and hesitant to respond." Furthermore, the police as well as the criminal justice system had been accused of trivializing the activities of such youths. The following are examples of criticisms, all too often heard from victims.

While 60 skinheads violently attacked 20 punks at a birthday celebration in Magdeburg (May 1992), seven police officers were within the vicinity of the attack but failed to intervene. The bartender at the scene reported police arrived one-half hour after the incident. The Police chief excused the actions on the part of his officers by stating that in order to be effective, 15 police officers would have had to intervene (others had been called away on a false alarm minutes earlier) (Löblich, 1992).

In Rostock (August 1992) the police were accused of withdrawing and standing idly by as hundreds of violent youths attacked homes in which Vietnamese workers and asylum-seekers lived. On the first day of the attacks, 60 police officers appeared, confronted by 150 youths and 1,000 spectators. Police defended their action during the initial attacks with the argument that they were not properly outfitted to intervene in such dangerous situations.[16] As violence escalated the number of police increased and at one point 1,600 police were battling 1,200 young radicals and their sympathizers. Over 100 officers were injured, some seriously.

Eberswalde, a small city about 40 miles northeast of Berlin. On November 24, 1990, 50 neo-Nazis, skinheads, and heavy metal rockers attacked three Mozambique and Angolan guestworkers with baseball bats, chains, and knives. The Angolan, Antonio Amadeu, died three weeks later as a result of his injuries. Newspaper accounts further documented that the police were forewarned of right-wing trouble. Their excuse for failing to intervene was due to "inferior technical equipment and uncertainty" (*Freitag*, 7/22/92). Farin and Seidel-Pielen (1992), however, report that a police officer responded to a friend's plea to help Amadeu with, "should we allow ourselves to be killed for an Angolan?"[17] A judicial inquiry is being conducted on three officers who failed to intervene; the charges: bodily injury resulting in death (manslaughter) as a result of failure to act (Thuillier, 1992).

The judicial system, as well, has been criticized by their own for being slow in responding to these acts of terror against foreigners (*Frankfurter Rundschau*, 12/1/92; *der Spiegel*, 49/1992). In the Frankfurt/Oder district court 16 trials against right-wing violent attacks have resulted in mild sentences of probation for those involved. The courts have consistently dismissed the right-wing extremist orientation of the acts and have emphasized the fact that they are dealing with youths acting spontaneously and under the influence of alcohol and peers (Farin & Seidel-Pielen, 1992). In August of 1991, 25 youths attacked and burned a home for Rumanian asylum-seekers. Eight of the youths between the ages of 16 to 19 were given sentences of incarceration from one year two months to one year seven months to be reduced to probation for the crime of disturbing the peace (*Freitag*, September 12, 1992). Three youths who attacked and burned to the ground an asylum hostel were sentenced to between six months and one year probation and community service for disturbing the peace (*Freitag*, 12/3/92; *IHT*, 10/3-4/92). In Hamburg charges were dismissed against a 32-year-old man charged with vandalism for smearing the door of a subway car with Nazi slogans. The court's rationale: the door had already been smeared with other graffiti and to write on top of graffiti did not cause further damage to the door; therefore no vandalism occurred (*Freitag*, August 15, 1990).

By American standards the sentences imposed by the courts are still relatively mild although the courts have shifted away from handing down sentences of probation. For the past two years the crimes have been investigated and prosecuted at the local level. When youths throwing Molotov cocktails set fires to refuge centers they were charged with vandalism and disturbing the peace. When deaths occurred as a result of firebombings or physical assaults, the perpetrators were charged with manslaughter. Additionally, the federal prosecutor had declined to get involved in previous cases in which foreigners had been attacked because there was no proof of a political motive (*IHT*, 11/24/92). The continuous belief that these were individual acts of violence carried out under the influence of alcohol and peer pressure allowed the courts to take a milder stance against the offenders.[18] In many instances in which foreign hostels were attacked the individuals, if caught, were charged with disturbing the peace. In a landmark case in November 1992, a Landauer court handed down sentences of three and one-half years for arson and attempted murder for the firebombing of a hostel that burned to the ground, but in which no one sustained injuries. This was the first time a court had brought charges of attempted murder against individuals involved in an arson attack (*TAZ*, 11/12/92). The Ministers of Justice in the various states have now demanded of their prosecutors that firebombings in refuge centers will be treated as felony arsons and attempted murder (*der Spiegel*, 50/1992).

Government proposals to aid police and prosecutors in clamping down on anti-foreign violence has included the use of preventive detention of "traveling serial rioters," tightening the laws against disturbing the peace (to prevent mob action such as that in Rostock), holding participants in mob action accountable for any (unanticipated actions committed by the mob), allowing police to use sophisticated electronic eavesdropping equipment to spy on people in their homes, and to expedite the deportation of foreigners convicted of crimes, particularly asylum-seekers (*CJ Europe*, 1992).

After the Mölln deaths the police and courts began enforcing laws which had previously been ignored. Numerous newspaper articles document cases in which individuals were arrested and prosecuted for using racial, ethnic, or anti-foreign slurs.[19]

On November 27, 1992 the German Minister for the Interior outlawed the right-wing extremist party the Nationalistic Front. The action was followed on December 10 with a prohibition against the German Alternative. The act of outlawing these two organizations allowed police to conduct searches of party offices and the homes of their members. Police raids in apartments throughout Germany have turned up weapons, membership and address lists, and large quantities of banned Nazi propaganda (*IHT,* 12/12-13/92; 12/11/92; *der Tagesspiegel,* 11/29/92). The Federal Minister of Justice called upon police and prosecutors to pursue musicians, authors, and publishers who spread or distributed rightist texts and emblems (*der Tagesspiegel,* 12/2/92). The Federal Inspection Office for Writings Endangering Youth banned three recordings by the German group "Störkraft" (Destructive Force). Another rightist group "Böhse Onkelz" (Evil Uncles) was banned from performing (*IHT,* 12/3/92). Shortly thereafter, five apartments of the members of a right-wing musical group "Kraftschlag" (Forceful Blow) were raided and records and compact discs with rightist lyrics were seized (*Berliner Morgenpost,* 12/11/92).

Permits to demonstrate have been denied right-wing groups (the Republicans were denied the right to meet over the weekend of November 28/29 on the grounds that it would endanger public security and order (*Freitag,* 11/28/92; *IHT,* 11/28-29/92) and when challenged or when groups have planned demonstrations without permits, police have stationed themselves at control points outside of town to prevent the arrival of rightwing radicals (*Freitag,* 11/14/92). Security experts in the government agreed that a special police unit would be formed to fight anti-foreign violence. They will receive special training in psychology and martial arts and be equipped with special bulletproof clothing. This special command will operate on a national level and be under the command of regional police when needed (*TAZ,* 8/31/92). *Freitag* (11/14/92) reports that the state criminal agency (Landeskriminalamt) Hamburg would create 12 new positions to observe the right-wing extremist scene and DM one million would be spent for better technical equipment. Germany's domestic intelligence agency (Verfassungsschutz) is watching the 76 rightist organizations to collect evidence that may allow the Interior Minister to have them banned (*der Tagesspiegel,* 11/27/92).

Asylum laws have recently been changed. In November 1992 Germany signed a repatriation agreement with Romania allowing for the return of 40,000 people (mostly gypsies) to that country. Under previous law, it was difficult to deport individuals without proper identity papers. This new agreement made it easier. Furthermore, anyone crossing into Germany from another European Community Country, from Poland, Czechoslovakia, Austria, or Switzerland was immediately turned back at the border. Individuals seeking asylum from war-torn countries may remain until peace has returned to their country and then must leave Germany, and asylum will not be granted to individuals from countries deemed free from political persecution (although individuals may still apply and cases will be judged on an individual basis).

Police razzias, while not new,[20] are occurring with greater frequency. The state has turned to more repressive tactics with crimes from the far right. Police have planned to double the number of anti-terrorist commandos from 43 to 85 in the eastern state of Sachsen-Anhalt. A national task force, under the command of the Verfassungschutz, will be established with the purpose of infiltrating extremist groups and raiding their offices (*Stars and Stripes*, 12/6/92).

A leading neo-Nazi leader of the German National Party was sentenced to two years and eight months in prison for making a racist, neo-Nazi speech (openly calling for violence against foreigners and Jews) at a right-wing rally in September 1992. Unrepentent, he repeated these same slurs in the courtroom. To further silence him and another leading neo-Nazi, the German government has applied to the Federal Constitutional Court to strip the two men of their civic rights. Two such applications made since Germany became a republic in 1949 were both denied in the past. Should the government succeed this time, both men would lose their right to vote, to hold public office, to make political statements or to take part in or organize political meetings for at least a year (*Stars and Stripes*, 12/11/92; *Süddeutsche Zeitung*, 11/30/92; *die Welt*, 11/30/92; *TAZ*, 12/10/92).

Further actions taken to reaffirm Germans' alliance with foreigners is exemplified in numerous pro-foreigner demonstrations throughout Germany. The largest, and to date most successful, was the December demonstration in Munich attended by over 350,000 persons. On Sunday, December 13, 1992 various German musicians performed at a free concert under the theme, "Today Them, Tomorrow You." The President of the Federal Association of German Industries reported that industries are determined to treat anti-foreign or extremist activities as grounds for dismissal from the job (*Freitag*, 11/11/92). And a federal program to counter influence from the right will be initiated. The three focal points of the program include (1) the prohibition of neo-Nazi parties, (2) the distribution of hundreds of thousands of pamphlets to children in schools throughout Germany explaining political radicalism, and (3) the provision of seminars for individuals working in the area of juvenile publications, teachers, counselors, and social workers to help them fight the problem (*Freitag*, 11/9/92).

The government's actions against extremist organizations, increased police razzias, and harsher court sentences has not gone without criticism. While this type of reaction may be appropriate and necessary for "hard core," committed neo-Nazis or habitual violent offenders, this is not necessarily the case for the majority of youths taking part in anti-foreign attacks who have been described as "Mitläufer" or those on the periphery. A percentage of those youths who attack refugee centers come from intact families; they have jobs. They are not committed to a national socialist ideology (*Freitag*, 12/21/92). Rabe (1980) puts forth a number of assertions concerning youths involved in right-wing activities: Youths involved in right-wing youth organizations are not schooled in the national socialist ideology but function on an emotional (rather than a political) level. What they desire is a sense of belonging, a sense of "community" which is strengthened through uniforms, symbols, rituals, and songs. Right-wing extremism is only one of many demeanors or attitudes that youths may adopt to react to situations with which they cannot cope (e.g., unemployment, failure in school). A high-ranking officer from the Berlin police department's unit concerned with Juvenile Group Violence reports that "in their search for a personal identity, it is not impossible for individuals within a group to change their philosophy of life and change from one group (skinhead to anti-fascist or the other way around) to another (Zirk, 1992). Therefore, it has been argued, the appropriate judicial response is dictated not only by the situation but also by the offender and his dedication, or lack thereof, to a cause. Hornstein (1990) takes the argument one step further and argues that formal criminal justice processing and harsh sentences for youths may, through a process of labeling and further exclusion from society, strengthen a commitment to a rightist ideology.

Heitmeyer, Seidel-Pielen and others warn that the current threat comes not from the right extremists but "from the core of society which is incapable of coming to grips with the current economic, social and political uncertainties."[21] According to Heitmeyer (1991b) right-wing extremist organizations are not the causes of such problems but rather the symptoms. These groups provide youths with a sense of belonging, power, certainty, excitement, and direction (1991a). He (1988) argues that any prophylactic work with youths with rightist tendencies is *reactive*. How, then, can these youths be reached before the onset of rightist tendencies, ideologies or behavioral patterns?

SOCIAL RESPONSES

The federal government, aware of the need for preventive work with youths, granted the five new federal states (and Berlin-East) 20 million marks for a three-year project to include further training for pedagogues and social workers and an "action program against aggression and violence" (*TAZ*, 1/9/92). This should include the use of streetworkers to approach skinheads on the streets, improvement and expansion of programs in youth clubs, and the establishment of living quarters for youths in various cities. A number of innovative programs have been implemented with an emphasis upon preventing youths from developing a rightist theoretical framework. Others focus their attention upon those youths who have already drifted into the skinhead or right-wing scene. The following section will provide the reader with a smorgasbord of programs throughout Germany.[22]

Hornstein (1990) characterizes these youths as isolated, insecure, and suffering from a lack of future perspectives. Both Hornstein and Schneider (*Freitag*, 12/21/92) argue they can best be reached through either the school or their cliques and informal groups. While programs exist to reach youths through schools (see

Dollmann, 1991; Teuscher, 1991) the remainder of the chapter will concentrate on preventive programs offered through the community. Particular emphasis will be given to streetworker programs that target youths most at risk.

Prophylactic programs offered through the community include the following:[23]

(1) In 1988 youths organized themselves into an umbrella anti-fascist group Jugendantifa-Koordination (JAKOB) within which independent "antifa" (anti-fascist) groups could cooperate. JAKOB concentrates its work on schools and special events where stands are set up and information is disseminated. A monthly publication deals with such problems as "right-wing extremism, nationalism, sexism, racism, xenophobia, and asylum laws."

(2) Between 1982 and 1985 the grocery chain Bolle in coordination with the Ausländerbeauftragte (the office that deals with the integration and problems of foreigners in Germany) created a model program to improve job possibilities for Turkish youths. A focus of the project was to promote improved relations between German and Turkish youths in the apprenticeship program, through intercultural training vacations and free-time activities sponsored by the company.

(3) The International Computer Club was founded in Cologne in 1989 by Turkish, Italian, and German youths with the threefold purpose of promoting (a) the "usability" of computers and software, particularly for disadvantaged groups who may not have easy access to such; (b) understanding of and cooperation between different ethnic groups; and (c) fighting the spread of racist and right-wing software.

(4) The Ausländerbeauftragte in Berlin currently has two programs[24] aimed at reducing violence among young people. This first program is aimed at youths before they become involved in violent activities. "Youths against Violence," begun in 1991, is comprised of people of different nationalities between the ages of 14 and 25. The size of the group varies from 30 to 50 individuals, and is open to anyone who is interested. The goal of the project is to work with other young people in providing them with alternatives to violence and discrimination. Rather than letting adults make decisions that concern youths, these young people want to take the initiative in finding solutions to problems that concern them. The program is multifaceted to reach youths from various backgrounds and with different interests. Over the past two years their varied activities have included: weekend seminars with the theme, "Causes and Consequences of Violence" with role-playing and group dynamic training. A contest was held in schools throughout the city to design the best logo for the group. Cooperation with the Berlin Public Transportation Department (BVG) led to the group's posters and advertisements being hung throughout the city in subway cars and stations. Through the "snowball effect" members of the group attempted to establish other anti-violence working groups in schools, youth clubs, and church circles. This group has had meetings with groups from the both the "right" and "left." They have set up stands to pass out materials at street festivals, have met with politicians to discuss their activities, and have visited a refugee center as well as a unit of Soviet military officers. They have staged "anti-violence" events

in youth clubs and have participated in school activities such as parents' evening and teachers' conferences. Additionally, this group has established contact with various agencies such as schools, sports clubs, police, youth clubs and the Berlin Transportation Department to help organized an "Anti-Violence Network."

(5) The second program, also sponsored by the Berlin Ausländerbeauftragte, is aimed at youths who, through some act of violence, have come into contact with the juvenile justice system. The Training Course Against Discrimination and Violence has been in operation for three and one-half years. While the majority of the participants are there as a result of a court order, a number have voluntarily returned for a second session. Over the course of a weekend, six to 10 youths come together with a social pedagogue to learn alternatives to violent behavior. The youths are assigned to one of two groups depending upon their age (14-17 or 18-21) and maturity level. The emphasis of the training course—making youths understand the consequences of their actions—is carried out differently with each group. Role-playing is emphasized with the younger youths; each participant is placed in the role of the victim. Among older youths the emphasis is on an emotional level where an attempt is made to confront them with the reality of their behavior (use of violence will bring them into contact with the police and court system resulting in a monetary loss, restitution, and possible prison time). While this program has worked with skinhead, rightist, and foreign youths, the director of the program refuses to bring these youths together. The program helps the youths recognize that their propensity towards violence has nothing to do with dislike of other racial or ethnic groups (skinheads or foreigners) but comes from within. Emphasis, then, is upon helping youths to recognize situations with which they cannot cope, causing them to resort to violence. Time is spent allowing the youths to discuss situations in which they have personally been exposed to violence (home, school, police, within their social group, with other groups, as both victims and perpetrators). The seminar emphasizes individual strategies to teach youths how to deal with their aggression and attempts to destroy some of the myths surrounding their discriminatory beliefs.

STREETWORKER PROGRAMS

Those youths who have already drifted into the skinhead and "right" scene are not lost, but are more difficult to reach. One of the problems experienced throughout Germany is that social workers, with their usual left-of-center political beliefs, drift between hesitancy and outward refusal to work with such youths. Streetworker programs with skinhead youths are limited and face numerous obstacles from the political arena, as well as from the leftist and foreign youths.

Within the past five years Berlin has experienced relatively few and sometimes short-lived programs with skinheads. Because they are often refused entrance to most youth clubs, contact with them must be established on the street. But to accomplish any long-term project with them requires that they have a place of their own.

In 1988, street worker Thomas Mücke began organizing meetings between

"West"-Berlin skinheads and the same students from a nearby school, that they had attacked: "With one another rather than against one another" (Miteinander statt Gegeneinander). The youths discussed such themes as fascism, violence, left-wing ideology. The program fostered understanding between the two groups. The participants found that they all shared something in common: boredom. With the financial help of the Berlin Senate for Youths, the group of skinheads organized two construction wagons which they renovated as their meeting place. The project provided the youths with an activity for which they themselves were responsible, a sense of pride, a sense of belonging. The project was also successful in driving away organized facist parties who soon lost interest in Mücke's youths. A fire one year later destroyed the cars; the perpetrator(s) left behind one word painted on the ruins: "Nazipack" (pack of Nazis). Shortly thereafter the group disbanded.

Another project with skinheads, in "East" Berlin is run by the social deacon, Michael Heinisch (von Zglinicki, 1992). Begun in 1992, his project was open to any youths who sought orientation and a sense of belonging. Predominantly skinheads, including some involved in right-wing organizations, joined his project. Given a house by the city, Heinisch and his youths set out to renovate it. Some of the youths were partially sponsored financially by the Berlin Senate. In addition to the work the youths have done on the house, Heinisch has also tried to broaden their horizons through various programs: meetings and discussions with leftist squatters, soccer games with Vietnamese, trips to exhibitions featuring Jewish culture and history (Goddar, 1991). His goal is not to resocialize the youths, rather to offer them a niche where they can begin the process of establishing a future for themselves. This house, too, was burned the day before the opening. In November of 1992, Heinisch was attacked and brutally beaten, requiring hospitalization. The police suspect it was the work of leftists, who view Heinisch as the leader of the Nazis.[25]

A third project with skinheads, also in "East" Berlin, is supervised by a street-worker who gained prior experience with skinhead youths in a pilot project two years earlier in an economically depressed area in "West" Berlin. Michael Wieczorek's philosophy in working with such youths encompasses the following: (1) acceptance by the group as a streetworker is imperative; (2) the aim of the project is not the dissolution of the group but rather to emphasize and strengthen the positive aspects of the group; (3) emphasis must be placed upon reducing the criminal activities of individuals or the group (music, video projects, sports events, trips keep the youths off the streets and out of trouble) (Mücke, 1990). Wieczorek's new project shares similarities with the previous two projects: the renovation of areas in their neighborhoods and the creation of a cafe; the goal: integration into their neighborhood (Rogalla, 1992).

Mücke (1990) emphasizes that pedagogical work with youths with rightist orientations must avoid stigmatization and exclusion from mainstream society. Further, emphasis upon antifascist work is not the solution to "winning these youths back from the right." Rabe (1980) argues that antifascist actions have side effects in that they may strengthen commitment to rightist beliefs.

Heitmeyer (1990) argues that the following must be emphasized in dealing with youths with rightist, extremist orientations:

(1) Politics
Youths must feel they are useful and are making a contribution to society. This is gained predominantly through work or career on the one hand, and involvement in socially acceptable "milieus" on the other. Any political decisions must create opportunities to give young people this chance.

(2) Work with Youths
"Stationary" work with youths, such as in youth clubs must be supplemented with "mobile" or street worker approaches, particularly with youths who have previously been excluded from such youth clubs.

(3) Youth Education
Antifascist work in the form of brochures, cultural studies seminars or films no longer suffice to counteract a rightist orientation. Heitmeyer emphasizes education that the youths themselves can experience.

Heinisch attempts this, education through experience emphasizing the dissolution of prejudices towards foreigners, by involving his youths in discussions, projects or sports activities with such persons. It remains to be seen whether he will be successful.

NOTES

[1] The 11 old federal states represent the former West Germany; the 5 new federal states represent the former East Germany. Throughout this chapter the author will refer interchangeably to the terms old federal states or "West" Germany when refering to the former West Germany, or new federal states or "East" Germany when refering to the former German Democratic Republic.

[2] Compare these figures to 256,000 applicants in 1991 and 193,000 in 1990 (*der Spiegel,* 36/1992; 28).

[3] The confrontations in Rostock-Lichtenhagen that began on August 22, 1992 triggered a wave of violence between neo-Nazis and police in towns throughout the new federal states. This will be discussed later in the chapter.

4   See Wilfried Schubarth, "Rechtsextremismus—eine subjektive Verarbeitungsform des Umbruchs?," in *Der antifaschistische Staat entläßt seine Kinder,* Köln: PapyRossa Verlag GmbH, 1992, pp. 80-81.

5   In January 1981 Rockers beat to death a 44-year-old Turkish man. In June 1982 sentences were handed down to followers of the German Actiongroup for the deaths and attempted murders of foreigners. During the same month, a sympathizer of the neo-Nazi group NSDAP shot to death six foreigners, and young Germans beat to death a Turkish man in a disco while yelling "foreigners out." For a further chronological assessment of such attacks see *der Spiegel* 50/12/7/92, pp. 24-25 and Zeitungsprojekt antirassistischer and antifaschistischer Gruppen, February 1992, pp. 30-33.

6   In October 1991 in Hünxe, youths threw Molotov cocktails into a refugee center setting fire to the apartment of a Lebanese family. Two young sisters (six and eight years old) suffered life-threatening burns; in January 1992 in Berlin skinheads attacked a 19-year-old Polish tourist, injected an anesthetic in his tongue, attempted to cut it with a pair of scissors, then finally succeeded in severing one-third of his tongue with a pair of garden shears.

7   *die Tageszeitung,* February 1, 1992.

8   See *Verfassungsschutz Bericht,* 1991, p. 76.

9   Interview conducted by author with an officer within the Staatsschutz in Berlin on July 14, 1992.

10 Compare Staritz, Dietrich, "Sieger der Geschichte" or "Gnade der späten Geburt" in German Studies, Aston University, 1989:2-6.

11 For a more complete discussion of Nazi or fascist organizations in Germany, refer to Benedict (1991b), Wolowitz (1990) and *Verfassungsschutz Bericht* (1991).

12 Information provided by a participant at a conference on "Right-wing Extremism, Antisemitism and Ausländerfeindlichkeit" in Berlin, sponsored by the Center for the Study of Anti-Semitism at the Technical University of Berlin. See Schmitz, 1991.

13 While eight of the victims were foreigners, two additional German victims belonged to the leftist movement. An additional five victims were homeless; one was killed because his attackers thought he was Jewish, and another victim was killed because he called Hitler a criminal (*der Spiegel,* 49, 11/30/92).

14 German Chancelor Helmut Kohl publicly acknowledges criticisms for the first time that he had acted too slowly to the wave of violence in Germany (*IHT,* 12/4/92).

15 *TAZ* (5/13/92) claims police watched as skinheads attacked guests at a party attended by left-wing youths. *TAZ* (6/28/91) reports that police and city government facilitated neo-Nazi activities in Dresden and that police initially refused to take eyewitness reports of the attackers involved in the serious injury—and subsequent death —of a Mozambican man. Polish tourists complained that police were uninterested in filing reports in which Poles had been attacked by right-wing extremists (*TAZ,* 2/6/92).

16 *der Spiegel* (August 31, 1992:24) reports that police were outfitted with thin plastic helmets and solid white riot shields. Officers were forced to lower their shields if they intended to move forward thus exposing their head and face to attack. A lack of protective covering for their knees left them exposed.

17 After the more than 800 African guest workers had been sent back to their home countries, the right-wing extremists found new targets for their attacks: the girlfriends and wives of these black Africans whom the neo-Nazis have marked as "Negerhur" and "Rassenschaenderin" ("nigger whore" and "one who has disgraced the race"). See Farin and Seidel-Pielen's *Rechtsruck* (Shift to the Right) (1992) for interviews with two such women.

18 In the trial involving their attack on the foreigners' hostel in Hoyerswerda in September 1991, 3 skinheads were sentenced to probation. The judge refused to recognize the political dimension of the attack and instead emphasized the offenders' social problems. See *die Tageszeitung* (2/27/92).

19 Berlin's *die Tageszeitung* (4/16/92) reports that eight men were fined for yelling out "Sieg Heil." A sentence of 5 months incarceration suspended to 3 years probation and a DM 500 fine was handed down to a man for yelling "Sieg Heil" and displaying a Hitler greeting at a Germany-Turkey soccer match (*die Welt,* 12/5/92). A known neo-Nazi was given a 16-month prison sentence for uttering numerous threats and disturbing the public peace (*die Welt,* 11/27/92).

20 In December 1991 police nationwide conducted raids in 32 cities and 114 apartments of right-wing radicals and skinheads believed to be involved in attacks on foreigners. Weapons and Nazi propaganda were confiscated leading to future arrest proceedings against 107 persons (*TAZ,* 12/14/91; *Het Parool,* 12/4/91, *IHT,* 12/4/91).

21 Interview with Eberhard Seidel-Pielen, *die Tageszeitung,* "Verbote rechtsextremer Gruppen keine Lösung" (11/21/92).

22 For a further description of projects refer to *Modelle and Projekte gegen Rechtsextremismus und Ausländerfeindlichkeit: Dokumentation ausgewählter Beispiele.*

23 For examples of other programs see *Modelle and Projekte gegen Rechtsextremismus und Ausländerfeindlichkeit: Dokumentation ausgewählter Beispiele,* Arbeitsstelle Neonazismus, Fachhochschule Düsseldorf: Düsseldorf (n.d.).

24 More information about the project "Youths Against Violence" can be found in a publication *Arbeitskreis "Jugend Gegen Gewalt,"* published by the Berlin Buro of the Ausländerbeauftragte. A description of the second project was obtained in a personal interview by the author with the project director at the Office of the Ausländerbeauftragte on December 16, 1992.

25 Interview with a Berlin police official from the unit Jugendgruppen Gewalt, December 10, 1992.

REFERENCES

Anarchistische Gruppe/Rätekommunistinnen, *Nazi Raus!*, (AG/R, EX-GJA/R) 2000 Hamburg 76: GNN-Verlag, July 1991.

Arbeitskreis "Jugend Gegen Gewalt," Office of the Ausländerbeauftrage Berlin, 1992.

Beck, U. *Risikogesellschaft—Auf dem Weg in eine andere Moderne*, Frankfurt am Main, 1986.

Benedict, L. "Die nackte Gewalt," *Freitag*, Nr. 41, October 4, 1991a.

_____ "Die Fahne hoch, die Reihe fest geschlossen," *Jugend und Rechtsextremismus in Berlin-Ost*, Berlin: Magistratsverwaltung für Jugend, Familie und Sport, 1991b, 39-49.

Berliner Morgenpost, "Extremisten sollen Rechte aberkannt werden," December 10, 1992; 1.

_____ "Bonn verbietet erneut rechte Partei; Bundesweit Razzien gegen Radikale," December 11, 1992; 1.

Bild am Sonntag, "RTL kaufte Nazi-Gruß," September 14, 1992.

Brück, W. "Skinheads—Verboten der Systemkrise," in Heinemann and Schubarth (eds.), *Der antifaschistische Staat entläßt seine Kinder*, PapyRossa Verlag: Köln, 1992; 37-46.

CJ Europe, "Kohl's Party Wants German Crackdown on Rightists, Crime," Volume 2, Number 6, November-December, 1992; 11.

Dollmann, T. "Was kann Schule gegen Rechtsextremismus, Neonazismus tun?," *Hakenkreuze auf der Schulbank: Berichte, Fragen, Gegenstrategien; Beiträge einer Tagung Bad Boll*, epd Dokumentation; GEP Vertrieb: Frankfurt am Main; 1991; 68-72.

Durkheim, E. *Suicide*, The Free Press: New York, 1951.

Eisenhammer, J. "Crackdown on neo-Nazis," *The Independent*, October 7, 1991.

Farin, K. & E. Seidel-Pielen *Krieg in den Städten: Jugendgangs in Deutschland*, Rotbuch Verlag: Berlin, 1991.

_____ *Rechtsruck: Rassismus im Neuem Deutschland*, Rotbuch Verlag: Berlin, 1992.

Frankfurter Rundschau, "Rechtsterror: Geltende Gesetze auch anwenden," December 1, 1992.

Freitag, "Verfassungsschutz rechnet mit 6,000 Skinheads," October 15, 1991.

_____ August 15, 1990.

_____ "Polizei hielt zich zurück," July 22, 1992.

_____ September 12, 1992.

_____ "Bundesprogram gegen rechts," November 9, 1992.

_____ "Industriepräsident rät zur Entlassung von Extremisten," November 11, 1992.

_____ "Polizei soll Neonazis stoppen," November 14, 1992.

_____ "Aus für Republikaner Treffen," November 28, 1992.

_____ "Brandstifter verurteilt," December 3, 1992.

_____ "Nazi-Gedanken frühzeitig in Elternhaus und Schule begegnen," December 21, 1992.

Funke, H. *Jetzt sind wir dran: Nationalismus in geeinten Deutschland*, Aktion-Suhnezeichen Friedensdienste E.V.: Berlin, 1991; 9.

Gast, Wolfgang, "Verfassungsschützer uneins," *die Tageszeitung*, November 26, 1991.

Goddar, J. "Keine Angst vor Glatzköpfen," *die Tageszeitung*, August 9, 1991.

Heitmeyer, W. *rechtsextremistische Orientierungen bei Jugendlichen*, Juventa Verlag: Weinheim und München, 1988.

_____ *Rechtsextremistische Orientierungen bei Jugendlichen*: Juventa Verlag: Köln, 1989.

_____ "Rechtsextremistische Orientierungen bei Jugendlichen in sozial akzeptierten Gruppen: Folgerung für Jugendpolitik, Jugendarbeit und Jugendbildung," *Materialiensammlung: Jugendarbeit gegen Rechtsextremismus*, Berlin: Senatsverwaltung für Frauen, Jugend und Familie, 1990; 59-70.

_____ *Warum handeln Menschen gegen ihre eigenen Interessen?*, Bund Verlag: Köln, 1991a.

_____ *Warum handeln Menschen gegen ihre eigenen Interessen?: Beiheft zum 'ran Handbuch für Jugendliche*, Bund Verlag: Köln, 1991b.

_____ "Die Widerspiegelung von Modernisierungsrückständen im Rechtsextremismus," in Heinemann and Schubarth (eds.), *Der antifaschistische Staatenläßt seine Kinder*, PapyRossa Verlag: Köln, 1992; 100-115.

Hornstein, W. "Jugendliche heute: vereinzelt—verunsichert—ohne Perspektive—vom Rechtsextremismus gefährdet?," *Rechtsextremismus and Ausländerfeindlichkeit: Eine Herausforderung für die Jugendarbeit*, Kreisjugendring München-Stadt, February, 1990; 22-34.

Huth, L. "Der braune Mob im neuen Staat," *d'Letzebureger Land*, Nr. 46/ November 15, 1991; 22.

IHT or *International Herald Tribune*

_____ "10 Germans get Suspended Terms in Hostel Attack," October 3-4, 1992.

_____ "Outrage as Violence Widens in Germany," November 24, 1992; 1.

_____ "Germany Cracks Down on Far-Right Groups as Turks Mourn Dead," November 28-29, 1992; 1.

_____ "Neo-Nazi Words and Music," December 3, 1992; 1.

_____ "German Police Seize Neo-Nazi Weaponry," December 4, 1991.

_____ "Protests Spread in Germany," December 4, 1992; 5.

_____ "Bonn Raids Rightists and Bans 2nd Party," Dec. 11, 1992; 4.

_____ "German Police Arrest 6 Neo-Nazis in Hostel Raid," December 12-13, 1992; 5.

Independent, "A Burden Europe Should Share," October 5, 1991.

Korfes, G. "Rechtsextremistische Orientierungen in der DDR-Jugend: wie sind sie entstanden?," *Jugend und Rechtsextremismus in Berlin-Ost,* Magistratsverwaltung für Jugend, Familie und Sport: Berlin, 1991, 9-18.

Letzebureger Journal, "Wiesenthal für Verbot rechtsradikaler Gruppen," 11/26/92.

Löblich, E. "Skin-Opfer in Magdeburg gestorben," *die Tageszeitung,* 5/13/92.

Madloch, N. "Rechtsextremismus in Ostberlin und in den Ländern der einstigen DDR," *Jugend und Rechtsextremismus in Berlin-Ost,* Magistratsverwaltung für Jugend, Familie und Sport: Berlin, 1991, 3-8.

Matussek, M. "Jagdzeit in Sachsen," *der Spiegel,* #40/ 9/30/1991; 41-51.

Modelle and Projekte gegen Rechtsextremismus und Ausländerfeindlichkeit: Dokumentation ausgewählter Beispiele, Arbeitsstelle Neonazismus, Fachhochschule Düsseldorf: Düsseldorf (n.d.)

Mücke, T. *Rechtsextreme Orientierungen bei Jugendlichen: Grenzen und Möglichkeiten der Jugendarbeit,* Unpublished Master's Thesis, Technical University, Berlin, 1990.

Neues Deutschland, 6/7 October 1990.

Parool, Het, "Duitse politie in actie tegen neo-Nazis," December 4, 1991.

Rabe, K.H., *Rechtsextreme Jugendliche: Gespräche mit Verführen und Verführten,* Lamuv Verlag GmbH: Bornheim-Merten 1980.

Rogalla, A. "Mit Streetworkern gegen Bandenbildung," *die Tageszeitung,* February 19, 1992; 3.

Runge, I. "Wer hat Angst vor'm Schwarzen Mann?," in Heinemann and Schubarth (eds.), *Der antifaschistische Staat entläßt seine Kinder,* PapyRossa Verlag: Köln, 1992; 132-139.

Schibli, P. "Bewaffnete Neonazi-Gruppierungen verbreiten Haß und Gewalt," *Tageblatt* (Luxemburg), Nr. 137, June 15, 1991.

Schmidt, I. "Ausländer in der DDR - Ihre Erfahrungen vor und nach der 'Wende'," in Heinemann and Schubarth (eds.), *Der Antifaschistische Staat entläßt seine Kinder,* PapyRossa Verlag: Köln, 1992; 64-76.

Schmitz, T. "Vom Schlagstock zum Molotowcocktail," *die Tageszeitung,* October 4, 1991; 6.

Schubarth, W. "Rechtsextremismus—Subjektive Verarbeitung des Umbruchs?", in Heinemann and Schubarth (eds.), *Der antifaschistische Staat entläßt seine Kinder*, PapyRossa Verlag: Köln, 1992; 78-99.

Schubarth, W. & T. Schmidt "Sieger der Geschichte: Verordneter Antifaschismus und die Folgen," in Heinemann and Schubarth (eds.), *Der antifaschistische Staat entläßt seine Kinder*, PapyRossa Verlag: Köln, 1992; 12-28.

Spiegel, der, "Ernstes Zeichen an der Wand," #36a, 8/31/92; 18-29.

_____ "Alle drei Wochen ein Toter," #36b, 8/31/92; 26-27.

_____ "Das ist politische Justiz," #49, 11/30/92; 16-17.

_____ "Hitlerjugend ohne Partei," #50, 12/7/92; 28-29.

_____ "Bestie aus deutschem Blut," #50, 12/7/92, 22-33.

Stars and Stripes, The, "Raid uncovers neo-Nazis' "hit list," November 27, 1992.

_____ "Germans plan task force to battle neo-Nazi groups," December 6, 1992; 1.

_____ "Unrepentent neo-Nazi sentenced," December 11, 1992; p. 7.

Strafgesetzbuch, Verlag C.H. Beck: Munich, 1991.

Süddeutsche Zeitung, "Seiters will weitere rechtsextremistische Vereine verbieten," 11/30/92.

TAZ or Tageszeitung, die:

_____ "Bundesweite Razzia gegen Rechtsradikale," April 4, 1991.

_____ "Kumpanei zwischen Neonazis und Polizei?," June 28, 1991.

_____ "Gewalt im Suff und aus der Laune heraus," October 25, 1991.

_____ "TV-Teams setzen Skinheads ins Bild," December 17, 1991.

_____ "1991 über 2.000 rassistische Straftaten," January 2, 1992.

_____ "Offene Jugendarbeit gegen Rechtsradikalismus," January 9, 1992.

_____ "Nur in Deutschland werden Polen angegriffen," February 6, 1992.

_____ "Progrom unter Aufsicht der Polizei," February 27, 1992.

_____ "Acht Männer zu Geldstrafen wegen 'Sieg Heil'-Rufen verurteilt," April 16, 1992.

_____ "Es geht darum, daß Leute umgebracht werden," May 13, 1992.

_____ "Neue Polizeitruppe in Vorbereitung," August 31, 1992; 2.

_____ "Polizei spielt Blindekuh," October 6, 1992; 4.

_____ "Brandanschlag: Dreieinhalb Jahre Haft," November 12, 1992.

_____ "Verbote rechtsextremer Gruppen keine Lösung," November 21, 1992.

_____ "Maulkorb für zwei Rechtsextremisten?," December 10, 1992; 1.

_____ "Ich bin erst Antifaschist, dann Skinhead," December 14, 1992; 23.

Tagesspiegel, der, "Ein Verbot von Neonazis muß hieb- und stichfest sein," November 27, 1992.

_____ "Seiters erwägt auch eine Einschränkung der Grundrechte," November 29, 1992.

_____ "Justizministerin: Rechtsextreme Texte und Embleme verbieten," December 2, 1992.

_____ "Die Listen der Opfer waren schon vorbereitet," December 6, 1992.

Teuscher, S. "Projektwoche an der Urspringschule in Schelklingen," *Hakenkreuze auf der Schulbank: Berichte, Fragen, Gegenstrategien; Beiträge einer Tagung Bad Boll,* epd Dokumentation; GEP Vertrieb: Frankfurt am Main; 1991; 73-80.

Thuillier, B. "Das Leben eines Schwarzen bedeutet nichts," *Frankfurter Allgemeine Zeitung,* August 26, 1992.

Verfassungsschutz Bericht 1991, Bundesminister des Innern: Bonn, 9/1992.

von Zglinicki, C. & E. Berthold, "Der Nationalsozialarbeiter," *Wochenpost,* #19; 4/29/92; 4-5.

Wagner, B. "Polizei und Rechtsextremismus," *Jugend und Rechtsextremismus in Berlin-Ost,* Magistratsverwaltung für Jugend, Familie und Sport: Berlin, 1991, 51-54.

Welt, die, "Weitere Schritte gegen Rechte," November 30, 1992.

_____ "16 Monate Gefängnis für Neonazi Thorsten de Vries," November 27, 1992.

_____ "Bewährungsstrafe für 'Hitlergruß' und 'Sieg Heil' Ruf," December 5, 1992.

Wippermann, W. "Neofaschismus in Vergangenheit und Gegenwart," *Materialiensammlung: Jugendarbeit gegen Rechtsextremismus,* Senatsverwaltung für Frauen, Jugend und Familie: Berlin, 1990, 3-7.

Winkler, B. "Spannungsfelder des Zusammenlebens," *Zukunftsangst Einwanderung,* Verlag C.H. Beck: München, 1992; 61-90.

Wolowicz, E. "Rechtsextremismus am Ende der 80er und Anfang der 90er Jahre—Eine Analyse der aktuellen Situation und ihre Entwicklungstendenzen," *Rechtsextremismus und Ausländerfeindlichkeit: eine Herausforderung für die Jugendarbeit,* Kreisjugendright München-Stadt, February, 1990; 50-65.

Zeitungsprojekt antirassistischer and antifaschistischer Gruppen, *Rechtsextreme Übergriffe,* DGB Antifa Gruppe: Berlin, February 1992, pp.30-33.

Zirk, W. "Gruppengewalt," *Berliner Anwaltsblatt,* Heft 1-2/1992; 9-16.

3

Legal Reactions to Racism: Law and Practice in Scandinavia

Tore Björgo
The Norwegian Institute of International Affairs

In the relatively homogenous Scandinavian countries of Sweden, Norway, and Denmark, racist harassment and violence also have become increasing problems, mainly as reactions to the rise in the number of asylum-seekers since the mid-1980s.[1] What legal measures have been taken to counteract these racist tendencies, and how do they work in practice? Is existing legislation adequate to handle racist violence and harassment, in both its organized and unorganized forms? Do the police and the prosecuting authorities make use of the legal means at their disposal to fight racism? If not, why?

RACIAL DISCRIMINATION AND AGITATION

All three Scandinavian countries have ratified the United Nations International Convention on the Elimination of all Forms of Racial Discrimination (CERD) and have committed themselves to complying with its provisions. These include prohibition of all forms of racial discrimination and racist statements as well as a more controversial ban against racist organizations (see Appendix for text of the relevant clause in the Convention).[2]

To fulfill these provisions, Norway, Sweden, and Denmark have adopted legislation to prevent discrimination and racist statements and agitation against ethnic groups. Thus, Sec. 135a of Norway's Criminal Code provides that:

> Any person shall be liable to fines or to imprisonment for a
> term not exceeding 2 years who by any utterance or communication
> made publicly or disseminated among the public threatens,
> insults, or subjects to hatred, persecution or contempt any per-
> son or group of persons because of their religion, race, colour,
> or national or ethnic origin [...] The same shall apply to any
> person who instigates or is otherwise accessory to any action men-
> tioned in the first paragraph.

Sec. 266b of Denmark's Criminal Code and Ch. 16 Sec. 8 of Sweden's Criminal Code have similar provisions. In addition, Sweden has included provisions in its Freedom of the Press Ordinance (Ch. 7, Sec. 4,11) banning media defamation against any ethnic group. Penalties in all three countries range from fines to two years' imprisonment. This Swedish provision was amended in 1989 to make it an offense to spread racist propaganda even within the confines of organizations and other restricted groups, and not only to the general public.[3]

Nevertheless, in Norway and Denmark, prosecution and conviction under antidiscrimination and antiharassment legislation have been rare, particularly in recent years. In Norway, several convictions for violation of Sec. 135a of the Penal Code, including four decisions by the Supreme Court, were handed down in the late 1970s and early 1980s. Paradoxically, prosecution under this provision has been rare after the mid 1980s—even though racism and xenophobia have become a more serious problem than before. Between 1982 and 1989 as many as 500 complaints of racism may have been filed in Norway without subsequent prosecution.[4] Many of these complaints concerned leaflets and statements of a far more grave nature than those resulting in conviction a few years earlier. In what appears to be the only case after 1984 where anyone was convicted in Norway for violation of the ban on racism,[5] a petty criminal youth gang hurled a burning cross at the wall of a store owned by an immigrant in 1988. The municipal court decision was remarkable in that it considered cross burning—well known as a ritualistic act of the Ku Klux Klan in the southern United States—to be a type of "statement" or "expression of opinion." In Sweden several convictions have been handed down for cross-burning as representing a violation of the ban on agitation against ethnic groups.

In Denmark too, racism and ethnic denigration appear to have become more common and explicit after the mid 1980s, but also there the prosecuting authorities and the police in recent years have refrained from criminal proceedings. More than 100 complaints have been dismissed, often without any investigation. When *Danmarks Nationalsocialistiske Bevægelse* (Denmark's National Socialist Movement, DNSB) was charged with making extremely malicious statements about Danish Jews who were mentioned by name, the case was dropped after being referred to the Minister of Justice. The somewhat far-fetched reason given was that section 266b of the Criminal Code related to statement directed against "groups of persons," whereas this case involved statements about named and well-known Jewish persons as individuals, not as a group.

Neither have virulent statements made by Mogens Glistrup, the founder of *Fremskridtspartiet* (the Progress Party), led to charges and prosecution. One example may serve to indicate the nature of these statements: "Just as our grandparents eradicated tuberculosis and our parents eradicated polio, the national cause for the present generation is to strive purposefully and with determination to make Denmark a country free of Muslims."[6]

The usual explanation for non-application of antiracism legislation, or for very restrictive interpretation of the law, is that there is a contradiction between a ban on certain types of statements, and the constitutional principle of free speech. It appears that prosecuting authorities give freedom of speech priority over protection against racial defamation.

In Denmark we see the paradox of restrictive interpretation of the racism clause becoming a protective shield for anti-immigration groups. In recent years, the clause has hardly ever been applied in line with its original purpose. Quite the contrary, *Den Danske Forening* (The Danish Association, the largest anti-immigrant organization) in several cases has won damages in libel proceedings against individuals, newspapers, and organizations who have claimed that *Den Danske Forening* is a racist organization. Thus, the newspaper *Extrabladet* was sentenced to pay compensation for quoting a member of the European Parliament who spoke of *Den Danske Forening* as being "culturally racist" in a statement from the rostrum. In applying section 266b, Danish courts have used a restrictive interpretation of "racism" based on a traditional, biological concept. By using this narrow definition as a guideline in libel cases as well, the courts to some extent also define what can be called racism in the political debate.

Norwegian law, on the other hand, has been quite restrictive in interpreting its section 135a as anything more than a minimum definition of racism—a definition setting the threshold for what constitutes such a gross level of racism that it qualifies for punishment. In other words, a statement may be racist in a conventional sense without being legally criminal.

In a libel lawsuit brought by an executive member of the Norwegian *Folkebevegelsen Mot Innvandring* (FMI, the People's Movement Against Immigration) against a local newspaper who had called FMI "racist," the Appeals Committee of the Supreme Court refrained from making a decision on whether section 135a may be interpreted to give a general definition of the concept "racism." However, the Appeals Committee did question whether accusing the FMI of racism might at all be seen as libelous.[7] Differences between Norwegian and Danish libel law may explain the different court practice in such cases.

In Sweden, legislation against denigration of ethnic groups (in the Penal Code and the Freedom of Press Ordinance) is used far more actively than in Norway and Denmark. In the period 1990 to 1992 the Chancellor of Law *(Justitiekansleren)*, who is the prosecutor in cases of violation of the Freedom of Press Ordinance (which covers printed material and radio/TV) instituted criminal proceedings in 10 cases out of 161 complaints. Among the accused were the two extreme right-wing organizations *Sverigepartiet* (The Sweden Party) and *Föreningen Sveriges Framtid/ Riksfronten* (The Future of Sweden Association/National Front) and the heavily anti-semitic *Radio Islam.*[8] Most of these cases resulted in convictions. Also, in several instances Public Prosecutors have filed indictments for breeches of Penal Code provisions on forms of agitation other than statements in print/radio/TV—for instance, cross-burning. However, even in Sweden, legislation on agitation against ethnic groups is relatively infrequently applied, particularly in view of the widespread racist activity that does *not* result in prosecution and conviction. Police and pros- ecution practice seem to vary considerably from district to district. Nevertheless, Swedish authorities and the prosecution appear to have been more actively engaged in mat- ters of racism and application of anti-racist legislation than has been the case in Norway and in Denmark. Thus, Sweden has a special *Diskrimineringsombud* (Discrimination Commissioner), with a secretariat to follow up concrete violations, and to take the initiative in general questions of racism. In Norway, because of specific events (a riot against anti-racist demonstrators instigated by anti-immigrant activists), the government has focused increasingly on this issue since 1991.

Discrepancies in the implementation of legislation on racism can partly be explained in terms of the fact that Sweden has more extreme racist groups than is the case in Norway and Denmark. Nevertheless, this cannot fully explain the major differences in application of the law.

Even if laws against racism are rarely applied in Norway and Denmark, the mere fact that these laws exist may nevertheless have a certain preventive effect. On the other hand, we may expect this effect to be weakened, the longer it is since the last time the provisions were used to ascertain the limits of the acceptable. To have a deter- rent effect, a threat must remain credible.

BAN ON RACIST ORGANIZATIONS?

The most controversial provision in the United Nations Convention on Elimination of all Forms of Racial Discrimination (CERD) is probably the obliga- tion of all signatory parties to ban racist organizations. The Scandinavian countries have been hesitant to follow upon this directly, although some aspects are covered indirectly by existing legislation, to a varying extent.

In Sweden, official commissions have delivered reports on legislation and on the extent of racist offenses. Several reports have proposed a ban on racist organi- zations. So far these proposals have not won political approval in *Riksdagen* (the Swedish Parliament), mainly because the constitutional right to freedom of orga- nization has been invoked. However, after the CERD Committee had repeatedly crit- icized Sweden's failure to ban racist organizations, a committee chaired by the Chancellor of Law *(Justisiekansler)* Hans Stark, presenting its report on "Organized Racism" in September 1991, proposed a ban on organizations involved in violent harassment:

> Anyone belonging to an organization which, by participating in, or inciting to, criminal offence involving violence, threat or coercion amounting to persecution of an ethnic group or other group of persons because of race, colour, national or ethnic origin or faith, shall be sentenced to fines or imprisonment of no longer than two years for organized racism. The same shall apply to anyone establishing an organization for the purpose of inciting to such persecution.
>
> Anyone leasing premises or giving economic or other support to an organization as described in the paragraph above shall be liable to the same sentence for support of organized racism. (Proposed new Ch 16 sec 7 in *Brottsbalken* (the Criminal Code).

The proposal is interesting in that it is directed against associations committing racist offenses involving violence, threat, or coercion—not against an association's racist orientation as such. In other words, actions and not opinions are to be the basis for prohibiting membership in or support of such organizations. Using violence and intimidation to promote racist views cannot in any case be defended as exercise of a democratic right. A more controversial part of the proposal is that it would make any form of support of such organizations a legal offense. According to the committee report (pp. 118-120) this includes not only passive membership in such organizations, but wearing an organization's label pin, leasing premises to it, or even buying its propaganda material. At present, it is still uncertain whether the proposed law banning violent racist organizations will pass the *Riksdag*.[9]

Denmark is the only Scandinavian country that may be seen as complying with the United Nations Convention on this point, at least formally. The Danish Constitution too emphasizes the freedom "to establish associations for any legal purpose without prior permit" (Sec. 78), but freedom of association does not include a right to establish association for unlawful purposes. Any act or activity that is prohibited for individuals is also prohibited for associations. Thus, an association with racist activity as its *purpose* may be dissolved. A single instance of violation of Sec. 266b of the Penal Code on Racism, on the other hand, does not call for dissolution. In practice, there has been no interference with racist associations since the end of the 1940s. An organization like *Denmark's National Socialist Movement* (DNSB), which has called for a "racially pure Denmark," does not seem to have been deterred by this rather sleeping provision. The Danish Constitution also allows dissolution of associations that pursue their goal through violence or incitement to violence. Neither has this provision been applied to racist organizations. However, organized racist violence has not so far been as much of a problem in Denmark as it has in Norway and Sweden.[10] Most of the organizations on the far Right in Denmark appear more concerned about maintaining an image of respectability. Links to violent groups have been disclosed on several occasions, but evidence of more direct involvement is meager.

In Norway, freedom of association is not inscribed in the Constitution, but secured through constitutional practice. Norwegian law does not provide for dissolution per se of political or racist organizations, nor does it ban participation in such groups. On the other hand, there are severe provisions against anyone establishing, participating in, or supporting "a private organization of military character," especially if the organization maintains supplies of weapons or explosives, or if its "aim is to disturb the social order or to obtain influence in public affairs by sabotage, the use of force or other illegal means" (Penal Code Sec. 104a). There is also penalty for any person "who establishes or participates in any association that is prohibited by law, or whose purpose is the commission or encouragement of offenses, or whose members pledge themselves to unconditional obedience to any person" (Penal Code Sec. 330). This latter provision has not been applied in practice. Today there is no "association that is prohibited by law," nor is there any authority in law to prohibit associations. However, nothing prevents the *Storting* (Norway's Parliament) from adopting a law to prohibit specifically named organizations that are involved in unlawful activities. In connection with the treason trials after the Second World War, it was established that membership in Vidkun Quisling's fascist party, *Nasjonal Samling* (National Unity) after April 8, 1940 was a crime—but that was because the party had aided and abetted the German occupying forces, and not because of its ideology.[11]

A committee appointed in 1990 by the Norwegian Ministry of Justice to make recommendations on whether there was a need for special legal provisions against terrorism advised *against* banning organizations on the basis of their ideologies or opinions. An outright ban on neo-Nazi organizations was considered countrary to democratic principles; furthermore, it would actually make it more difficult to fight neo-Nazi tendencies, it was argued. Existing legislation was considered adequate to handle organized political violence and similar offenses.[12]

A ban on political organizations, such as neo-Nazi parties, has not been on the political agenda in Norway after the second half of the 1970s, when *Norsk Front* (Norwegian Front) was highly active. At that time the Labor Government declined to propose a ban on opinions and parties.[13] Instead, the Government attempted to prevent *Norsk Front* from registering as a political party—even if this was not explicitly admitted. Several registration applications were turned down on strictly formal and sometimes dubious grounds—insofar as two left-wing parties had recently been allowed to register with less stringent application of formal requirements. Furthermore, in 1976 requirements in the Election Code for registration of parties were tightened by increasing the requisite number of individual signatories from 1,000 to 3,000. *Norsk Front* would not be able to meet this requirement; and consequently the group had to relinquish hopes of participation in the political process through election. According to a leading NF-activist, this caused *Norsk Front* to start the "underground struggle" that was to lead to the bombings on May 1, 1979, when a NF activist threw two small bombs at left-wing demonstrators.[14]

Various arguments have been advanced both in support of and against an outright ban on racist organizations:

One main line of argumentation in favor of such a ban is that prohibiting organizations that promote racism and racist violence will act as a powerful signal that the State will not tolerate such incursions on the fundamental rights of minority groups in society. The criminalization of racist organizations will also be an effective means to bring such activities to an end, it is claimed.

A more formalistic argument raised in favor of adopting such legislation is that when a country has signed the United Nations Convention calling for a ban on racist organizations (CERD), it is also obliged to implement such a ban. In the report from the Stark Commission in Sweden, it is apparent that the proposal to ban violent racist organizations is motivated more by a desire to comply with international obligations than by a belief that banning such organizations is necessarily the best means of suppressing racism and racist violence.[15]

When arguing before the United Nations CERD Committee that it is not necessary to adopt a legal ban on racist organizations, the Scandinavian countries generally have claimed that existing legislation prohibiting agitation against ethnic groups makes it impossible for racist organizations to function at all. In view of the very limited application of this legislation in the judicial system, however, this argument hardly seems tenable.

The main ideological argument against banning racist organizations is that this runs counter to the right to freedom of association, which is a fundamental part of the democratic system. Consequently, limitation of that freedom could be seen as a defeat of democracy. It is better that such attitudes are exposed to the light of day and countered in public debate, rather than being suppressed by bans and threats of punishment, it is argued.[16] A ban on one type of organization could also result in demands for a prohibition against other organizations that regularly violate legal provisions, such as activist environmental groups or leftist revolutionary organizations. Counter to this, one may argue that *all* basic rights in society will have to be balanced against other basic rights that serve to protect citizens from ruthlessness and harassment.

A more pragmatic argument against prohibiting extremist political organizations is that it—despite the good intentions of fighting racism—would probably prove counterproductive or have negative side effects that outweigh the positive ones. By preventing undesirable views from being voiced in public, and by preventing radical groups from participating in the normal political system, one may create a "pressure-cooker effect"—with an explosion once the steam has no outlet. There is a risk that such restrictions may drive undesirable political groups underground and lead to acts of terrorism instead of open political activity.

In this regard, we may cite the case of *Norsk Front*, described briefly above. Although the organization was not formally banned, it turned to violence and terrorism after it had been effectively prevented—by somewhat dubious methods—from taking part in the democratic process of parliamentary election.

Counter to this, it may be argued that by being precluded—by banning or not—from achieving the legitimization implicit in participation in parliamentary elections along with normal parties, this fascist grouping was not able to build itself into a seemingly "respectable" political force with a mass basis—as Jean Marie Le Pens' *National Front* had done in France and Franz Schönhuber's *Die Republikaner* in Germany.

The Netherlands—which in terms of political culture is quite similar to the Scandinavian countries—has had quite a positive experience with legislation prohibiting political organizations that advocate national socialism and racism. The Dutch ban has been particularly effective against parties and organizations that seek mass support, and desire to act in the public political arena. For these organizations the threat of being labeled Nazi and being ordered to dissolve has led them into a precarious balancing act. Time and again this has resulted in internal splits between "radicals" who feel that the party or organization is compromising its ideological principles so much as to become indistinguishable from the mainstream, and "moderates" who fear that the organization will be discredited and prohibited for being Nazi. The threat of banning and fear of being criminalized is more important than the actual banning.[17] But this, of course, will depend on the credibility of the threat.

On the other hand, there is ample reason to believe that criminalizing an organization and branding it as racist or Nazi will have a rather different effect on political parties seeking mass support, and on militant, elitist groups that base their political strategy on violence and terrorism.

To political parties like *Sverigedemokraterna* or *Nationalpartiet Danmark*, a ban would mean an absolutely devastating blow to their efforts to win legitimacy and mass electoral support. A credible threat of banning, or of being convicted for racist incitement, would also serve to keep their racism within bounds and prevent it from being expressed openly. However, once a party has been able to establish a base of mass support, such as *National Front* or *Die Republikaner*, it may be too late to ban the party without causing a major political turmoil and possibly alienating a large section of the electorate from the democratic system. At an earlier stage, however, a ban—or the mere threat of a ban—will in most cases be an effective measure. Even large and established parties can be hit by legislation against racist incitement or similar provisions. Le Pen was badly damaged politically when he was convicted and fined heavily for making remarks that denigrated the magnitude of the Nazi Holocaust of the Jews.[18]

In organizations on the far right there is often disagreement between those who wish primarily to work politically and those who seek a more militant course. Rigid restriction of the opportunity to participate in "normal" political activity could lend support to actionist and violent elements. Although potentially very effective against political parties, criminalization may not have the same preventive effect upon more informal and violence-oriented organizations and groups that act underground and do not care whether they may be branded as Nazi or racist. Such groups tend to have a loose network structure, often based on friendship rather than formal membership. Obviously, it is easier to ban a formal organization than a network of old pals. A ban may, however, make it possible to prosecute the leaders and members of such organizations in cases where it is not possible to produce evidence linking them directly to specific acts of violence perpetrated by members of their group.

In Germany, four militant German neo-Nazi organizations were banned in December 1992 and January 1993 after a series of vicious terrorist attacks and pogroms against foreigners. A firebombing in Mölln, killing a Turkish woman and two girls, shocked the German public sufficiently to force the authorities to take drastic action against violent groups on the far right. At the time of writing, the number of violent actions against immigrant and asylum-seekers has been reduced, and the extremist organizations seem to be keeping a lower profile. However, it remains to be seen what the long-term effects of the bannings will be. The German police and courts apparently find it very difficult to apply against violent right-wing groups the far-reaching anti-terrorism legislation which was implemented and used with such a great force against the left-wing *Rote Armee Fraktion* during the 1970s. The main reason is that the right-wing extremist groups behind some of the racist violence are much looser and more informally organized than their terrorist counterparts on the far left.[19] If they are banned, they tend to reemerge under another name. Like in Scandinavia, much of the racist violence in Germany is carried out by people who are not members of organizations.

THE PROBLEM OF BANNING: THE CASE OF "VITT ARISKT MOTSTÅND"

A closer look at a militant racist group such as Sweden's *"Vitt Ariskt Motstånd"* (VAM, "White Aryan Resistance")[20] may enable us to evaluate the potential effects of a ban like that proposed by the Stark Commission. VAM is not a formal organization but rather a network consisting of a core of trusted activists of about 50, with wider circles of some 500 to 600 activists and supporters. The latter are involved mainly in VAM's open propaganda activities, such as selling the magazine *Storm* and taking part in demonstrations. The core activists, most of whom are friends who have been active together on the extreme right scene for many years, are directing VAM's open activity, but are also responsible for the illegal and secret part of its activities. This involves weapons thefts, bank robberies, intelligence, and probably also other actions of a more terrorist nature. However, associates in the outer circle at times also carry out violent actions on their own, most of the time probably without any direct orders or clearance from above. There are also "freelancers" who carry out violent acts in the name of VAM, but are not really part of the network. They act without any approval of the organization. According to inside sources, these uncontrollable "psychopaths and nuts" cause VAM much trouble.

VAM propagates a virulent and violent form of racism, based on national socialist ideology, and ideas and concepts imported from United States racist movements, such as Aryan Nations, Ku Klux Klan and the White Aryan Resistance. Their main role model is a United States terrorist organization, The Order, and its fictional predecessor in the ideological novel *The Turner Diaries*.[21] A central concept is the notion of the "Zionist Occupation Government" and its lackeys, whose aim is said to be the destruction of the white race by promoting immigration and race-mixing. According to this ideology, it is therefore necessary to conduct an all-out "racial war" to annihilate "traitors and defilers of the race," to cleanse the white race of impurities (including people of mixed race and homosexuals) and, ultimately, to make the world inhabited by Aryans only. This "racial war" is to be fought in the fields of birthrates, propaganda, and armed struggle.

At the present stage, VAM activists claim to be preparing for the armed stage of the "racial war" by focusing their actions on bank robberies and weapons thefts— a series of which have been carried out with varying degrees of success. As of January 1993, no less than 23 VAM activists are under arrest, some sentenced to four to six years in prison. However, many of the key activists are still at large. More important, large parts of the network are gradually cutting their ties to society and going underground.

If the proposed law-banning organizations engaging in or inciting to violence against ethnic minorities were implemented, what would be the likely effects on a group like VAM?

This possibility has been discussed in VAM's own internal and external magazines, newsletters and ideological writings. One of VAM's main leaders comments from prison, where he is jailed for bank robberies, on the proposals of banning in the VAM magazine *Storm* (1991:5-6):

> There are two proposals to a ban. 1. A ban against "racist organizations." 2. A ban against membership in "racist organizations" (which may give two years in prison).

> [...] What will this "ban" really mean to our noble struggle? [...] Which of the two proposals they chose does not really matter. It will have about the same consequences. Will it stop VAM, or make us "play down" our message and become "respectable"? *Definitely not!* It will neither stop us nor make us become the "racist poodles" of society. The only difference is that we will have to take the network "underground." Others have succeeded, then we can succeed here!

> Could this ban even be useful to us? *Certainly!* At least a part of the population would then have their eyes opened to see the repression under which we are forced to live! The repression which goes under the name "democracy". [...]

> But will not many [activists] defect because of fear? I do not believe many will defect. Some might. But do we really need such weaklings? [No! ...] *Militant activists* will take the places of these cowards. [...] Remember that it is better to have a small but hard group, than a large and weak one. (Signed: Christopher Ragne, ZOG Gulag in Östersund).

The consensus appears to be that VAM would not be particularly damaged by such a ban, and some would even *welcome* a ban. A ban would imply the immediate start of the underground, armed stage of the "racial war" for which they have been preparing. The defection of "soft" members in the face of a ban is seen as a positive cleansing in terms of their elitist ideology. It is also sometimes argued that a ban would mean more *political* trials, rather than the almost purely criminal proceedings VAM members have been subjected to until now. Thus, a ban would sharpen polarization and confrontation with the "Zionist Occupation Government," which is one of VAM's political goals.

Clouded as these arguments may be by ideology and wishful thinking, it is nevertheless clear that there is little deterrent effect in the proposed ban. Criminalizing membership in such an organization might slow down recruitment and keep some individuals away, but the hard-core members would probably become tougher and more extremist in their illegal operations. It seems quite inconceivable that the most strongly motivated ideologs in the circle around the periodical *Storm* or such organizations as VAM could be pacified by a legal ban, or that they would become more moderate in order to stay within the limits of law. These leaders are revolutionaries who have more or less grown up in extreme rightist circles, and have declared war on what they term "ZOG." They have already taken the step into illegality, with most of them having several convictions for violence and other offenses on their records. Indeed, from their ideological point of view, social stigmatization is desirable.

On the other hand, a ban against the organization would give the police a legal tool to strike against known VAM leaders and activists—people who so far have gone free because it has not been possible to link them to specific criminal offenses. It is a problem that VAM has been set up more as a network of friends than as a formal organization with membership records. However, in the course of its two years of operation, VAM has increasingly acquired sufficient organizational structures to make it possible to ban.

One important argument against a ban is that as long as VAM is allowed to engage in some open activity through publications and meetings, it is possible to keep an eye on their activity, support, and development. A ban would reduce the opportunity to monitor their activities, without necessarily bringing their racist publications to an end. These would get a more limited circulation, and be harder to obtain for outsiders such as journalists, researchers, and the police. On the other hand, banning may also limit their opportunity to reach a wider audience of possible recruits.

It is possible that a ban would force VAM to reorganize to such a degree that its activities will be seriously hampered for an extended period. It is more likely, however, that a ban would cause large parts of the network immediately to take a further step into illegality by going underground and increasing their more direct terrorist activities. Such a terrorist campaign is not likely to last long, but it might well prove to be costly in terms of human lives. VAM's partly cell-based organizational structure has been chosen for the purpose of surviving a ban. The Swedish police do, however, appear to have reasonably good intelligence on who the activists are, and would probably be able to round up most of the network relatively fast. Although there is no question about the extremism and dedication of VAM activists, some of their previous actions have been marred by blunders. VAM may score high on *intention* to carry out large-scale terrorist violence, but low to moderate on *capability* to carry out such operations.

Thus, the effects of banning organizations will depend largely on the type of organization in question. Political parties seeking mass electoral support and legitimacy within the political system may very effectively be disbanded and discredited by a ban. In most cases, the mere threat of a ban against organizations promoting racism will suffice to keep them within bounds—at least as long as the threat is seen as credible. On the negative side, there is a danger that banning a political party will serve to alienate parts of its electorate from the democratic system, and possibly cause them to join more extreme groupings.

From the viewpoint of democracy, banning militant groups that attempt to pursue racist aims through violence, threats, or coercion against persons or property is less problematic, but the effects of a ban are less certain. A ban will have little or no deterrent effect on others than the less dedicated members. Groups already prepared to move their members and activities underground may survive relatively intact, at least for a while. In such cases, they will be much more difficult to monitor than before. There is also a sizable risk that they may step up their terrorist activities, perhaps with high tolls in terms of human life. On the other hand, a ban on such organizations will give the police the legal tools necessary to arrest and persecute leaders and activists who cannot be linked directly to specific criminal acts. However, experience from Germany indicates that many violent groups on the far Right may have such elusive organizational structures that they are impossible to ban effectively.

UNORGANIZED RACISM

A common misconception sometimes held by the police and the prosecuting authorities is that racism and racist violence are normally associated with explicit and clearly elaborated racist ideologies and membership in right-wing organizations. Several studies from different European countries show that this is generally not the case.[22] Although right-wing and anti-immigrant organizations are behind most of the racist propaganda, day-to-day harassment and violence is in most cases carried out by unorganized perpetrators.

In Scandinavia, most violent attacks on asylum reception centers, immigrant-owned shops and similar targets have been committed by local youth gangs *not* affiliated to racist or right-wing organizations. They "don't like foreigners," and may employ racist slogans and symbols, but they generally lack any formulated racist or political ideology. In many cases, these gangs have been feared and despised in the local community for their random violence and criminality. However, they sometimes discover that by turning their violent aggression against the unpopular "foreigners," they can win support and prestige from other young people in the community—and even from some adults. By carrying out spectacular acts of violence, such as throwing dynamite or firebombs, they make the headlines in both the local and the national news media. To achieve such media coverage can even be one of the motives for the action. In their own eyes—and of a few others as well—they have become local heroes. The media tend to describe them as dangerous racists and neo-Nazis, and sometimes even give them a name and an image to live up to, such as "The Clan" or "The Green Jackets." Although they may have been unorganized when they carried out the actions, at a later stage these gangs are regularly contacted—and sometimes recruited—by racist organizations.

A closer examination of the circumstances leading up to firebombings and dynamite attacks also reveals several other motives and factors than just "racism" which influence the course of events. A recurring feature is that a group of young men are having a drinking party. During their drunken discussion the issue of immigrants arises. Everyone agrees as to their negative influence, often citing arguments propagated by anti-immigrant organizations. Someone then suggests a violent action against a symbol of the despised foreigners, often getting the idea from a similar action recently covered in the news media. There is often an implicit contest among the participants to outdo each other in reckless proposals, together with the desire to show off—especially from the new and marginal members of the gang, whose status within the group is not firmly established. They promptly put together a simple firebomb or explosive charge, and carry out the action. A good measure of booze acts to quell any second thoughts.

Thus, internal group dynamics and a competition to express and fulfill central values in gang culture seem central in determining the course of events that lead up to acts of violence. When these group factors are combined with a prevalent hostility against immigrants and asylum-seekers, such violent tendencies take a specific direction.

Violent actions may not just give prestige to individual perpetrators in relation to the rest of the group. When criminal youth gangs direct their violence and harassment towards unpopular "foreigners," the group as a whole often experiences a dramatic change in social status in the eyes of the community. From being a bunch of nobodies, group members become *something*: dangerous racists and neo-Nazis in the eyes of some, local heroes and patriots in the eyes of others.[23]

RACIALLY MOTIVATED VIOLENCE

Norwegian law has established racist motive as an independent aggravating circumstance in certain types of violence. An amendment in 1989 to sec. 232 in the Penal Code increased the maximum sentence by three years. Here it is stated:

> ... In deciding whether other especially aggravating circumstances exist, special regard shall be paid to whether the offence has been committed against a defenceless person, whether there was a racial motive, whether it was unprovoked, whether it was committed by several persons acting together, and whether it constitutes molestation.

Sec. 232 deals with assault and battery of persons, and normally will not include racially motivated damage of property, bombings, arson, or similar acts where persons are not physically injured. However, in serious cases such acts may be seen as attempted assault and thus fall within the purview of sec. 232. Amendments have also been made to Penal Code sec. 222 on coercion and to sec. 227 on threats. In both instances, maximum sentence may be increased by three years if a crime is committed under especially aggravating circumstances. Racist motive is listed as one such aggravating circumstance. The preparatory works on sec. 232 on serious assault state:

> 1.5.3. Secondly, racially motivated violence generally should be regarded as an especially aggravating circumstance. Racism here is used as a collective term for humiliating or hostile attitudes toward persons or groups on the basis of race, colour or national or ethnic origin.

> The reason for including racially motivated violence in this connection is a need to emphasize that public authorities take a very serious view of offences that have been directed against immigrants, asylum applicants and refugees from Third World countries. The provision may also be important in connection with violence directed e.g., against the Sami people [the indigenous minority in Norway].

> It may be argued that it may be difficult to prove ex post facto what was the real psychological motivating force behind such acts as beating and kicking. This is true if the violent act is the only base for judgment. However, physical violence will often be accompanied by verbal exclamations that will make it easier to determine if there was a racist motive. Moreover, it is

not decisive that racism is the only motive of the act—one may
find cases where racism has been prevalent and clearly has left
its mark on the offence. (From the Department of Justice preparatory document of February 10, 1989 on legal measures to combat violent crime.)

This document provides guidelines to the courts in the interpretation of this provision. In principle racism is here defined in the same manner as in the "racism clause"
sec. 135a. The intention of establishing racism as an aggravating circumstance in
violent crime was undoubtedly to cover such cases as when someone criticizes a person because he "does not like foreigners," "they take our jobs" or similar reasons—
in cases not necessarily motivated by specific reference to e.g., race or color. As discussed
above, sec. 135a has been rarely and restrictively applied in Norway. A main reason for this is that the prohibition of racist statements has to some degree been
seen as conflicting with the constitutional principle of freedom of expression.
However, such conflict with freedom of expression cannot be invoked in cases of
racist violence. Consequently, we may expect that the courts will lower the threshold for defining acts of violence as racist, in comparison with the case of verbal or
written statements.[24]

If the provision is to serve as an effective instrument for prosecuting racially
motivated violence, it should be defined in terms of acts of violence where the victims are targeted because they are "foreigners" or members of ethnic, racial, religious, or cultural minorities. Victims are attacked not in their capacity of individuals,
but as representatives of such minorities. Such a definition of "racially motivated
violence" does not presuppose that the perpetrator subscribes to any formulated racist
ideology. Rather, the decisive factor should be whether the attack was fully or
partly motivated by a general dislike for this category of people.

Current Danish and Swedish law lacks comparable provisions concerning
racially motivated violence. However, the Swedish Stark committee examining
"organized racism" has proposed the introduction of a similar provision for increased
penalty for racial motivation and racist elements in crime.[25]Unlike the Norwegian
provision, this proposal is not limited to violent crime, but includes criminal damage to property.

Police Handling of Racially Motivated Violence

The main problem may not be lack of legal means to combat racially motivated
violence, but rather lack of will from the local police to confront it as such, or lack
of understanding of the phenomenon.

In Norway, there has been a clear policy from the Director General of Public
Prosecution to give priority to the investigation of such offenses, and to apply the
provisions concerning racist motives. He has repeatedly instructed police chiefs that
investigation of racially motivated mistreatment and arson are to have priority.

This applies also when "the individual act per se is not very serious, but when several acts together will be threatening to such degree that the offense must be included on the list of priorities." On this basis the Director General instructed "police and the prosecuting authority to thoroughly and consistently pursue all illegal acts that may appear to be racially motivated."[26]

Implementation of these instructions appears to have varied, however. In some regions, police headquarters and local police do regard racist violence and attack on foreigners as a very serious matter. Thus, the police in Hamar used the trial resulting from a series of violent attacks on an immigrant-owned store in the small town of Brumunddal in 1987/88 to take on an open confrontation with racist violence and condemnation of racist attitudes motivating violence.

In other districts, police still seem to prefer to treat attacks on immigrants on equal terms with other "ordinary" crimes of violence. Such acts of violence have been dealt with as isolated cases, and possible racist or political connections and dimensions have been played down. In many cases the police have been very quick to state that a particular act of violence against an immigrant or a dynamite attack on a reception center for asylum-seekers has nothing to do with racism or politics. In such connections, "boyish tricks and drunken pranks" have much been used as characterizations. In the course of the first three years after the new provisions concerning racially motivated violence were introduced in 1989, these provisions have been applied only in a few cases.

There may be several reasons for the police to tone down and show little interest in investigating possible racist motives. A desire not to provoke copycat actions, and to prevent violent groups from gaining prestige through media coverage and presentation of the event as being "political" may to some extent explain the way the police handle such matters. Furthermore, it may be difficult to find sufficient legal evidence that a criminal act is racially motivated in a legal sense. Experience from the implementation of similar legislation in the United States has shown that it is very difficult to prove such motives in court. Motives are buried in the culprit's psyche, character, and beliefs. As James Morsch argues, "when the accused's action clearly suggests only one explanation, racial motivation, prosecutors may have a decent chance of securing a conviction of hate crime. Conversely, when circumstantial evidence indicates the existence of mixed motives, the prosecutor's burden of proof can be nearly impossible."[27] My own research findings on racist violence in Scandinavia referred to above indicate that mixed motives are the rule rather than the exception. However, at least in the Norwegian provisions concerning racially motivated violence, the existence of several simultaneous motives should not preclude a conviction where a racist motive is considered an aggravating circumstance.

Nevertheless, the police seem to prefer to concentrate on other aspects of the case where it may be less difficult to secure a conviction, or simply to drop the case due to lack of investigation capacity. In cases where the police have been quick to deny that acts of violence have been racially or politically motivated—often before any real investigation has been carried out—concern for the reputation of the local community seems to have been a major factor. An indicator of this is that police spokesmen have often argued that "there isn't any more racism here than other places."

Moreover, the police are trained to be nonpolitical. Generally this will be an advantage in a democratic society, but it may be a handicap in investigations if police are blind to the fact that some criminal acts do in fact take place in political contexts (e.g., opposition to immigration).

It would be most unfortunate if, for these reasons, police and prosecution should refrain from investigating indications that racist motives and xenophobia may motivate specific acts of violence. If this comes to pass, the new provision that has made racist motivation an aggravating circumstance in cases of violence may easily be reduced to a sleeping provision only.

APPENDIX

The central clause in the United Nations Convention on the Elimination of all Forms of Racial Discrimination (CERD) of 1963 (revised in 1978) is Article 4:

> State Parties condemn all propaganda and all organizations which are based on ideas or theories of superiority of one race or group of persons of one colour or ethnic origin, or which attempt to justify or promote racial hatred and discrimination in any form." They undertook to adopt "immediate and positive measures ... to eradicate all incitement to, or acts of, such discrimination." To this end they would take the following measures:
>
> (i) Declare as an offence punishable by law "all dissemination of ideas based on racial superiority or hatred, or incitement to racial discrimination, as well as all acts of violence or incitement to such acts against any group of persons of another colour or ethnic origin."
>
> (ii) Declare illegal and prohibit "organizations, and also all propaganda activities, which promote and incite racial discrimination." Participation in such organizations and activities would constitute an offence punishable by law.
>
> (iii) Not permit public authorities or public institutions, national or local, to promote or incite racial discrimination.

By the end of 1992 this Convention had been ratified by 132 countries. Unlike almost all other Western democracies, the USA has not ratified the convention, but merely signed it. Article 4 was considered to be in conflict with the Constitutional right to free speech.[28]

NOTES

1 This study is part of a research project on racist violence in Scandinavia, financed by the Norwegian Research Council for Applied Social Research (NORAS).

2 The standard work on the CERD is Natan Lerner: *The United Nations Convention on the Elimination of all Forms of Racial Discrimination* (Alphen aan den Rijn: Sijthoff & Noordhoff, 1980). A more recent work is Sandra Coliver (ed.): *Striking a Balance: Hate Speech, Freedom of Expression and Non-Discrimination* (Human Rights Centre, University of Essex, 1992).

3 Cfr. the Swedish public report *Organiserad rasism: EDU:s delbetänkande om Åtgärder mot rasistiska organisationer* (Organized racism: EDU partial report on measures against racist organizations) (*SOU*, 1991: 75), and Gro Nystuen: *Rett mot rett: Rasistiske ytringer og organisasjoner sett i lys av FNs rasediskrimineringskonvensjon* (Right versus Right: Racist statements and organizations in terms of the United Nations Convention against Racial Discrimination) (Oslo: Antirasistisk Senter, 1991), which provide useful information on law and practice.

4 Estimate by Gro Nystuen: *Rett mot rett: Rasistiske ytringer og organisasjoner sett i lys av FNs rasediskrimineringskonvensjon* (Oslo: Antirasistisk Senter, 1991) p. 74.

5 There may have been a few more cases that have not come to the public attention, or where racist harassment was an additional offense and not the major cause for conviction.

6 *Z-Bladet*, November 1990.

7 Supreme Court Appeal Committee (October 8, 1987) overruled a decision by the Municipal Court of Senja, Norway. In the new trial in the Municipal Court the newspaper editor was also acquitted for libel.

8 This local radio station in Stockholm was closed down in 1992 after lengthy court proceedings. The director of the local radio, Ahmed Rami, a Moroccan who is a leading historical revisionist, has close connections with Swedish extreme rightists. Other recent convictions concern material produced by the strongly racist *Kreativistens Kyrka* (Church of the Creator)—which promotes violence against "racial enemies."

9 It is, however, not at all certain that this proposal will be adopted by the current nonsocialist government. Generally, the nonsocialist parties in Sweden have been even more skeptical than the Social Democrats to support a ban on such organizations. The present proposal, however, is not as far-reaching as former proposals, which would have banned racial organizations on general grounds.

10 Tore Björgo: "Racist Violence in Scandinavia: Patterns and Motives," in Björgo & Witte (eds.): *Racist Violence in Europe* (Basingstoke: Macmillan, 1993).

11 Vidkun Quisling and 24 other Norwegians were executed for war crimes and treason after World War II. And 46,000 others received convictions for collaboration with the German occupying forces and for membership in the fascist party *Nasjonal Samling* (National Unity), which was banned by the Norwegian government in exile (in London) during the war.

12 *Penal Law provisions in the Suppression of Terrorism*, Norwegian Public Report (*NOU*, 1993:3), pp. 46-47.

13 This was made clear by Prime Minister Oddvar Nordli in *Stortinget* (Norway's Parliament) on May 5, 1976.

14 Quoted by Per Bangsund: *Arvtakerne: Nazisme i Norge etter krigen* (Oslo: Pax, 1984) pp. 163-172.

15 "Organiserad Rasism," *SOU*, 1991, pp. 9-11, 103-106.

16 *NOU*, 1993:3, p. 47.

17 Jaap van Donselaar: "Post-war fascism in the Netherlands," *Crime, Law and Social Change*, No. 19, pp. 87-100, 1993; Donselaar: "The Extreme Right and Racist Violence in the Netherlands," in Björgo & Witte (eds.): *Racist Violence in Europe*, Basingstoke: Macmillan, 1993 (in press).

18 Jean-Marie le Pen was convicted in March 1991, see Glyn Ford: *Fascist Europe: The Rise of Racism and Xenophobia* (London: Pluto Press, 1992), p. xiii.

19 According to *der Spiegel* (pp. 38-39, No. 1, 1993), several judges argue that many of the violent groups who are behind the recent attacks on asylum centers in Germany have very weak structures and do not qualify as "criminal associations" in a legal sense. Even militant right-wing extremists have to be set free if the judges are unable to demonstrate that they have built a firm organization.

20 For a more thorough analysis of VAM, see T. Björgo: "Militant neo-Nazism in Sweden," *Terrorism and Political Violence* (in press).

21 Andrew Macdonald (pseudonym for William L. Pierce, a leading figure in American racism): *The Turner Diaries*, Hillsboro: National Vanguard Books, 1980. A later novel by the same author, *Hunter* (1989), about a man who conducts a series of killings of Jews, blacks, and "racial traitors," is also an important ideological source of inspiration to these groups.

22 Tore Björgo & Rob Witte (eds.): *Racist Violence in Europe* (Basingstoke: Macmillan, 1993), in particular the contributions of Jaap van Donselaar ("The Extreme Right and Violence in the Netherlands"), Tore Björgo ("Terrorist Violence against immigrants and Refugees in Scandinavia: Patterns and Motives" and "Role of the Media in Racist Violence"), Erik Jensen: ("International Nazi Cooperation: A Terrorist Oriented Network"), Heléne Lööw ("The Cult of Violence—The Swedish Racist Counter-Culture") and John Klier ("The Pogrom Tradition in Eastern Europe").

23 This process is described in more detail in my two chapters in Björgo & Witte (1993).

24 This assessment is based on conversations with the Director General of Public Procecutions, George Fr. Rieber-Mohn and Assistant Director General Tor-Axel Busch, and an interview with the Director General in *Aftenposten* May 15, 1992.

25 "Organiserad rasism," *SOU* 1991:3, pp. 130-131.

26 From the address of the Director General of Prosecution at the annual meeting of Police Chiefs, 1989.

27 James Morsch: "The Problem of Motive in Hate Crimes: The Argument Against Presumptions of Racial Motivation," *Journal of Criminal Law and Criminology*, Vol 82, No. 3, 1992.

28 See *Hearings Before the Committee on Foreign Relations, U.S. Senate*, November 14-19, 1979 (Washington, DC: U.S. Government Printing Office, 1980), pp. 511-514.

4

Comparing State Responses to Racist Violence in Europe: A Model for International Comparative Analysis

Rob Witte

University of Utrecht—The Netherlands

INTRODUCTION

In the 1970s and 1980s racism and xenophobia increasingly came to the surface in Western Europe. Particularly since the major political and socioeconomic changes in the late 1980s overt racism became part of everyday public life too in Eastern Europe. In addition to political mobilization including a growing support for xenophobic parties, this is clearly indicated by an increase in racist violence all over Europe. This violence is directed at people not as individuals, but as members of more or less clearly identifiable groups (often minorities) within society based on their skin color, religion, national, ethnic, or cultural origin. Nowadays racist violence in Europe is directed especially at immigrants and their descendants, asylum-seekers, Roma-gypsies and Jewish people.

In the 1990s some cases of racist violence attracted international attention, like the racist attacks on African street vendors in Florence, Italy (1990); the desecration of Jewish graves in Carpentras, France (1990); the shootings at asylum-seekers in Sweden (1991-1992); the racist siege of asylum-seekers centers in Hoyerswerda (1991) and Rostock (1992) in Germany; the assassination of immigrants from the Dominican Republic in Spain (1992); and the murderous arson attack in Mölln, Germany (1992). Yet, many racist attacks never reach the international stage of public attention. Neither do most of the violent attacks get national publicity. Nevertheless, there exists an enormous list of examples of racist violence in Europe, from Britain to Russia and from Sweden to Italy.

Although racist violence increasingly came to the surface all over Europe, this does not mean it occurred and developed everywhere in the same way and at the same time. Every country has its specific history, circumstances, developments, and discourses. The same holds true with respect to the racist violence itself. Countries differ with respect to (groups of) perpetrators, to groups of potential victims, and to the responses by various sections of society. Yet, in addition to differences similarities are present too.

In most European countries national and local authorities find themselves confronted with this violence and are forced to formulate policies and to take measures. At first glance, state responses appear very different from one another. This may have all kinds of historical, political, social, and ideological causes. Yet, it is also due to differences in time with respect to the moment(s) racist violence became a prominent social phenomenon in a country. One thing is clear: state responses to racist violence are an important, if not decisive factor with respect to future developments. Will the level and the scale of racist violence increase even more? Or will it decrease? Or will it be regulated in some other way? An international comparative analysis of state responses to racist violence may give a better insight in the variety and the influence of these responses to this violence. Such an analysis should include both similarities and differences of the various states and responses.

There are many ways to execute such an analysis. Often the situation in one country is compared with that in other countries. The first country is used here as a frame of reference. Differences in discourses are often neglected in this way. Yet, these differences are important because other perceptions and definitions of a situation will lead to other policy definitions and practices (Bovenkerk, Miles & Verbunt, 1990a). Starting with an abstract theory is another possibility to describe the situations and developments in several countries. This holds constant the danger of neglecting the specific historical circumstances of individual countries. For this reason, an abstract model will be described in this chapter, which enables an analysis of several countries and state responses while maintaining the specific historical circumstances and the specific discourses of each country. This model of types of state responses is developed with the help of the so-called "political agenda approach." Before explaining this approach, some remarks have to be made with respect to the concept of the state used here.

THE CONCEPT OF THE STATE

The concept of the state refers to an institutional complex of a series of institutions or state machineries. "These collectively claim and use power to structure a particular ensemble of economic, social, and political relations within a specified spatial unit to mediate the impact of exterior forces upon that unit" (Bovenkerk, Miles & Verbunt, 1990b:479-480). The most important state machineries are the central governmental apparatus, the bureaucratic administration, the police and military, the judiciary, (national and local) representative institutions, and a series of permanent advisory institutions (Stuurman, 1978). The relatively autonomous state, in which freedom of action is limited by economic, political, and ideological developments (Stuurman, 1985), should not be perceived as a monolythic unity. State activities comprise a complex series of actions by persons within one or more of the state machineries mentioned. State activities are the result of internal struggle and compromises (Bovenkerk, Miles & Verbunt, 1990b). External pressures are of influence too. The state machineries, including individuals and institutions, will be called "internal actors." "External actors" are those institutions, organizations, and individuals outside of the state machineries, such as nongovernmental organizations, pressure groups, social movements, lobbyists, etc.

The state has three main roles (Bovenkerk, Miles & Verbunt, 1990b:482): (1) the "gatekeeper role" (Who is allowed in and who is not?); (2) the welfare or collective consumption role (Who is included or excluded from the distribution of certain resources, goods, and services?); and (3) the role of maintaining law and order. This third role is of eminent importance with respect to racist violence. In Western democracies the state has monopolized the use of violence. Any act of violence by others will challenge the state in its role of maintainer of law and order. The way in which the state will respond to the violence in general and to racist violence in particular will differ by state, by situation, and through time.

With respect to state responses a distinction has to be made between the national and the local level. Of course there are major differences between these levels with respect to power, influence, range, and variety of response possibilities. Another distinction is that between policies and practices. The practical implementation of policies will not always correspond with the intentions of these policies. The concrete, practical response to racist violence will often occur at the local level. At the national level we will deal with more abstract formulated policies. State authorities on a national level have an important influence on the political, social, and ideological climate that may or may not be supported by activities and policies opposing racism and racist violence.

Since the main objective of this chapter is an international comparison, the main focus will be at the national level. If racist violence is no issue (yet) in a society, the focus will turn more to the local level, the only level with direct concrete responses to racist incidents. If racist violence is a political issue of the first order, the focus will be at the national level, although the local level will be taken into account with respect to the practical implementation of national state responses.

THE POLITICAL AGENDA

What makes racist violence a political issue? Why are certain social phenomena transformed into political issues while others are not? Why does a phenomenon become a political topic at a certain moment in time? How is it tranformed into a political issue? Social phenomena like racist violence, as well as incest, child abuse, domestic violence, rape, environmental pollution, etc. existed throughout the twentieth century and before. Yet, it was not until the 1970s and 1980s that they were transformed into political issues in Europe and policies were formulated and measures were taken. The degree to which a social phenomenon occurs cannot explain this transformation, because some of the phenomena mentioned occurred at a much larger scale earlier this century. Yet, not until the last 20 years have they received massive public, media, and political attention.

"Social problems are only then problematic, when (groups of) people define them as such" (Brants & Brants, 1990:23). An individual may experience racist violence, but that does not make this violence a social problem. Even if a certain group has the same experience, racist violence does not have to be perceived as a social problem. The position of the group(s) within the power relations of society plays an important role here. This is important with respect to the question of whether the violence is perceived as a social problem, and to the causes of this violence. This power position is crucial with respect to the success or failure of people to strive or prevent a social phenomenon, and to attract the public and political attention necessary to be perceived as a social problem.

Perceptions concerning the need to solve a specific social problem may be transformed into political demands and it may become a political issue. Often this coincides with a social event, which leads people to develop initiatives and to attract broader public attention. Usually these events are considered shocking, like incendiarism, besmirching of graves and places of worship, riots, assassinations, and certain international developments. In relation to racist violence one may think of the public outrage in France after the desecration of Jewish graves in Carpentras (1990) or in Germany after the three Turkish women burned to death in an arson attack by neo-Nazis in Mölln (1992). Events that surely were not the first signs of racist violence in both countries, nevertheless shocked the majority of the population and led to more attention for and state responses to racist violence.

Demands to solve a social problem like racist violence may be heard by decisionmakers when large groups of people support the demands. Not all supporters have to experience the violence themselves. They may share different motives to support the demands. This may be motivated by the idea that racism in general and racist violence in particular threaten the value system of society. Another motive may be that a certain definition of racist violence and the demands to combat this violence may bring other comparable phenomena to the forefront, for instance anti-homosexual violence and rape.

Large groups may demand action to solve the problem. In many cases people will consider it within the boundaries of state authority to do something about it. Their opinion may be adopted by internal actors, like politicians. These actors may themselves venture the opinion that the state has to take action. In these cases Cobb and Elder refer to the entrance of an issue on the public agenda. This agenda includes "all issues that are commonly perceived by members of the political community as meriting public attention and as involving matters within the legitimate jurisdiction of existing governmental authority" (Cobb & Elder, 1972:85). These authors mention three conditions for an issue to be posited on this public agenda: (1) broad attention by the public; (2) shared concern by the public that action is required; and (3) shared opinion that proper action is needed by the state and that this lies within the boundaries of state authorities. These conditions surely apply for issues brought to the surface by groups of people with a marginal power position. Issues presented by groups and individuals in the power centers will be less restricted by these conditions before entering the public agenda (van der Eijck, 1975).

A place on the public agenda is no guarantee for state action. The agenda includes a list of issues on which (part of) the public and the political community agree that attention of authoritarian decisionmakers is needed. Many of these issues are rather abstractly formulated and put in general terms, like "fight unemployment," "oppose pollution," "improve security for women," "combat discrimination." Issues that get serious active attention by decisionmakers shape the formal or political agenda. This agenda includes more specific, concrete issues and these are often small in number. Benyon (Benyon, 1987:169) distinguishes three ways in which an issue may be placed on this agenda. The first two refer to initiatives by internal actors. An internal actor may initiate to put an issue on the political agenda straight away with the explicit intention to keep it from the public agenda. This may be done in the form of legislation. Or, initiatives by internal actors may be carried out to mobilize public attention to get the issue on the public agenda first, and then find entrance to the political agenda. Thirdly, external actors may initiate activities to put an issue on the political agenda. One may think of organizing mass demonstrations, publishing documents, and many other ways to attract massive attention and turn up the pressure. When an issue is finally placed on the political agenda, the state may implement measures to "solve" the problem.

The role of the media in this process is of unequivocal importance. In addition to their contribution in raising general consciousness about a specific problem, the media's role is important with respect to the perception and definition of a problem and its "popularity." The media, as well as science, may play an important role in bringing a certain issue to the surface. The media play the same important role in hindering or preventing a phenomenon from being perceived as a social problem or as a political issue.

This "process" or "path of stages," as mentioned above, does not picture the route that a social phenomenon has to follow all the way before it reaches the political agenda. Not all issues on the political agenda have gone through all the stages. Some of those issues may have been put on the political agenda directly. Neither will all social phenomena in the end reach to the political agenda. A phenomenon may often enter a certain stage and then disappear from public view. The process described is also not a continuous process. An issue may reach to the political agenda, action may be taken and the issue may disappear from the agenda, only to recur at a later moment. This may be the case when the state actions do not have the results expected and demanded by the relevant audience. This may be due to differences in problem definitions between initiating actors and official decisionmakers. With the realization of the different agendas and with respect to the series of stages mentioned, the problem definition plays an important role. Within the scope of this chapter it will not be elaborated upon in detail. Yet, some remarks must be made.

THE PROBLEM DEFINITION

A definition of a problem not only mirrors problem experiences, it also indicates real or imagined causes of the problem. The problem of definition is of eminent importance in every stage mentioned. The likelihood of reaching a certain stage, or moving to another stage, will depend partly on the definitions used. This is particularly true for groups that occupy marginal power positions in society. Any "progress" will depend on activities to attract attention of other "new" groups to support the demands made. In the case of racist violence one might think of broadening the definitions to include violence against people who are discriminated against on other than ethnic, cultural, religious, or national grounds (e.g., to include anti-homosexual violence).

Problem definitions are important for more than to get an issue placed on the political agenda. The way the problem is defined is also of importance once an issue is placed in this agenda (van der Graaf & Hoppe, 1989). Differences in definitions may be one cause of the situation in which one fraction of the state machineries argues that the problem is dealt with effectively, while others and external actors disagree.

Symbolic presentations shape an important part of problem definitions: "The key to success in each case is to put the appeal in a symbolic context that will have a maximum impact on followers, potential supporters, the opposition or decisionmakers" (Cobb & Elder, 1972:150). The use of these symbolic presentations is important to attract attention, and the role of the mass media is essential. Symbolic presentations shape a continuing part of the political life. Expressions like "freedom," "justice," "tolerance," "integration," "security," etc. are often used without consensus about the content of these terms. Yet, they are very important in mobilizing people, formulating demands, contacting decisionmakers, and opposing resistance.

At a certain stage, at a certain moment different definitions of racist violence may coexist. For instance, in the British context there are differences in the definitions of racist violence. These differences exist among internal actors as well as between internal and external actors. One definition points at the violence where the perpetrator(s) and the victim(s) are of different "races" and racist motives are supposed to exist. A second definition points at the violence where the perpetrator is white and where the victim thinks racist motives were involved. A third definition points at all the violence in which racist motives have been proven to exist by court. These are just three examples of the definitions used in one country at the same time. In the European context, the variety of definitions is even much larger. In the 1990s terms are heard like "extreme right violence," "racist violence," "anti-immigrant violence," "racial violence," "violence against foreigners," "neo-Nazi violence," etc. Of course, different definitions point at least at different aspects of the violence.

The definitions used are important in the way people respond to racist violence. For instance, "anti-immigrant violence" can direct and/or limit the discussion to the issue of immigration, leaving out violence perpetrated against natives with a skin color different from the majority of the native population. Another example is "extreme right violence," which may include violence against homosexuals, women, and physically disabled persons without implicitly giving attention to the specific characteristics of racist violence. "Neo-Nazi violence" may only look at the violence perpetrated by people organized in neo-Nazi organizations, leaving out racist violence perpetrated by the "next-door-neighbor." These are just some examples of different definitions and their influences on possible responses. This shows the importance of defintions.

TYPES OF STATE RESPONSES TO RACIST VIOLENCE

With the different stages in mind in which a social phenomenon like racist violence can occur as a more or less idealized process, one may distinguish various types of state responses to racist violence. These state responses may be put in a similar idealized process from state responses to "racist-violence-being-an-individual-problem" to state responses to "racist-violence-as-a-political-agenda-issue." This is a purely idealized process. It does not mean that racist violence has to follow the whole process stage by stage, before it will be placed on the political agenda. Certain events may cause a sudden appearance of this violence at any stage. And it is also possible that racist violence never reaches the political agenda.

Yet, this idealized process enables us to look at the situation in different countries over a longer period of time. It also enables us to look at the main causes of shifts in this process. For instance, why did racist violence enter the political agenda? How did racist violence attract more attention and how did it become recognized as a social problem? What caused its entrance to the public agenda? The state responses in all these stages can be structured and analyzed this way. What were the main state responses when racist violence was not perceived as a social problem? How did the state respond to the issue once it entered the political agenda? Which measures were taken and which definitions were used? It should be noticed that different state responses may exist and may be contradictory to each other.

The diagram in Figure 4.1 is derived from the earlier mentioned process of political agenda building and sums up different types of state responses to racist violence.

Figure 4.1
A Theoretical Model for International Comparative Analaysis

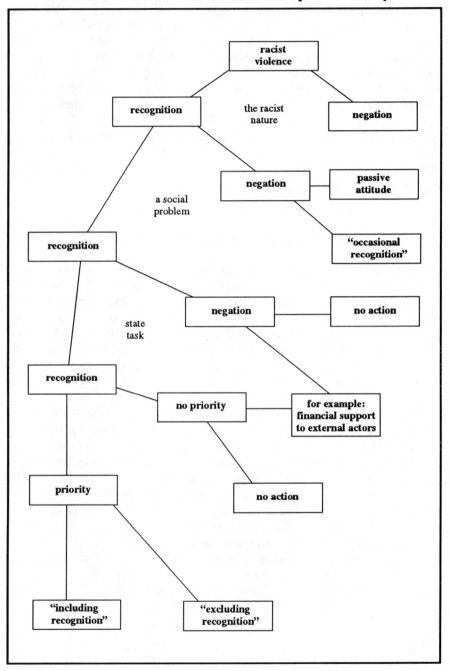

Source: Rob Witte.

The first distinction of state responses is made in the case of the individual incident of racist violence and/or in the situation where racist violence is not perceived to shape a social problem. The main focus will be directed at the local level of state authorities. The distinction concentrates on the question of whether the racist character of the incident is recognized. This recognition does not have to be expressed explicitly. It sometimes may be concluded from a lack of further practical action. If the racist character is denied, the question stands whether the violence meets any response. The maintenance of law and order is, as mentioned, one of the main functions of the state. It is likely that the state will respond to the violent act itself. There are many examples in which the perpetrator is prosecuted for violence, but the racist aspect of this violence is left outside the prosecution. Still, even action against the violence itself is not assured. This is illustrated by the fact that the police sometimes refuse emphatically to report racist violence. In 1981, for instance, an Asian shopkeeper in London, Britain suffered a five-week period of persistent racial harassment, including having his windows broken on two occasions. A racist leaflet was pushed through his letter box in between these attacks. Police said there was no evidence to suggest that the attacks were racially motivated (IRR, 1987:57). Cases are also known in which the police did not take notice of the racist violence and even prosecuted the victim because of his or her provoking behavior. This especially seems to be the case when victims have tried to defend themselves. In April 1977, the Virk brothers were repairing their car outside their home in east London when they were attacked by a gang of white youths. The brothers defended themselves with the tools they were using. When the police arrived, called for by one of the brothers, they arrested the Virk brothers, allowing the attackers to go free. In court, defense arguments about racism were dismissed as "irrelevant" (Gordon, 1990).

If the racist character of the violent incident is recognized, the question follows whether racist violence is perceived to constitute a social problem. Two ways of state responses can be distinguished if this is not the case. First, the racist motives of the violent perpetrator can be recognized with clear reference to the incidental, occasional character of the act. Racist violence as a social problem is denied. In this situation one may speak of "occasional recognition." Structural measures by the state are not considered necessary. The "incident" is handled by the judicial machinery without further state action. This "occasional recognition" occurs especially when racist motives are clearly stated by the perpetrator in a situation in which the predominant discourse in society denies that racist violence is a social problem.

A second way to respond is through action that follows from the opinion that racist violence does not deserve any (special) attention. This passive attitude can be motivated with reference to the real or imagined danger of overexposure and of the possible influence of this on potential perpetrators (e.g., copycatting). The racist character of the incident is not denied, and sometimes it is even explicitly recognized. Yet, no further state action is taken, except maybe by the judicial machinery.

If racist violence is recognized as a social, structural problem in society, then state responses seem to be inevitable. Yet, to counteract the racist nature of this violence may be perceived to be outside the boundaries of the state authority. Therefore, the state can reject further direct action. For the same reason, it can support a third party that propagates anti-racism activities. One could think of an increase in the financial support to organizations of potential victims, anti-racism organizations, and institutions concerning cross-cultural education. The main object for this support is combatting discrimination and racism in general.

If racist violence is recognized as a social problem that is to be dealt with by the state and is placed on the public agenda, two ways of state responses may be distinguished. The question is whether priority is given to combatting this violence? There can be many reasons why this is not the case. On the one hand one may refer to other issues on the political agenda, which explicitly or implicitly have been given higher priority. On the other hand one may argue that it is a case of "being watchful." For the moment no further measures are implemented, nor any other action has to be taken. Another possible response by the state in which no immediate action is taken, is the establishment of a special inquiry commission. This is often a policy to let off steam and gain some time to decrease any "panic." Whether any action will be undertaken at a later stage, and whether racist violence will actually be put on the political agenda, is still uncertain.

If priority is given and racist violence is placed on the political agenda again two types of state response may be distinguished. These two types of response are called "including recognition" and "excluding recognition." The racist nature of the violence is basically recognized in this stage. Racist violence is perceived to constitute a social problem in society, which has to be dealt with by the state. Yet, responses and measures may either be directed at the (potential) perpetrators or at the (potential) victims. The terminology "including-excluding" refers to the question of whether the potential victims are perceived as groups belonging to society. If so (= inclusion), racist violence is directed at an inextricable part of society and measures will be directed at the perpetrators and the circumstances in which this violence may flourish. If potential victims are perceived to form separate, more or less isolated groups, partly outside of society (= exclusion), measures will mainly be aimed at their increasing presence. Some examples of both types of state responses will be given.

An example of "including recognition" is one in which the racist motives play an important role in the prosecution procedure, and which are seen explicitly as aggravating circumstances. "Including recognition" does not always have to involve new legislation. Sometimes it can be dealt with by a stricter enforcement of existing legislation. In some European countries performing a "Hitler salute," carrying around swastikas and shouting racist slogans is prohibited. Yet, hardly any policeman in Europe arrests people when they salute in that way, when they wear t-shirts with swastikas, or when these slogans are shouted out loud during marches of neo-Nazi's or by soccer-supporters. Another example of "including recognition" is the way in which the police in Rotterdam, the Netherlands, handled the rumors of an expected, illegal concert by a British Nazi skinhead band. During the weekend, 29 skinheads, mainly from Germany, were stopped and arrested and sent back home. Nazi writings, tins with tear gas, and a knife were confiscated. This can be called "including recognition" because it occurred at a time when racist violence was a political issue all around Europe. The main causes of this were the recent racist attacks at asylum-seekers in Rostock, Germany (August 1992), which were broadly covered in Europe. By taking measures against all kinds of aggressive racist utterances, the state authorities in these examples combat the circumstances in which racist violence can flourish. Another direct state response in the context of "including recognition" is the example of President Mitterrand who headed a main demonstration against racist violence in Paris, France, after the desecration of Jewish graves in Carpentras (1990). By participating in the demonstration, the French President showed that the violence had to be taken seriously, and that the desecration was not only directed against the Jewish population but against the whole French state. A last example of "including recognition" is the way in which the German authorities prohibited certain extreme right organizations at the end of 1992. By doing so, they showed their intention to fight those organizations that were at least partly responsible for the racist violence in the 1990s in Germany.

Not every example of "including recognition" has to mean that the racist violence has disappeared. By heading an anti-racist demonstration racist violence is not diminished. Yet, the individual response gives notice that the violence is recognized as racist and that it is directed against an included part of society, and therefore it is called "including recognition."

"Excluding recognition" is also a type of state response in which the racist character of the violence is recognized. Yet, the main measures are not directed against the perpetrators and the circumstances that give rise to racist violence. Measures are directed against assumed causes of the violence lying within the presence of the groups of potential victims. In 1958 Britain was shocked by the so-called Notting Hill riots. These riots were caused by series of incidents of racist violence. Yet, looking back at the main responses to these riots one has to conclude, that the presence of the immigrant population was perceived as the cause of the riots (see, e.g., Miles, 1984). Migration control became the main issue after these riots, instead of any measures against the racist violence itself.

A more recent example of "excluding recognition" occurred in 1992 in Germany. Just a few weeks after the racist siege of an asylum-seekers center in Rostock, the German government announced the signing of a treaty with Rumanian authorities, in which they agreed to remove some 40,000 Rumanian asylum-seekers from Germany to Rumania. Sinti- and Roma-gypsies from Rumania constitute the majority of the Rumanian asylum-seekers and they were among the first targets of the Rostock-siege. They were living in tents outside the center because there was not enough room to give them shelter inside. In a period in which the German authorities showed they did not know how to respond to the racist attacks effectively, this treaty was one of the first concrete measures after the Rostock events. Because it is only directed against the presence of certain groups of asylum-seekers, and because these groups of people constituted the main targets of the racist attacks, this state response can be called "excluding recognition." It pretends to take away "the cause" of the violence, namely the potential victims. Other examples of "excluding recognition" are responses in which the violence is trivialized and in which understanding is asked and given to the perpetrators.

CONCLUSIONS

In this chapter a model has been described to structure and analyze state responses to racist violence. With the help of the "political agenda approach," an idealized process is reproduced in which a social phenomenon may move from a stage of solely individual experience to a stage in which it constitutes an issue on the political agenda. It should be noticed that this process is not an inevitable process that a social phenomenon has to go through before reaching the stage of political issue. A social phenomenon may appear and disappear in any stage without any certain continuation.

This idealized process of social phenomena is transformed into a model of types of state responses to the social phenomenon: racist violence. In every stage particular state responses may be distinguished. Different state responses may and will occur next to each other. These may even be opposing each other. This is partly because the state is no monolythic unity. The main questions that can be used to make a distinction among state responses, are:

- Is the racist nature of the violent incident recognized?
- Is racist violence recognized as a social problem?
- Is the combat of racist violence perceived as a state task?
- Is priority given to this combat?
- Is racist violence perceived as caused by the perpetrators or by the presence of the groups of potential victims?

The model enables a comparison between state responses to racist violence among different countries over a period of time. State responses may be structured and analyzed and main influences in and causes of sudden changes in the way racist violence is perceived by the political community may be distinguished. Executing such an international comparative analysis may give a better insight into state responses and their influence on racist violence and a better insight in the ways to bring racist violence to the political agenda and to combat this violence effectively.

REFERENCES

Benyon, J. (1987). "Unrest and the Political Agenda." In J. Benyon & J. Solomos (1987), *The Roots of Urban Unrest,"* pp.165-179. Pergamon Press, Oxford.

Bovenkerk, F., R. Miles & G.Verbunt (1990a). "Comparative Studies of Migration and Exclusionism on the Grounds of 'Race' and Ethnic Background in Western Europe: A Critical Appraisal." *International Migration Review,* vol. XXV, no. 2, pp. 375-391.

_____ (1990b). "Racism, Migration and the State in Western Europe: A Case for Comparative Analysis." *International Sociology,* vol. 5, no. 4, December 1990, pp. 475-490.

Brants, C.H. & K.L.K. Brants (1990). *"De Sociale Constructie van Fraude,"* Gouda Quint, Arnhem.

Cobb, R.W. & C.D. Elder (1972), *Participation in American Politics. The Dynamic of Agenda-Building,"* Baltimore MD: John Hopkins University Press. (Second Edition, 1983).

Gordon, P. (1990). *"Racial Violence and Harassment,"* The Runnymede Trust, London.

Institute of Race Relations (1987). *"Policing Against Black People,"* IRR, London.

Miles, R. (1984). "The Riots of 1958: Notes on the Ideological Construction of 'Race Relations' as a Political Issue in Britain," *Immigrants & Minorities,* 3, 3, pp. 252-275.

Stuurman, S. (1978). *"Kapitalisme en Burgerlijke Staat. Een Inleiding in de Marxistische Politieke Theorie,"* SUA, Amsterdam (Third Edition, 1981).

_____ (1985). *"De Labyrintische Staat. Over Politiek, Ideologie en Moderniteit,"* SUA, Amsterdam.

van der Eijck, C. (1975). "Politieke Participatie. Een overzicht van Recente Literatuur," *Acta Politica,* 10 jrg (1975), pp. 341-363.

van der Graaf, H. & R. Hoppe (1989). *"Beleid en Politiek. Een Inleiding tot de Beleidswetenschap en de Beleidskunde,"* Coutinho, Muiderberg.

5

A Modified Social Control Theory of Terrorism: An Empirical and Ethnographic Assessment of the American Neo-Nazi Skinheads

Mark S. Hamm
Indiana State University

Theories that directly link social processes with the emergence of terrorism (Gurr, 1971; O'Sullivan, 1986; Redlick, 1979) have recently become the topic of controversy (e.g., Laqueur, 1987; Merkl, 1986a). More than simply asserting that social processes "are not precisely definable or objectively measurable" (Wilkinson, 1986: 35), critics also downplay the salience of social factors such as alienation, religion, and the cultural transmission of terrorist values from one society to another, or from one generation to the next (Dror, 1983; Gibbs, 1989; Laqueur, 1987). I argue that such an assessment is misguided in suggesting that social processes either cannot be measured or are unimportant for understanding terrorism. Consistent with those who criticize the social process perspective, I conceptualize nonstate terrorism as violence employed for sub-revolutionary purposes of intimidation, vengeance, or punishment. My argument draws on Gibbs' (1989) theory of terrorism but qualifies and extends it to arrive at a *modified deterrent vicarious social control* approach. In this chapter I derive predictions from this approach and test them empirically. Specifically, I examine whether an array of social processes affect the incidence of terrorism among a group of white neo-Nazi youths.

I begin by noting that critics rely on one type of research to dismiss social processes as unimportant: historical analyses. For example, in his historical interpretation of the West German Baader-Meinhof gang, the Weathermen in the United States, the Japanese United Red Army, and the Angry Brigade in Britain, Wilkinson

(1986) concluded that "much of the politically motivated terrorism in liberal democracies for the past decade has been committed by the spoilt children of affluence ... young people from comfortably-off middle class homes and with the 'advantages' of higher education" (Wilkinson, 1986:93; see Handler, 1990). Other critics argue that even if extreme levels of alienation and frustration plague certain members of a society, such factors are not necessary or sufficient causes of terrorism (e.g., Gross, 1987; Laqueur, 1987; Lupsha, 1971). Similarly, Merkl's (1986a) historical review prompted him to conclude that terrorism is often "strikingly *unpolitical*" (Merkl, 1986a:40, emphasis in original; see Wardlaw, 1990:8-9). In one of the most comprehensive reviews conducted in recent years, Laqueur (1987) reported that terrorism is "usually resorted to by small groups of people whose motives may not necessarily be connected with observable 'objective' political, economic, social, or psychological trends" (Laqueur, 1987:157). More to the point, Duvall and Stohl contend that "Motives are entirely irrelevant to the concept of political terrorism" (quoted in Schmidt, 1983:100). Even if certain social processes could be directly linked to terrorism, Dror (1983) argues that the idea of controlling them "exposes the basic intellectual difficulty of coping with a problem whose basic causes are largely beyond understanding and beyond treatment" (Dror, 1983:70).

There is another body of historical research, however, that stands in contrast to these conclusions. First, studies examining a wide variety of conditions associated with the emergence of terrorism provide little evidence that social processes are benign. Redlick (1979) examined the Québecois and the Irish Republican Army of the 1970s to show that "A critical factor in the development first of discontent and then of political violence is information. Information may be transmitted via international travel ...; the import of books, films, journals, and so on" (Redlick, 1979:77). Similarly, Wasmund (1986) notes that West Berlin youth groups of the early 1970s were drawn into a counterculture of political violence "through underground leaflets and pamphlets" (Wasmund, 1986:196). Waldmann (1986) argues that material dissatisfaction led to "an increased preparedness for armed attacks on society" by left-wing Guatemalan and Nicaraguan guerrilla bands during the late 1970s. Weinberg (1986) shows how groups claiming inspiration from neo-fascist ideologies have recently "sought to throw Italy into a state of turmoil and undermine the incumbent political regime" (Weinberg, 1986:145). Bell (1975), Capitanchick (1986), and Post (1987) note that religious fanaticism—derived from beliefs in vengeance—often provides groups with internal power that allows them to take terrorist actions. Moreover, Crenshaw (1981) presents historical evidence to show that "terrorist organizations possess internally consistent sets of values, beliefs, and images of the environment" (Crenshaw, 1981:385). Additionally, some evidence suggests that social psychological models of authoritarianism help to explain the dynamics of political radicalism and the transformation from protest to terrorism (Lichter, 1979).

Second, even those critics who dismiss or downplay social processes recognize that they are not necessarily irrelevant. Wilkinson (1986) concedes that "Most social scientific attempts at theory of terrorism suffer from a fatal flaw: they neglect the role and influence of terrorist ideologies and beliefs in...nurturing hatred and violence" (Wilkinson, 1986:96). Although he does not include social processes in his theory, Gibbs (1989) notes that "reference to internal behavior is essential" (Gibbs, 1989:337). Gross (1987) suggests that antecedents for terrorism may include a state of anomie and the existence of a leadership with a potentially attractive ideology. Merkl (1986b) argues that "the depths of alienation" among German youth has recently produced terrorism (Merkl, 1986b:248). Dror (1983) predicts that informal international networks that support terrorism will permit or encourage terrorism in the future, and Laqueur (1987) acknowledges that there is "great value in understanding the specific counterculture in which the terrorism process is embedded" (Laqueur, 1987:164; see Wardlaw, 1990).

In summary, I believe that it is premature to characterize social processes as unmeasurable or to dismiss them as unimportant in the identification of propitious circumstances for a general theory of terrorism. On close examination I find less than convincing much of the evidence that critics offer to support their position. In fact, critics often appear to contradict themselves. Thus, I reject the pessimistic notion that the complexities of Western culture make it impossible to synthesize an explanation of the "basic causes" of terrorism that may be used to justify public strategies to prevent terrorism in the future (Dror, 1983). Though such studies appropriately question some of the strongest claims of terrorism research, typically they do not explain why persons turn to terrorist action. Building on this observation, I offer a model for understanding how social processes can contribute to terrorism. Since this framework extends Gibbs' (1989) path-breaking theorizing, I refer to the model as a modified deterrent vicarious social control approach.[1]

A MODIFIED DETERRENT VICARIOUS SOCIAL CONTROL APPROACH

Statement of the Approach

Gibbs' Model. As an introduction to my approach, I specify central elements of Gibbs' theory (1989) by considering his main points on the consequences of social control (see Figure 5.1a). Gibbs argues that "in all instances" (i.e., in all settings and across all social contexts in which terrorism takes place), "the first party (e.g., the terrorist group) attempts to punish the third party (e.g., the victim or victims of terrorist violence) ..., or somehow rectify the third party's behavior, always presuming that such action will influence the second party's (e.g., the government's) behavior (e.g., by attempting to control the third party). Vicarious social control is the basis of general deterrence, ... terrorists ... often resort to deterrent vicarious social control as an integral component of their intimidation strategy" (Gibb, 1989:337).[2] Gibbs then outlines the role of the state in responding to terrorism, and terrorists' reactions to that response: "Because nonstate terrorists resort to violence, they are

Figure 5.1   Diagrammatic Representation of Gibbs' Approach and the Modified Approach

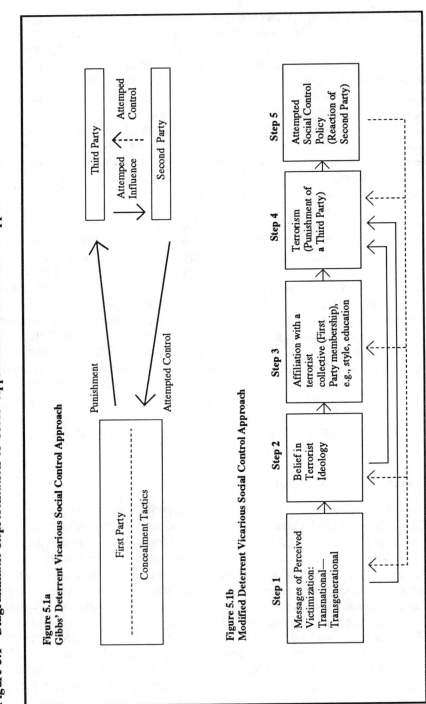

Figure 5.1a
Gibbs' Deterrent Vicarious Social Control Approach

Third Party

Second Party

Attempted Influence

Attempted Control

Punishment

First Party

Concealment Tactics

Attempted Control

Figure 5.1b
Modified Deterrent Vicarious Social Control Approach

Step 1
Messages of Perceived Victimization: Transnational—Transgenerational

Step 2
Belief in Terrorist Ideology

Step 3
Affiliation with a terrorist collective (First Party membership), e.g., style, education

Step 4
Terrorism (Punishment of a Third Party)

Step 5
Attempted Social Control Policy (Reaction of Second Party)

certain to be targets of attempted control by the police and/or the military ... Various
tactics of concealment—all types of countercontrol—offer the only hope of survival
[for terrorist groups]" (Gibb, 1989:338).

Step 1: Messages of Perceived Victimization. A modified deterrent vicarious
social control approach begins with the idea that individuals internalize deeply
held beliefs about what it means to be the victim of social injustice (Figure 5.1b).
As Mannheim (1936) observed, social myths and ideologies often have the requisite power to manifest surrogate religions and guides to deviant conduct. Those
who construct such religions and guides, according to Mannheim, are "incapable
of correctly diagnosing an existing condition of society" (1936:36). Mannheim
emphasized the features of blindness to the existing order, a tendency to simplify
social events and conditions, and an obsessively Manichean view of history and society that divides people into camps of friends and enemies. Following Mannheim I
note that American white supremicism is based on an "us versus them" mentality
that exaggerates perceived injustices (Kushnick, 1981), and that such a mentality
has been sewn into the fabric of extreme Christian fundamentalism, which has
played a central role in the organization and violence of groups such as the Ku
Klux Klan, the Order, and The Covenant, The Sword, and The Arm of the Lord (Flynn
& Gerhardt, 1989; Toy, 1989). In this vein, Blumenthal (1975) notes that "the idea
of justice or fairness may be more centrally related to attitudes toward violence
than are feelings of deprivation. It is the *perceived injustice* ... that gives rise to
anger or frustration" (Blumenthal, 1975:108, emphasis added). Similarly, Redlick
(1979) argues that once an individual in an ethnic group perceives a link between
their ethnicity and their relative deprivation, that person may become dissatisfied
and frustrated with the political system responsible for such victimization. Moreover,
a target (i.e., Gibbs' third party) must be singled out to blame for this suffering.

Perceived victimization includes two important components: the *transnational*
flow of information that can affect significantly the tensions in an open, ethnically
polarized society, and the *transgenerational* flow of information that fosters discrimination and prejudice. Either, or both working in tandem, give expression and
form to the perceived victimization and provide the initial enabling factor(s) necessary for terrorism to happen. "Transnational" flow of information comes from
Crenshaw's (1981) and Redlick's (1979) ideas on modernization in communications
and the subsequent creation of a multinational atmosphere in which violence, especially terrorism, appears justifiable and acceptable. "Transgenerational" is suggested by the extensive social cognition research on persuasion which shows that
extreme forms of prejudice and racism are passed from one generation to the next
through a processing of the "us versus them" mentality in which "them" are assigned
roles as negative agents and "us" are represented in a stereotypical victim role
(e.g., Allport, 1954; van Dijk, 1987). My interest in transnational-transgenerational
is the extent to which people choose models for their overgeneralized beliefs about
third parties through subjective rather than objective dimensions of social interaction (Liska, 1987). Following Gibbs (1989), I expect these forms of persuasive

communication to transmit knowledge supporting a strategic psychological model of terrorism. However, since numerous factors are likely to affect beliefs in perceived victimization, people will almost certainly vary in the extent to which they embrace terrorist goals and, therefore, in their extent of involvement in terrorism.

Step 2: Belief in Terrorist Ideology. A belief in an ideology that makes terrorism a purposeful activity is important because it brings personal relevance to a person's views about deterrent vicarious social control, and it creates the basis for examining the extent to which transnational and transgenerational communications affect negative attitudes toward third parties. This ideology must be capable of increasing the tendencies of persons to aggress against outgroups—racial and ethnic minorities, the weak, people who hold different values, and so forth (Crenshaw, 1981). This ideology also provides an enabling or permissive factor necessary for terrorism to happen.

Step 3: Affiliation with a Terrorist Collective: First Party Membership. I consider two possible responses to deterrent vicarious social control and argue that a tendency to endorse them indicates that persons (a) embrace a terrorist ideology, and (b) possess the necessary social support to act on it. This process begins when persons join a "secret society" dedicated to redressing perceived injustices (Crenshaw, 1981). The first response, then, is the adoption of a subcultural *style* that is a direct manifestation of the secrecy of such a closed group. By subcultural style, I mean the "spectacular means of expressing lived relations in which distinct objects [e.g., weapons], symbols [e.g., regalia], and rituals [e.g., violence] congeal into a system of meaning" for members of a terrorist collective (Kingsman, n.d.:2). Second is the attempt at *educating* others in hopes of enlightening them so as to increase hostility toward third parties. Their need to educate is important because it suggests that group members consider transnational and transgenerational communication likely, a possibility that critics of the social process perspective deny. Style and education create yet another pair of enabling factors that are similar to what Gurr (1971) refers to as social facilitation—or the subcultural traditions that sanction terrorism, making it morally and politically justifiable.

Step 4: Terrorism: Punishment of a Third Party. Terrorism may arise directly from transnational and/or transgenerational attitudes about a third party (Step 1); it may follow from a belief in ideology (Step 2); or, it may follow from affiliation with a terrorist collective (Step 3). With respect to affiliation, Crenshaw notes that the act of terrorism "may serve internal organizational functions of control, discipline, and morale building" (Crenshaw, 1981:387). Yet terrorism may also produce negative consequences for terrorists themselves. While punishment of a third party may provide terrorists with some positive aspects of affiliating with a terrorist collective, it may also limit individual liberty. For example, it was his affiliation with a terrorist collective that led 18-year-old Sean Terrant of the Confederate Hammerskins (CHS) to place two cyanide gas pellets into the air-conditioning system of the Dallas Jewish Community Center in the Spring of 1989 (Thornburgh, 1990). Today, Terrant is serving a 10-year sentence in the U.S. Bureau of Prisons for this crime.

Definition of Terrorism. This example meets the criterion for an act of terrorism as conceptualized by Gibbs (1989:330). He stipulates that "terrorism is illegal violence or threatened violence directed against human or nonhuman objects," provided that it: (1) was undertaken with a view to maintaining a putative norm in at least one particular territorial unit; (2) had secretive, furtive, and/or clandestine features that were expected by the participant to conceal their personal identity; (3) was not undertaken to further the permanent defense of some area; (4) was not conventional warfare; and (5) was perceived by the participant as contributing to the normative putative goal (described in point 1) by inculcating fear of violence in persons other than the immediate target of the actual or threatened violence and/or by publicizing some cause.

Placing Terrant's crime clearly within the definition of terrorism provided by Gibbs is important for the discussion to follow and warrants further explanation.[3] At his trial, the Texas Attorney General with assistance of counsel from the U.S. Attorney General, demonstrated that Terrant and his four co-defendants had attempted to commit a mass homicide (*threatened violence*) against members of the Dallas Jewish Community Center for the purpose of communicating a political message. Led by Terrant, CHS had undertaken their crime as an expression of violent rebellion against the state. The state was known among Terrant and his co-conspirators as the "Zionist Occupied Government"—or *ZOG* (*maintaining a putative norm*). Their attempted violence was limited to the city of Dallas (*one particular territorial unit*). The crime was committed at night when the Community Center was vacant; Terrant's plan was to have the air-conditioning system circulate the cyanide gas throughout the Center, thus rendering horrible deaths to an undetermined number of Jewish citizens as they entered the building for activities on the following morning (*secretive and clandestine*). Although Terrant and his accomplices left behind swastikas and other Nazi slogans painted in graffiti on the Community Center walls, CHS did not publicly claim responsibility for the attempted mass murder, nor did Terrant and his companions reveal their identities to the Dallas Jewish community, the media, or the police (*concealing personal identity*). The attempted mass murder was the first (and last) crime committed by Terrant against the Dallas Jewish community (*he was not seeking a permanent defense of the area*). (However, between 1989 and 1991 more than one dozen CHS members, including Terrant, were found guilty of using baseball bats, steel-toed boots, fists, knives, brass knuckles, Oriental throwing stars, and clubs wrapped in barbed wire to assault some 50 Mexican and Vietnamese immigrants in the Dallas area—e.g., other third-party victims.) Cyanide gas, blown through the atmosphere by an air-conditioning system, *is not a conventional weapon of war.* (And neither, importantly, are bats, boots, fists, knives, brass knuckles, throwing stars, and clubs.) Finally, the motive for Terrant's crime, as established by the prosecution, was to strike out against ZOG—the enemy (*contributing to the putative goal*)—thereby inculcating fear in the awareness of a larger human audience, the U.S. Government. Shortly after attempting his symbolic violence, Terrant appeared on the FBI's Ten Most Wanted Criminals List and CHS was featured in *The New York Times* (Aug. 4,

1990) and other international media outlets (*publicizing their cause*). Sean Terrant was a self-described neo-Nazi skinhead. His crime is properly defined as terrorism.[4]

Step 5: Attempted Social Control Policy: Reaction of the Second Party. If the processes outlined in Steps 1 through 4 operate, public administrations will be offered four counterterrorist strategies. Gibbs argues that "a theory's validity is jeopardized if it does not recognize that variation in terrorism may to some extent reflect variation in the *effectiveness* of attempts to control it" (Gibbs, 1989:339, emphasis added). The success of the attempted social control policy suggested by my approach, then, is dependent on the effectiveness of public administrations to: (1) hunt down, arrest, prosecute, and incarcerate known terrorists; (2) dismantle terrorist collectives; (3) mitigate against the formulation of terrorist ideology; and (4) interrupt the transmission of messages that lead to perceived victimization. While the effectiveness of these strategies rests on public administration's understanding of terrorism's antecedents and its resolve to do something about them, the strategies ignore the importance of latent problems associated with concealment tactics. As Horowitz (1983) observes, "If the causes of terrorism can be established and eradicated, then study of its consequences become moot" (Horowitz, 1983:39). Yet such attempts at social control, especially strategies 2-4 (*supra*), may run counter to the sensibilities of a constitutional republic. Crenshaw (1981) shows that nonstate terrorism does not occur in communist dictatorships. Instead, terrorism exists in modern liberal democracies that strive to protect civil liberties (Gurr, 1989). Such protections, in turn, may undermine the effectiveness of attempted security efforts to control terrorism. Put another way, "Policy options take on meaning only in the context of what elements of its political soul a society is willing to risk" (Horowitz, 1983:51).

Comparisons to Gibbs' Model. The differences between my approach and Gibbs' are related to emphasis and elaboration. First, although Gibbs recognizes the importance of "purposiveness" and makes reference to "all major types of internal behavior, such as perception and belief [and how] such behaviors enter into the pursuit of goals" (Gibbs, 1989:336), he does not explain how terrorist goals are developed in the first place. As such, Gibbs does not specify how perceptions and beliefs are developed, nor does he recognize the variability in internal behavior and its relative effects on the propensity of persons to pursue terrorist goals. By contrast, in Steps 1 and 2 I provide a way of thinking about the formulation of terrorist goals by focusing on transnational and transgenerational forms of communication that may congeal into a coherent ideology for persons who are likely to become terrorists. Second, Gibbs' model does not answer the question of how terrorist goals are implemented, and I highlight processes associated with the dynamics of terrorist collectives (Step 3). Third, Gibbs provides one public response for the attempted social control of terrorism: law enforcement and/or the military. In Step 5, I offer three additional responses which suggest that civilian security bureaucracies and citizen action groups may play a role in effective counterterrorism. Finally, my ideas intersect with Gibbs' at one important juncture (Step 4): neo-Nazi skinheads are terrorist-prone individuals.

The Neo-Nazi Skinheads

The neo-Nazi skinheads evolved in Great Britain amid the social and political
contentions of the Thatcher administration. At the time (there had been nonpolitical "skins" in Britain since the early 1970s), London skinheads were flirting with
the reactionary symbols of Nazism (Brake, 1985; Marcus, 1989). This subcultural
development began to inform the world of popular culture, and soon London youth
were introduced to a new brand of rock music called white power heavy metal. This
genre included acts such as Vengeance, Brutal Attack, No Remorse, White Power,
and the most popular all, *Skrewdriver*—who created a contemporary musical alloy
based on the racist belief that Anglo-Saxon England was being overrun by immigrants. It has been said that "Skrewdriver turned the clock back hundreds of years
and glorified the age where life was a day to day battle for survival, disease was rife,
war ever present, and the mass of people lived as virtual slaves" (*Cable Street Beat
Review*, n.d.:4). In 1982, White Noise Records of London (a subsidiary of the British
National Front—a neo-fascist organization with offices in Berlin, Paris, Rome and
more than 30 other European cities) released Skrewdriver's premiere white power
album titled *Hail the New Dawn*. The album cover displayed a group of Vikings
standing on a beach in front of a glorious sunrise. *Hail* featured songs that would eventually constitute a pantheon of white power anthems for racist skinheads throughout the Western world. These included "White Power," "Nigger, Nigger," "Race and
Nation," "Rudolf Hess (Prisoner of Peace)," and "Dead Paki in a Gutter." Following
the rise of Skrewdriver and white power heavy metal, one journalist wrote that
"Armies of skinheads tattooed their faces with swastikas and taunted onlookers
with *Sieg Heil* salutes, and many joined Britain's right-wing resurgence" (Coplon,
1989:86).

By decade's end, neo-Nazi skinheads throughout Europe had amassed a highly
publicized record of vandalism, racial assaults, and murder. In Britain alone, the number of racial attacks committed by skinheads (along with other right-wing activists)
reportedly increased from 10,000 a year between 1982 and 1985, to 70,000 a year
between 1985 and 1988, including 74 murders of Afro-Caribbean, Asian, and
Pakistani men (Brown, 1984; Gordon, 1990; Hiro, 1991). One study of London's
East End found that one-fourth of all black residents had been the victim of some
form of racial harassment committed by skinheads in the previous 12 months
(London Borough of Newham, 1986). On May 8, 1985, skinheads from Denmark,
Belgium, France, and Britain instigated the Brussels soccer riot leaving 38 dead and
more than 200 wounded, most of whom were racial minorities (Cooper, 1989).
Since the fall of the Berlin Wall, German neo-Nazi skinheads have used clubs,
knives, beer bottles, brass knuckles, ball bats, Oriental throwing stars, explosives,
and guns to assault (and sometimes murder) an estimated 3,000 *Auslanders*—or
foreigners—from the Third World nations of Nigeria, Uganda, Mozambique,
Vietnam, Pakistan, and Turkey (Bensinger, 1991; Jackson, 1991; Seidel-Pielen,
1991). Such terrorism continues to this day. During the Persian Gulf War, for exam-

ple, neo-Nazi skinheads were implicated in the firebombing of some 20 mosques in the London area (Hamm, 1993).

THE AMERICAN SKINHEADS: APPLYING THE MODIFIED TERRORISM THEORY

Unlike European sociologists (e.g., Brake, 1985; Mücke, 1991), U.S. scholars have not subjected the skinheads of their nation to even the most rudimentary analysis; hence, there is no social scientific evidence upon which to base assessments and formulate predictions concerning the modified terrorism theory as it relates to the American skinhead movement. There are, however, two alternative sources of information that can be used for these purposes: official documents and the research publications of civil rights groups.[5] Consistent with Step 4, in 1989 the U.S. Department of Justice reported that skinheads were responsible for a sudden increase in right-wing terrorist-type incidents in the nation, as the U.S. Attorney General decried the "shocking reemergence of hate group violence" (quoted in Barrett, 1989:12) and directed federal prosecutors to initiate some 40 investigations into suspected terrorist activity of skinhead groups (Thornburgh, 1990). Skinheads were subsequently implicated in a majority of the violent assaults against gays and lesbians in the United States (Berrill, 1990; National Gay & Lesbian Task Force, 1991) and were responsible for a reported 41 percent rise in anti-Semitic acts nationwide, including arsons, bombings, and cemetery desecrations (Anti-Defamation League of B'Nai B'rith [ADL], 1989a). By 1990, skinheads were reportedly involved in more than one-half of the violent racial assaults committed in the United States, including more than a dozen murders (ADL, 1989b; Klanwatch, 1991). Relying further on these reports, it is possible to assess the efficacy of the other four steps in the modified approach, and to make predictions concerning each step.

Assessments and Predictions

Table 5.1 summarizes the predictions to be tested in this research. All of these predictions are derived from Figure 5.1, but additional theoretical specifications are required to test Steps 3 and 4. Table 5.1 is divided into two parts, Preliminary Predictions and Key Predictions.

Preliminary Predictions. Part 1 of Table 5.1 is built on the following conclusion drawn by the U.S. Department of Justice: "Skinheads in the United States are split into 2 factions of opposing philosophies. One faction believes in racial harmony; these are known as 'straight-edge' skins. The other faction follows the extreme right-wing philosophies of racism ... neo-Nazism and hatred of Blacks, Jews and Hispanics" (1988:26). According to this official report, it is the second group—the racist skinheads—who are responsible for acts of domestic terrorism. Hence, the first part of Table 5.1 represents a double-cell of terrorists (i.e., racist skinheads) and non-terrorists (i.e., straight-edge skinheads). Critics of the social process perspective would predict no important differences between these factions, because they claim that social processes "defy objective measurement" (Laqueur, 1987:165), or that terrorism is a spur-of-the-moment idea that lacks any significant social, political, or economic justification (Dror, 1983; Merkl, 1986a; Wilkinson, 1986). In contrast, I contend that social processes are measurable, and predict that the two skinhead factions will differ significantly in terms of the distinguishing features of Steps 1 through 3.

Step 1: Assessment and Predictions. In keeping with Step 1, reports show that the skinheads emerged in the United States as a result of transnational communication. The U.S. Department of Justice (1988) notes that "Skinheads first appeared in the United States around 1980, as certain British rock groups, some of which are racist oriented, gained followers here. These British rock groups have song titles such as 'White Power' and white racist philosophy appears in their song lyrics" (1988: 26). Accordingly, I propose that terrorist skinheads will score higher than non-terrorist skinheads on a measure of preference for the music of Skrewdriver.

Also consistent with Step 1, reports show that two transgenerational sources of information have legitimized racism and prejudice among the American skinheads. First, the U.S. Department of Justice (1988) notes that "Skinheads are being recruited by white supremacist groups whose philosophy includes racial violence" (1988:26). Other reports suggest that this recruitment effort has been conducted by the far-right through an elaborate network of desktop publications and telephone hotlines (ADL, 1989c; Klanwatch, 1991). I predict that terrorists will score higher than non-terrorists on measures of exposure to this communications network. The second source is occult religion. Yet here the literature is interestingly divided. On one hand, a report shows that skinheads have been influenced by the teachings of Christian Identity, a religious movement that blends extreme anti-Semitism with prophecies of a racial revolution (Klanwatch, 1991). On the other hand, a report reveals that skinheads are influenced not by Christian Identity, but by the occult teachings of Satanism (ADL, 1988). I predict that terrorists will score higher than non-terrorists on a measure that examines beliefs in Satanism.[6]

Step 2: Assessment and Prediction. Numerous reports characterize American skinheads as neo-Nazis (e.g., ADL, 1989b; Center for Democratic Renewal, n.d.; U.S. Department of Justice, 1988). Therefore, I predict that terrorists will score higher than non-terrorists on a measure examining beliefs in neo-Nazi ideology.

Step 3: Assessment and Predictions. Evidence also speaks to the efficacy of Step 3 concerns about style, education, and affiliation. The U.S. Department of Justice (1988) concludes that "Skinheads are recognizable by their shaved heads and a 'uniform' consisting of...flight jackets and black English work boots" (1988:25). Other reports show that skinheads often wear Nazi and Viking regalia, white power T-shirts, and red suspenders (ADL, 1989b; Klanwatch, 1991). There is unanimous consensus among these reports that gun ownership and beer intoxication are also part of this style. With respect to educating others, reports show that skinheads are often frequent contributors to the white power press through the production of editorials, poems, and cartoons (ADL, 1987, 1988); and other investigations show that skinheads have formed their own white power rock bands (ADL, 1988; Thornburgh, 1990). Last, there is evidence to suggest that violence against third parties serves an internal function of control within skinhead collectives (ADL, 1989b).

My Step 3 predictions center around the idea that terrorists will be more tightly affiliated with one another than non-terrorists. I predict that terrorists will demonstrate (a) a more consistent subcultural style as expressed in hairstyle, costume, and regalia; (b) higher levels of gun ownership (another facet of style); (c) higher levels of educating others through the artistic expression of racism; (d) lower levels of intra-group conflict; and (e) lower levels of social alienation. Underlying these predictions is a theoretical perspective on youth subcultures developed by British researchers who argue that subcultural youths engage in violence as largely symbolic acts of resistance against the power-elites who are responsible for establishing cultural hegemony. When youths join a subculture, they inherit a positive reference group that supplies social support that allows for the emergence of a counterculture ideology. This ideology is manifested in subcultural style that represents the active resistance to hegemony. Among British skinheads, this style is read in the text of contemporary music, hairstyle, costume, jewelry, and weapons; and in excessive beer drinking, involvement in the arts, and symbolic violence (see Brake, 1985; Hebdige, 1979; Marcus, 1989).

Key Predictions. The second part of Table 5.1 is dedicated to a more rigorous test of the modified theory. Because the individuals to be studied in this research are members of the same known group (i.e., they are all members of the international skinhead movement) they can be studied for variation within that group (i.e., a single cell) to map more precisely the connections between Steps 1 through 4. Extending the conceptions of Figure 5.1, I predict that transnational and transgeneration messages of perceived victimization (i.e., preference for Skrewdriver, exposure to racist publications/hotlines, and beliefs in occult religion) will correlate significantly with neo-Nazi ideology, collective dynamics (i.e., hairstyle, etc., gun ownership, educating others, levels of group conflict and social alienation), and with acts of terrorism. I predict that neo-Nazi ideology will correlate significantly with collective dynamics and terrorism. And, of course, I predict that collective dynamics, including the style of beer intoxication, will correlate significantly with terrorism. These predictions are based on the work being done in the sociologies of music (e.g., Prinsky & Rosenbaum, 1989), religion (e.g., Stark, 1985), and deviance (e.g., Ben-Yehuda, 1990) on why individuals join cults/sects and engage in behaviors consistent with the beliefs of those subcultures; and on current research in the area of intoxication and aggression which shows that sociocultural factors can often channel the arousal affects of alcohol into behaviors that may include violence (Fagan, 1990).

It is beyond the scope of this analysis, however, to test predictions about the fifth and final step of the approach concerning the attempted social control of terrorism. My intent is to identify the relative influence of social processes in the pursuit of terrorist goals. I intend to do this through a study of what Wilkinson (1986) refers to as the "mental re-enactment of terrorist thought in each tiny terrorist group"

Table 5.1
**Summary of Modified Deterrent Vicarious Social Control Predictions:
Two Groups That Differ in Their Experiences with
Social Processes and General Predictions About Terrorism**

Part 1: Preliminary Predictions
Distinguishing Features of Modified Approach

	Terrorists	Non-Terrorists
Step 1		
1a. Favorite musical group	Skrewdriver	Other (not white power rock)
1b. Exposure to racist communications network		
1b1. publications	High[a]	Low
1b2. telephone hotlines	High[a]	Low
1c. Level of beliefs in occult religion	High[a]	Low
Step 2		
2a. Level of beliefs in neo-Nazi ideology	High[a]	Low
Step 3		
3a. Consistency of style (i.e., hairstyle, costume, regalia)	High[a]	Low
3b. Levels of gun ownership	High[a]	Low
3c. Levels of educating others	High[a]	Low
3d. Levels of intra-group conflict	Low	High[a]
3e. Levels of social alienation	Low	High[a]

[a] The term "High" is used in a relative sense, meaning that between-group differences will be statistically significant.

Part II: Key Predictions
Expected Correlations Between
Distinguishing Features
of Modified Approach

	Neo-Nazi Ideology	Style (i.e., hairstyle, etc.)	Gun Ownership	Educating Others	Group Conflict	Social Alienation	Terrorism
Preference for Skrewdriver	+	+	+	+	−	−	+
Racist publications	+	+	+	+	−	−	+
Racist hotlines	+	+	+	+	−	−	+
Occult religion	+	+	+	+	−	−	+
Neo-Nazi ideology		+	+	+	−	−	+
Style							+
Gun ownership							+
Beer intoxication							+
Educating others							+
Group conflict							−
Social alienation							−

(1986:97). To the extent that I capture this re-enactment empirically, the findings can be considered relevant to the plausibility of the full five-step model.

METHODS

The Research Problem. It is impossible to determine the number of skinheads living in America. In the late 1980s, the U.S. Department of Justice estimated that "there are approximately 500 to 1,000 skinheads in the United States belonging to about 10 major gangs each having several subgroups" (1988:25). Two sampling problems emerge from this estimate: (1) How many skinheads are necessary for a systematic analysis of terrorism? and (2) How many groups must be studied to make generalizations about the skinhead movement? Gaining access to skinheads represents a more formidable problem. In the United States, right-wing extremist groups present a built-in barrier that transcends the problems encountered by criminologists who attempt to gain access to the lives of gang members who engage in savage forms of street violence (e.g., Jankowski, 1991). In both cases, among gang members and white extremists, there is a well-developed code of silence wherein persons are naturally prone to conceal information about their violence. Yet with extremists, like the skinheads, the code of silence assumes a more functional role. Evidence of a politics of silence within the far-right is well-documented (e.g., Dees, 1991; Langer, 1990). Moreover, withholding information—silence—is a political tool: Not only does silence add to the mystique of extremist groups, but the less outsiders know about these groups, the safer they are from attempts to control them.

Procedures and Sample

I began the study in 1989 by conducting a series of confidential interviews with FBI agents and officials of anti-racist organizations responsible for investigating and monitoring the criminal activities of the far-right. The purpose of these interviews was to determine those areas of the U.S. where skinhead groups were most active. Through this process, I created a list of approximately 50 skinhead organizations, including the "10 major gangs" and their various subgroups referred to by the U.S. Department of Justice. With two exceptions, all subjects in this research were members of the groups appearing on this list.

I then chose seven major U.S. cities and began fieldwork in an attempt to track down the identified skinheads in the course of their routine activities (e.g., in public parks, on street corners, in front of liquor stores, at rock concerts, and in coffee shops, bars, record stores, motorcycle shops, and survivalist outlets). I used these procedures, on and off, for a period of three years (1989-1991) and conducted 10 structured interviews. Each interview was conducted using a questionnaire that addressed issues of theoretical and practical concern. Unanticipated topics that emerged in the interviews were also explored, such as the role of religion in the skinhead movement. These comments were noted verbatim on the questionnaire itself, and this procedure was repeated throughout the research. The 10 questionnaires were based on interviews with skinheads from the San Francisco Bay Area (two interviews with subjects from two different organizations), Seattle (two interviews/two organizations), Indianapolis (two interviews/two organizations), Phoenix, Chicago, Cincinnati, and Louisville (one interview/one organization in each city). These subjects were not difficult to identify: They all had shaved heads and wore white power and/or Nazi regalia (e.g., the SS badge, the Iron Cross, etc.). Two skinheads, for example, were tattooed in the middle of their foreheads with the mark of the swastika. I simply approached these youths and asked them to participate in the structured interview. No attempt was made to mislead them. I presented myself as an independent social scientist unaffiliated with law enforcement or social service. To gain their trust, I promised complete anonymity. I presented the research as an attempt to set the record straight on the skinhead movement, and at no time were subjects asked to speak into a tape recorder.[7]

Next, I wrote to the leaders of 26 skinhead groups who had published their addresses in the white power press. Each leader was invited to make a collect, long-distance telephone call to me for the purpose of conducting the structured interview. Again, I made clear my intention of setting the record straight and promised complete anonymity. This method yielded 12 questionnaires on skinheads from New York City; Dallas; Birmingham, and Montgomery, Alabama; San Diego; Milwaukee; Washington, D.C.; Detroit; Cincinnati (a different organization than the one referred to previously); Austin, Texas; Orlando, Florida; and Point Pleasant, New Jersey. For those leaders who did not respond to the telephone interview, I sent follow-up letters and a copy of the questionnaire under a simple, innocuous cover. Once more, I promised objectivity and anonymity. I invited leaders to fill out the questionnaires and return them to me. This procedure produced eight completed questionnaires on skinheads from Austin, Texas (a different organization from the one referred to previously); Portland, Oregon; Taveras, Florida; Memphis, Tennessee; New Brunswick, New Jersey; Grand Rapids, and Southfield, Michigan; and Racine, Wisconsin.

Having gained access to the skinheads through the white power press, I then tried my luck with the far-right electronic media by logging onto a well-known computerized bulletin board. I identified myself as a social scientist "with no axe to grind against anybody" and again guaranteed complete anonymity. This procedure produced two completed questionnaires on skinheads from Alabama (city unknown and the first exception to the aforementioned list) and Buffalo, New York. Last, I used prison field study methods. Assisted by prison guards and correctional educators, questionnaires were completed by skinheads from Los Angeles; Atlanta; Carbondale, Illinois (the second exception to the list); and a small town in South Carolina. Two of these individuals were incarcerated for racially motivated homicides and two were incarcerated for attempted homicides of minorities.

In summary, 36 questionnaires and related interview data were gathered on skinheads from 36 organizations in 30 locations across the United States. The sample consists primarily of group leaders, or core members who are likely to display the highest rates and severity of violence against third parties. I solved the problem of gaining access to white extremist groups by presenting myself to subjects as a social scientist with an academic interest in their lives, and by promising objectivity and anonymity. To the extent that the original list of groups was an accurate estimate of the most active skinheads in the United States, and to the extent that these 36 individuals have been selected from that list, then the sample—roughly 3.5 percent (i.e., 36 out of 1,000) to 7 percent (i.e., 36 out of 500) of the total number of officially estimated skinheads in the nation during the late 1980s—can be considered representative of the U.S. skinhead movement.

Measures

Transnational-Transgenerational. These measures began with a single item answered on a two-point scale. Those who answered Skrewdriver were coded 2, those who answered otherwise were coded 1. The item is listed below, along with the sample mean, standard deviation, and frequency counts of those who either selected Skrewdriver or another band.

> Perhaps the most important aspect of youth culture is music. List your favorite bands, beginning with your most favorite (Skrewdriver=23, other=13; mean=1.63; sd=.48)

Three measures examined transgenerational influences. The first was exposure to the *WAR* magazine, published by the White Aryan Resistance of Fallbrook, California. Exposure to *WAR* was measured by an item answered on a three-point scale. Those who answered that they were *WAR* readers only were coded 3, readers of other white power magazines were coded 2, and non-readers of racist magazines were coded 1. (Multiple responses, of which there were only three, were coded 3. *WAR* readers only=26; readers of other white power magazines=9; non-readers=1; mean=2.65; sd=0.54). The second was exposure to the WAR (telephone) Hotline, measured by a single question answered on a two-point scale. Those who answered that they were WAR Hotline users were coded 2, non-users were coded 1. (WAR Hotline users=20; non-users=16; sample mean=1.54; sd=.50.)

The third measure tested for the presence of Satanic beliefs among subjects. Support for Satanism was measured by five items derived from the religious principles set forth in *The Satanic Bible* (LaVey, 1969:25). The principles appear in Appendix A, followed by the corresponding items, response options, frequency counts, sample means, standard deviations, and item-total correlations. When subjects' scores were summated, the five items show internal consistency overall (Cronbach's alpha=.41; sample mean=8.70; sd=2.11), justifying the creation of an occult religion scale.[8]

Neo-Nazi Ideology. This measure was the seven-item authoritarian aggression scale designed by Adorno and Associates (1950) in their attempt to dissect fascistic mentality within broad populations. As conceived by Adorno et al., fascism was interchangeable with the term authoritarianism which was used to describe the character structure (or personality) of lower-middle-class Germany during the 1930s. It was the authoritarian character structure, according to this theory, that served as the basis for the ideas and emotions forming the nucleus of Nazism (Dillehay, 1978). The seven items were answered on a three-point scale: Agree (3); uncertain (2); disagree (1). The items, frequency counts, sample means, standard deviations, and item/total correlations are displayed in Appendix B. When summated, responses to the seven items also revealed adequate internal consistency (alpha=.56; sample mean=17.61; sd=2.30), justifying the creation of a neo-Nazi ideology scale.[9]

Dynamics of Collective Affiliation. Two single-items began the examination of subcultural style. In the first, subjects were studied in relation to hairstyle, clothing usually worn, and jewelry. Those who displayed traditional skinhead hairstyle (i.e., the shaven head), clothing (i.e., Doc Marten work boots, flight jackets, and/or white power t-shirts), *and* jewelry (i.e., images of Nazism) were coded 2; those who did not display such trappings were coded 1. (Traditional style=15; nontraditional=21; sample mean=1.58; sd=.50.) The second measure was gun ownership. Gun owners were coded 2 and non-owners were coded 1 (Gun owners=17; non-owners=19; sample mean=1.47; sd=0.51). One item measured the extent to which subjects educate others through the artistic expression of racism. Those who played in racist bands, wrote poetry, articles, or drew cartoons for the white power press were coded 2; and those who did not were coded 1. (Artistic expression of racism=33; no expression=3; sample mean=1.86; sd=.18.) Intra-group conflict was examined by a single item answered on a three-point scale. Response options were no problems, low conflict (3); few problems, moderate conflict (2), and "a lot of problems," high conflict (1). The item is listed below, along with frequency counts, sample mean, and standard deviation.

> No matter what group we join, the group will have problems. Someone will always disagree with another over things like power and control of the group. What are the problems of your group? (Low conflict=22; moderate conflict=14; high conflict=0; mean=2.61; sd=.49)

One item, derived from Srole's (1956) measure, examined levels of social alienation, defined as "a separation between self and others, a fundamental failure to achieve reciprocity thinking" (Nash, 1985: 124). The item was answered on the same three-point scale as the neo-Nazi ideology measures.

These days a person doesn't really know whom he can count on.
(Agree=17; uncertain=3; disagree=16; sample mean=2.02;
sd=.97)[10]

Terrorism. Schmidt (1983) presents evidence of 109 different definitions of political terrorism used by various writers between 1936 and 1981; Laqueur (1987) points out that "there is every reason to assume that there have been more since" (1987:143). I rely on an integration of two such definitions. First, although my measure does not permit the full application of Gibbs' rigorous definition,[11] it does permit a partial application. I measure illegal violence directed against human objects "undertaken with a view to maintaining a putative norm ... [which is] perceived by the participant as contributing to the normative putative goal" (Gibbs, 1989: 330). Second, my measure relies on this definition provided by the U.S. Department of Justice:

> Terrorism is a violent act or an act dangerous to human life in
> violation of the criminal laws, to intimidate or coerce a government,
> *the civilian population, or any segment thereof,* in the furtherance
> of political or social objectives" (1989:25, emphasis added).

Three items were used to measure these definitions of terrorism. The first examined "a putative norm" or a "political objective." The item, response options, frequency counts, sample mean, and standard deviation are as follows:

Item: Why did you join your group?

Response Options: to make money (1);
                      to protect myself against other groups
                      or gangs (2);
                      to fight for my neighborhood (3);
                      to fight for my race (4);
                      other (5)

Responses: to make money=0;
                      protection=0;
                      fight for neighborhood=0;
                      to fight for race=32;
                      other=4
                      (mean=4.11; sd=1.0)

When considered in light of responses to this item, the other two questions measured the concept of "maintaining and contributing to the normative putative goal" or "the furtherance of political objectives" through the use of illegal violence.

Item:	How many fights have you been in during the past two years?
Response Options:	none (1); one or two (2); three or four (3); five or more (4)
Responses:	none=7; one or two=10; three or four=7; five or more=12 (sample mean=2.67; sd=1.14)
Item:	How many of these fights were against people of another race?
Response Options:	none (1); about half of them (2); all of them (3)
Responses:	none=14; about half=14; all=8 (sample mean=1.83; sd=.77)

In total, the 36 skinheads were involved in approximately 120 acts of violence. Roughly 42 percent (n=51) were against persons of another race, including two homicides and two attempted homicides. An inspection of the questionnaires revealed that 22 subjects committed these racial assaults, and each reportedly joined their group to fight for their race. It is the third item, then, (self-reported assaults against persons of another race) that serves as the initial basis for the study's design. That is, the sample can be divided into two groups: 22 terrorists and 14 non-terrorists. These groups will be used to test the preliminary predictions in Table 5.1. The key predictions will then be tested by including all subjects in a single analysis, ultimately treating racial assaults as the dependent variable.

Finally, the ADL (1989b) argues that "The heavy consumption of beer very likely has contributed to the skinhead propensity toward violence" (1989b:30). To test this, those 22 subjects who reported racial assaults were asked to identify those intoxicants, if any, they had usually ingested prior to their fights. Response options were amphetamines/barbiturates (1); PCP/cocaine (2); marijuana (3); gin/vodka/other hard liquor (4); beer (5); and sober (6). (Vodka=1; beer=17; sober=4; mean=4.94; sd=.23.)

Sociodemographic and Control Variables

In Table 5.2, I show significant differences between terrorists and non-terrorists on three important sociodemographic measures. Such differences suggest the importance of controlling these variables while testing predictions about differences between groups. However, my key predictions involve the effects of social processes on the pursuit of terrorist goals *within* the skinhead movement. While it is necessary to bear in mind the significant between-group differences, their control is not as central as it is to testing within-group predictions. Therefore, I shall use the three significant sociodemographic measures as control variables because they are potential confounders of the association between social processes and terrorism in the within-group analysis.

Table 5.2
Control Variables and Demographic Variables in Two Groups

	Terrorists (n=22)	Non-Terrorists (n=14)	X^2 Test of Group Differences
Age	19.6	19.8	$X^2_9=15.52$
(mean age in years)			
Sex			
males	20	7	$X^2_1=7.63*$
females	2	7	
Class Origin: Father's Occupation			
white-collar	4	10	$X^2_3=16.44*$
blue-collar	17	2	
unemployed	1	0	
Family Experiences			
non-friction with parents	16	14	$X^2_2=4.58$
friction	5	0	
pattern of violent abuse	1	0	
Educational Status[a]			
college student	7	3	$X^2_3=.38$
high school graduate	10	9	
high school student	2	2	
high school dropout	3	0	
Occupational Status[a]			
white-collar employed	2	7	$X^2_2=12.33*$
blue-collar employed	18	3	
unemployed	2	4	

a Incarcerated subjects were asked to list their most recent educational and occupational accomplishments.

*p < .05

NOTE: Number of subjects permit the calculation of X^2 coefficients only at the 5% level of confidence with an 80% chance of predicting statistical differences (see Kraemer and Theimann, 1987).

RESULTS

The results are organized into two parts. Table 5.3 presents evidence concerning Steps 1 through 3 of the modified theory for between-group predictions. In Table 5.4, I present evidence concerning Steps 1 through 4 for within-group predictions. Major findings are highlighted with interview data.

Evidence Concerning Step 1: Transnational and Transgenerational Messages of Perceived Victimization

Preference for Skrewdriver. The modified approach posits that terrorists perceive themselves as victims of social injustice. I argue that this is a learned perception. Among the American skinheads, I contend that this perception is learned—first and foremost—through the prism of music. I suggest that this occurs at a metaphysical level through a sort of seat-of-the-pants shamanism wherein ordinary musicians transform themselves into extraordinary ones by expressing highly forbidden messages of racial and ethnic hatred. These messages convey an elaborate fantasy in which racial minorities, immigrants, and Jews are portrayed as agents in a conspiracy to threaten the well-being of working-class whites. This fantasy is transmitted to American youths by British rock bands via white power heavy metal music.

White power heavy metal was created by Skrewdriver through a blending of three distinct musical forms. First, Skrewdriver took its roots from British "Oi" music: 1930s pub sing-alongs about the glories of the British state set to male surge-chanting (*Oi! Oi! Oi!*). Skrewdriver then crossed the nationalism and patriotism of Oi with the banality of 1970s punk music, à la the Sex Pistols. On top of this, Skrewdriver then layed the din-of-battle threonodies of heavy metal in the tradition of Led Zeppelin. This musical amalgamation created a mystical, occult-oriented "bully-boy" appeal for a "clean white Britain" in which the Viking—an age-old mythological warrior known for horrendous acts of raping, burning, and pillaging—once again emerges to conquer the British Isles. The net effect was this.

> *Nigger, nigger, get on that boat*
> *Nigger, nigger, row*
> *Nigger, nigger, get out of here,*
> *Nigger, nigger, go, go, go* (Skrewdriver, 1982).

I argue that songs such as this emit emotions so powerful in the minds of certain American white youths that they begin to link song lyrics to their focal concerns about employment and quality of life. Through exposure to anthems such as "Nigger, Nigger," "Race and Nation," and "Dead Paki in a Gutter," youths then transform themselves from their ordinary realities to something wider, something that enlarges them as people. They become skinheads armed with the emotional capacity to commit violence against third parties.

Table 5.3
Frequency Counts, Group Means, and Chi-Square Tests of
Between-Group Differences Showing the Extent to Which Terrorists
and Non-Terrorists are Influenced by Social Processes

	Terrorists	Non-Terrorists	X^2 Test of Group Differences
Preference for Skrewdriver	20	3	$X^2_1=17.90*$
(other preference)	(2)	(11)	
Exposure to *WAR*	19	4	$X^2_2=10.59*$
(other racist magazines)	(2)	(7)	
(non-exposure)	(1)	(0)	
Exposure to WAR Hotline	16	4	$X^2_1=6.21*$
(non-exposure)	(6)	(10)	
Occult Religion			
Beliefs in:			
Self-indulgence	1.18	1.00	$X^2_2=1.43$
Vital existence	2.00	1.35	$X^2_2=4.91$
Selective compassion	2.40	2.71	$X^2_2=4.24$
Vengeance	2.22	1.71	$X^2_2=7.63*$
Man-as-animal	2.18	1.57	$X^2_2=3.04$
Occult Religion scale	9.17	6.91	$X^2_{10}=4.25$
Neo-Nazi Ideology			
Attitudes toward:			
"people with bad manners, habits and breeding"	2.71	1.71	$X^2_2=16.36*$
"family and country"	2.95	2.64	$X^2_2=4.33$
"honor"	2.40	2.35	$X^2_2=3.08$
"sex crimes"	3.00	2.71	$X^2_2=3.32$
"respect for parents"	1.90	1.71	$X^2_2=180$
"immoral, crooked, and feebleminded people"	3.00	2.57	$X^2_2=11.31*$
"homosexuals"	2.72	2.00	$X^2_2=15.50*$
Neo-Nazi Ideology scale	18.33	15.69	$X^2_{14}=7.95$
Style:			
hairstyle, costume, regalia	1.31	1.57	$X^2_2=2.25$
gun ownership	16	1	$X^2_1=14.76$
(non-ownership)	(6)	(13)	
Educating others	21	12	$X^2_1=5.50$
(no expression)	(1)	(2)	
Intra-group conflict	2.40	2.92	$X^2_1=9.71*$
Social alienation	1.68	2.57	$X^2_2=8.50*$

*p < .05

These ideas mirror a growing body of research on European skinheads showing that white power heavy metal, with its intense social content, serves to raise the
political consciousness of youths allowing them to display their resistance to cultural hegemony by committing violence against immigrants and racial minorities
(Brake, 1985; Douglas, 1993; Mücke, 1991). Consistent with this, Table 5.3 confirms the between-group prediction: 20 out of 22 terrorist skinheads selected
Skrewdriver as their favorite band, while only 3 of 14 non-terrorists selected
Skrewdriver ($X^2=17.90$, df=1, p< .05). In another section of the questionnaire, subjects were asked to respond to an item measuring frequency of exposure to their favorite
band. Of the 20 terrorists who selected Skrewdriver, 17 reported that they were
daily listeners. The interviews confirmed this level of intensity. For example, a terrorist who claimed to be the leader of a collective numbering more than 250 members said:

> Back in 1985 [when we started], Skrewdriver *was* the skinhead
> movement. They provided the ideology for what we did back
> then.

Exposure to WAR and the WAR Hotline. The modified approach further stipulates
that perceived victimization is transmitted transgenerationally. This occurs by way
of the following logic: If X likes Y, and Y hates Z, then X will also hate Z; where
X is a youth, Y is an adult, and Z is the member of a third party.

At the time of this research, the White Aryan Resistance was operated by a 52-
year-old white male, a father of eight children, and a well-known figure in the
racist underground. But he was not a skinhead. Unlike other white extremist groups
in the United States (e.g., the Invisible Empire of the Knights of the Ku Klux Klan),
WAR was not a membership organization either. It did not hold meetings, it did not
require membership cards, nor did it require members to wear costumes. *WAR*
operated solely through the technology of computer bulletin boards, telephone hotlines, cable-access television, and the *WAR* magazine. The stated goal of WAR, in
the words of its founder, was "to inject some ideology into the skinheads" (quoted
in Coplon, 1989:85). This ideology was called the Third Position, described as an
"international pan-Aryan movement dedicated to an emerging global struggle of whites
against Jews and mongrels" (see Langer, 1990). *WAR* offered vibrant and electric
presentations of this point of view. Each issue contained clear and highly resoluted
photographs of skinheads "injured in the line of battle"; an "Aryan Entertainment
Section" featuring mail-order services for Skrewdriver tapes, Nazi regalia, Viking
posters, racist videos, and hard-to-find racist books; and a "POW Section" listing
the mailing addresses of incarcerated right-wing terrorists and assassins in Britain,
Germany, France, and the United States. But the most outstanding feature of *WAR*
was its extravagant cartoons. These cartoons sought to breathe humor into the
Third Position manifesto by glorifying skinheads who committed racial violence.
In these cartoons, blacks were drawn grotesquely and referred to as "Niggers,"

"Black-Assed Coons," "Spooks," "Congoids," "Monkeys," "Black Baboons," and "Mud People." Hispanics were called "Brown Rot" and "Spics." Jews were drawn as "Kikes" and "Jewish Lesbians." Gays were referred to as "Pathetic Queers" and "AIDS-Ravaged Faggots."

This transgenerational outreach to white youth is consistent with European studies showing that the National Fronts of Britian, Germany, and France have all sponsored projects to recruit skinheads into their ranks (Bowling, 1990; Hiro, 1991; Seidel-Pielen, 1991). And once recruited, these skinheads were known to commit violence against immigrants and racial minorities (Douglas, 1993; Mücke, 1991). In keeping with this, Table 5.3 again confirms the between-group prediction: 19 terrorists were readers of *WAR*, whereas only 4 non-terrorists were *WAR* readers (X^2=10.59, df=2, p=<.05). When examined for frequency of exposure, 17 of the 19 terrorists reported that they read *WAR* on a regular basis (i.e., weekly or monthly). The persuasiveness of such communication is evidenced by responses to the item measuring exposure to the WAR Hotline. These taped telephone call-in bulletins offered general information about the Third Position, such as "Skrewdriver News" and declarations of solidarity with the Order—the most violent right-wing terrorist organization of the American twentieth century (U.S. Department of Justice, 1988). The between-group predictions are once again confirmed: A total of 16 terrorists were Hotline users, compared to only 4 non-terrorists (X^2=6.21, df=1, p< .05), and the majority of terrorists used the Hotline on a weekly basis.

Religion. With respect to the religious orientation of subjects, three conclusions can be drawn from Table 5.3. First, skinheads are not Satanists. The "golden rule" of the religion, as defined by LaVey (1969), is "Do What Thou Wilt Shall Be The Full of The Law" (1969:25). Yet fully 100 percent of the skinheads rejected a belief in self-indulgence, the essential principle of the Satanic paradigm (see Appendix A for frequency counts).[12] Second, terrorists are distinguished from non-terrorists only by their beliefs in vengeance (X^2=7.63, df=2, p<. 05). And third, the occult religion scale scores show no difference between groups. Thus, the findings do not confirm the preliminary prediction overall. We are left, then, with a sample of young persons who tend to embrace a morality that values vengeance over forgiveness, selective compassion over unconditional compassion, and conceives of man as a potentially vicious animal rather than a spiritual being; yet this morality also rebukes self-indulgence and recognizes a spiritual afterlife (together, these beliefs comprise the defining characteristics of the occult religion scale.) But we are also left with the questions of (a) How do youths come to embrace a set of beliefs (i.e., vengeance, conditional compassion, and man-as-animal) that run counter to the morality of Western religion? (b) How is this alternative morality linked to terrorism? and (c) How is conventional morality (i.e., beliefs in self-restraint and the promise of a spiritual afterlife) also associated with terrorism? I suggest that these questions can be answered through reference to *Nazi Occultism.*

Nazi Occultism. A total of seven terrorists referred to themselves as a Reverend in the Church of the Creator. Four other terrorists reported that Creativity is at the very core of American skinheadism, and the original list contained nine groups who used the name Creativity Skins. The Church of the Creator is part of the Christian Identity movement. Its major text is *The White Man's Bible*, published in 1971 by member of the South Carolina Knights of the Ku Klux Klan, though supplemental readings include *Mein Kampf, The Negro: A Beast, The International Jew,* and *The Holy Book of Adolf Hitler*—a work that elevates Hitler to sainthood (see ADL, 1983; Coates, 1987). *The White Man's Bible* is based on a reinterpretation of Genesis. It maintains that God made all races, except one, on the third day of Creation. These races were seen as inferior in the eyes of God, however. And so it was on the final day, according to this scenario, that God made the perfect human creation—Adam, a white man. Hence the term Creativity. Aryan supremacy is viewed as an "eternal law of nature" and devotees of the religion are promised a spiritual afterlife if they make certain sacrifices and commitments. Similar to the strategy employed by WAR in developing an appeal for its Third Position, Creativity is based on historical revisionism promulgated by an adult white racist.

Creativity sermons are preached in the comfort of homes where walls are typically decorated with swastikas, SS insignias, and portraits of Hitler, Rudolf Hess, and Robert Mathews, slain leader of the Order. This comfort seems to allow Creativity's born-again men and women to practice with clear moral conscience the bigotry and hatred that have traditionally been denied to them as sinful. Through this redefinition process, devotees conquer their moral beings and come to believe that violence is an exalted virtue. This is the prerequisite for a belief in vengeance.

Creativity has three targets for its vengeance. First is the African-American male, referred to in sermons as a "monkey" or a "beast." Devotees consider race mixing the most sinful act known to humankind. Yet it is sanctioned by the U.S. Government; hence, they become the second target of vengeance. Allowing the ultimate sin is a firm indication that the United States is being administered by a Zionist Occupied Government. Race mixing is, therefore, viewed as a state-organized Jewish effort to dilute the sacred white progeny and inevitably turn the Aryans into a race of mongrels. The third target is the gay community. To devotees, gays represent a putrefaction of all manner of human morality. Creativity has been described as "a religion by sociopaths, for sociopaths. It turns their sickness into virtue" (Coates, 1987:92). Yet one preacher in this research—a terrorist who regularly preached to a congregation of some 70 disciples—described the religion like this.

> Most of the youth in the white power movement are involved in salubrious living. It is part of our religion of Creativity. It means to have a clean mind, body, and soul...Most of these kids [in the movement] actually look more like Young Republicans than skinheads. Nobody uses drugs and we all have strong family ties. We're a positive culture. We go by the eternal laws of nature.

Evidence Concerning Step 2: Neo-Nazi Ideology

The modified approach posits that terrorists must embrace an ideology that is capable of increasing their tendencies to aggress against third parties. Table 5.3 confirms the between-group predictions on three counts. First, responses to the authoritarian aggression measure indicate that terrorists are more likely to focus hostility against people they perceive to have "bad manners, habits, and breeding" ($X^2=16.36$, df=2, p< 0.05). This is the essence of racism, and the finding is consistent with the seminal work of Adorno et al. (1950) who found intense levels of inter-group prejudice among criminals. Second, terrorists are more likely to advocate "getting rid of immoral, crooked, and feebleminded people" ($X^2=11.31$, df=2, p<.05). This finding confirms the research of Hofstadter (1967) who argues that those who espouse fascistic beliefs will be especially responsive to conspiracy theories of social, political, and economic events. Dillehay (1978) suggests that "[t]he essence of conspiracy theories is that they forecast imminent doom for cherished values and institutions, with the impending disaster attributed to a carefully conceived plan of action surreptitiously controlled and conditioned by a diabolical enemy" (1978: 112). The diabolical enemy of American skinhead folklore is, of course, ZOG. Third, terrorists are more likely to hold extreme opinions about homosexuals ($X^2=15.50$, df=2, p<.05), a finding that is not only in keeping with the research of Adorno et al. who demonstrated that authoritarians typically hold negative attitudes toward a broad range of outgroups, but it is also consistent with research showing that a revolt against the decadence of homosexuality was an important historical correlate of fascist and Nazi youth movements in Europe (e.g., Linz, 1976).

In summary, Table 5.3 does not confirm the predictions about neo-Nazi ideology overall inasmuch as the scale scores failed to discriminate between groups. Terrorists are no different than non-terrorists in their beliefs about family and country, honor, sex crimes, and respect for parents. Yet, Table 5.3 does show that the defining characteristics of terrorists' ideology are racism, anti-Semitism, and homophobia. Taken together, these beliefs comprise the core value of biological determinism—the heart of National Socialism (Fromm, 1941; Sternhell, 1976; Von Maltitz, 1973). Interviews confirmed this finding. For instance, a terrorist (also a Creativity preacher) who claimed to be the leader of a collective with more than 50 members reported that:

> I've been a racist since I was 15. I started out reading Nietzsche,
> then I read German history books about the ancient Aryans. I
> became a National Socialist at about 17. I read Hitler's *Mein Kampf*
> three times in a row, and began to appreciate his brilliance. I saw
> that the racial cohesiveness of the Jews had allowed them to gain
> power for their own purposes. I began to think: Why can't
> whites do the same thing? [Then] I started listening to Wagner
> and the classic German marching bands. After that, Skrewdriver
> came along and that's when I started the skinheads in [this city].

Evidence Concerning Step 3: Style, Education, and Affiliation

According to the modified theory, subcultural style is considered the linchpin to understanding affiliation within a terrorist collective because style embodies the true patterns of life in the group. Two accoutrements of the European skinhead style are paramilitary uniforms and weapons (Hiro, 1991; Mücke, 1991). Therefore, it is important to determine the manner in which this style operates as a means of bonding terrorists to one another in their pursuit of goals.

Contrary to the prediction, however, Table 5.3 shows no difference between terrorists and non-terrorists with respect to hairstyle, costume, and regalia. Yet the measure of gun ownership does confirm the prediction concerning style: terrorist were more likely to own firearms (X^2=, 14.76, df=1, p<.05). These weapons included a variety of hunting rifles, shotguns, and handguns; the most popular of which was the Smith & Wesson .357 magnum revolver. Consistent with Crenshaw's (1981) finding that terrorists possess "internally consistent images of the environment" (1981: 385), the interviews revealed that terrorists viewed gun ownership as largely a defensive strategy to protect themselves against outside antagonists. Moreover, the presence of guns represents a group process that seems to heighten the aggressive effect on subjects' behavior, thereby entrenching terrorism as a collective norm (see Yablonsky, 1990).

British researchers have also found that skinhead subcultures are typically dominated by working-class artists. These ideas are consistent with Table 5.3 findings concerning the education of others through the artistic expression of racism: both groups are dominated by artists. Yet since there is almost no variation in the between-group analysis, terrorists do not differ from non-terrorists; hence, again the preliminary prediction is not confirmed. The preliminary prediction is also refuted with respect to group conflict. Although no one in the sample reported high conflict, terrorists were more likely to experience moderate levels of conflict in their groups (X^2=9.71, df=1, p<.05). Despite this modest conflict, and consistent with the prediction, terrorists nevertheless experienced lower levels of social alienation than did non-terrorists (X^2=8.50, df=2, p<.05). Moreover, this finding confirms the ADL's (1989b) finding that "Skinheads provide their members with a substitute family....This sense of kinship is strengthened even further if the gang has been involved in violence together" (1989b:29).

In summary, Table 5.3 presents evidence to confirm a number of important between-group predictions. Terrorists are distinguished from non-terrorists by their preference for Skrewdriver, exposure to *WAR* and the WAR Hotline, gun ownership, and levels of social alienation—that is, terrorists are more likely to have someone in this world on whom they can rely. Although important differences exist between groups with respect to beliefs in vengeance, racism, the conspiracy theory concerning Jews, homophobia, and group conflict—the roles of religion, ideology, and collective dynamics in the pursuit of terrorist goals are less clear. These issues are clarified by the within-group analysis.

Table 5.4   Correlation Matrix Showing Extent to Which Terrorist Goals Are Influenced by Social Processes and Sociodemographic Factors (Only Significant Pearson's r's reported).

| | Step 1 | | | Step 2 | Step 3 | | | | | | Step 4 |
Step 1 Measures	WAR	Hotline	Occult	Neo-Nazi	Hair, etc.	Guns	Beer[a]	Educating	Conflict	Alienation	Terrorism
Preference for Skrewdriver	.64	.60	.50	.57	—	.60	.68	—	.36	—	.67
Exposure to WAR		.58	—	.47	—	—	—	—	—	—	—
Exposure to W.A.R. Hotline			.30	.40	—	—	—	—	—	—	—
Occult Religion Scale				.45	.38	.48	.53	.56	—	—	.53
Step 2 Measure											
Neo-Nazi Ideology Scale					—	.65	—	.32	.42	-.35	.57
Step 3 Measures											
Style:											
Hair, costume, regalia						.35	—	—	—	—	.33
Gun Ownership						—	—	.42	—	—	.71
Beer Intoxication						—	—	.36	—	—	.77
Educating others								—	—	—	—
Intra-Group Conflict									—	—	.39
Social Alienation										—	—
Control Measures											
Sex											.46
Class Origin											—
Occupational Status											—

[a] n=22

NOTE: All coefficients are significant at the .05 level.

Key Predictions of the Modified Theory

The most global test of the modified theory is whether the three sets of measures (transnational-transgenerational, ideology, and collective dynamics) have an effect on the pursuit of terrorist goals *within* the skinhead movement. I predict that each set will be associated with others and with terrorism. In the main, these predictions are confirmed by Table 5.4.

Evidence Concerning the Associations Between Step 1 and Steps 2 through 4

As a prelude to discussing the major results, I note that the Step 1 measures approach construct validity: Table 5.4 shows that transnational influence (Preference for Skrewdriver) is correlated positively with transgenerational influences (Exposure to *WAR,* the Hotline, and occult religion). Skrewdriver and WAR transmit messages of perceived victimization subjectively through technology, and occult religion is transmitted subjectively through hard-to-find racist books. This implies that perceived victimization is not a (set of) personal opinions. Rather, they are opinions that belong to others about the negative role of third parties.

Table 5.4 shows that these transnational-transgenerational influences have a uniformly positive effect on the development of terrorist ideology. Preference for Skrewdriver, exposure to the WAR materials, and occult religion all correlate positively with neo-Nazi ideology. Hence, social cognition, shaped by the opinions of others, is manifested in ideological orientation. Because of the persuasiveness of technology and the mystique of religion, transnational-transgenerational messages are highly structured and attractive. This seems to allow for a fast and effective application of perceived victimization into the evaluative beliefs of skinheads (see van Dijk, 1987:194).

Transnational-transgenerational also affects the dynamics of terrorist collectives. Yet this effect is selective. Preference for Skrewdriver is correlated with gun ownership, beer drinking, and low levels of group conflict; occult religion is correlated with educating others through artistic racism and all facets of the skinhead style. But the WAR materials uniformly have no effect on internal dynamics. Although WAR's messages facilitate the move toward neo-Nazism, they have no effect on the internal dynamics of groups. This finding was vociferously conveyed during the interviews. For example, one terrorist said that:

> Metzger [the WAR founder] is a joke. His whole thing is naive.
> He's using people to do his dirty work. I think that's really
> wrong.

Another said:

> The job done on European-Americans will not be cleared up
> overnight. It will take a racialist struggle. The vast majority [of
> adults] in the racial right only want skinheads to do their dirty
> work. I am a National Socialist and a European-American with
> strong family ties. I am not a "disciple" of Tom Metzger.

And to re-confirm the lack of effect WAR has on the internal dynamics of
skinhead groups, a terrorist reported:

> WAR and the Klan are associated. I don't believe they are well
> organized, however. They only deal with the ignorant people...
> Did you hear about that meeting in British Columbia? The
> meeting of the British National Party? Metzger's people were
> thrown out. They're a joke!

This is confirmed in Table 5.4 by examining the effect of WAR materials on
the incidence of terrorism. Neither exposure to *WAR* or the WAR Hotline produced
significant correlations. In contrast, the Table 5.4 implies that terrorism can arise directly
from exposure to Skrewdriver and beliefs in occult religion.

Evidence Concerning the Associations
Between Step 2 and Steps 3 and 4

Table 5.4 shows that neo-Nazi ideology directly effects the pursuit of terrorist
goals. Ideology is correlated with the style of gun ownership, educating others,
low group conflict, low social alienation, and terrorism. Consistent with Gibbs'
(1989) theory, the interviews revealed that skinhead ideology supports a strategic
psychological model of terrorism wherein skinheads assume the role of the first party,
racial and ethnic minorities are the third party, and the government—conceived as
ZOG—is the second party. Two examples suffice to make this point.

> Why'd I become a skinhead? 'Cause the Jews are takin' over.
> The Jews, spics, and niggers, and nobody's watchin' out for
> whitey. But the day will come when ZOG will fall.

* * *

> The system enforces your right to blow dope, turn queer, marry
> a nigger, kill the unborn, and do anything else to destroy America.
> Some may be sick enough to accept this, but not us. We want
> to smash this system and replace it with a healthy white man's
> order!

Evidence Concerning the Association
Between Step 3 and Step 4

Last, Table 5.4 shows that three collective processes effect terrorism. The first
is style. The traditional skinhead paramilitary style (the shaven head, Doc Marten
boots, Nazi regalia, etc.) is correlated positively with the style of gun ownership,
educating others, and with terrorism. Gun ownership is also positively correlated
with educating others and with terrorism. And the style of beer intoxication is correlated with terrorism. In fact, the consumption of beer immediately preceding a racial
assault is the strongest correlate of terrorism displayed in Table 5.4. The second process is bonding: low levels of group conflict are correlated positively with terrorism. The final process is gender, terrorism is a male-oriented crime.

According to the modified theory, these processes interact to create the decisive antecedents of terrorism. Similar to Mexican-American barrio gangs (see
Jankowski, 1991; Vigil, 1988), skinheads appear to value beer drinking as a means
of demonstrating their masculinity. These young white males share a common style
of dress, a fascination with weapons, and a sense of belonging with one another. In
their state of intoxication, skinheads engross themselves in style and male-bonding
to engage in what they call the ceremony of beserking.

The term *beserking* is derived from eighth-century Viking mythology. This
mythology, as we have seen, is communicated to skinheads through a musical fantasy created by Skrewdriver. According to the *Anglo-Saxon Chronicle*, going beserk
meant that Vikings were "raging, half-made, and insensate. They went into battle
without armor, like mad dogs or wolves, biting their shields, strong like bears or bulls,
mowing down everything in their path" (quoted in Portner, 1971:152). During the
field-study, I witnessed three acts of beserking. In each case, a small group of
shaven-headed white males—festooned with Nazi regalia and armed with loaded
Smith & Wesson .357 magnum revolvers—combined their masculinity with beer
intoxication to take part in a gang beating of a lone black male. In these terms,
going beserk behind the psychoactive impetus of beer can be viewed as an instru-
mental stylistic creation of the American skinhead movement. The following quote,
taken from a terrorist who was typically intoxicated on beer during his racial
assaults, vividly portrays this style.

> Sometimes they [his enemies] provoke it. Like they'll say
> some shit about white power. That's when we throw
> down. I beat one nigger in the head with a beer bottle.
> Fucked him up good! Just goin' beserk on that nigger's
> skull.

DISCUSSION

The results are consistent with the following explanation of the effects of social processes on the pursuit of terrorist goals, based on a modified theory of deterrent vicarious social control. In the course of being socialized, individuals develop the idea that they are victims of social injustice and thus form reified beliefs about how minority groups have caused that victimization. These beliefs form the social reality within terrorist collectives. With time, individuals tend to endorse terroristic orientations of the group, such as style and education. As a result, their beliefs about the implications of being victimized and group processes of dealing with it shape the nature of their response to minorities (i.e., terrorist goals are formed). This response is then triggered by beer intoxication and male-bonding. The outcome is a pagan-like act of violence derived from a morality of vengeance which is intended to capture the attention of a larger human audience (i.e., ZOG). This is the essence of terrorism within the American skinhead movement. These results are generally inconsistent with positions taken by critics of the social process perspective and are not easily dismissed by those investigators' alternative explanations of terrorism. This is true for transnational-transgenerational messages of perceived victimization (Step 1), ideology (Step 2), and collective affiliation (Step 3). However, my results are highly consistent with the critics' description of the crime of terrorism itself (Step 4).

With respect to persuasive communication, critics suggest that messages of perceived victimization may have little bearing on terrorism beyond the borders of a single nation-state (Dror, 1983; O'Brien, 1983; Wilkinson, 1986). Others argue that conversion to occult religion does not necessarily lead to terrorism (see White, 1991). Instead of these transnational-transgenerational factors, critics argue that terrorism is a contagious phenomenon driven by "ultranationalistic" factions that gain media coverage for their political violence (see Crozier, 1974; Parry, 1976; White, 1991). However, because these findings are based exclusively on historical analyses, the studies offer no social scientific evidence that can be used to support an adequate test of the relevance of ultranationalism in the pursuit of terrorist goals. Furthermore, these studies do not identify the specific means by which individuals become caught up in the contagiousness of terrorism. Thus, this research is merely hypothetical and does not fully specify the communication processes that support terrorism.

In contrast, I identified a real transnational form of communication (white power heavy metal) that was consistently associated with the emergence of ideology, group dynamics, and terrorism. Yet my results do not confirm the notion that all forms of transgenerational communication are associated with terrorism. Although transgenerational communication may contribute to the development of terrorist ideology, young terrorists themselves often react negatively to adult-instigated attempts to exploit them for political purposes. And in this sense, transgenerational communication has no effect on terrorism. The results show that transgenerational influences are uniformly important only when they are communicated through occult religion. Thus, my results directly contradict the findings presented by critics of the social process perspective and cast serious doubt on the conclusions that (1) transnational communication and occult religion are unimportant for understanding terrorism, and (2) that all forms of ultranationalism are important for a contagion thesis.

The results concerning ideology also support a social process perspective over an anti-social process position. Critics argue that commitment to ideological beliefs enter the lives of terrorists "through the back door" and are not important in shaping terrorist careers (Laqueur, 1987; Wilkinson, 1986). With respect to right-wing terrorism, critics claim that ideology is especially unimportant (Merkl, 1986a). Instead, critics point to the salience of a "seriously flawed personality" to explain why individuals turn to terroristic violence (Laqueur, 1987:245; see Freedman, 1986). For example, Merkl's (1986a) historical analysis of youths recruited into the Baader-Meinhof gang prompted him to conclude that the "recruits, with their insecure personalities and weak egos, were given a sense of political direction solely by ... recruiters or protectors who took charge of their failed personal lives (many were students or other dropouts) and told them to read a certain political literature" (1986a:42).

The only result that might support this view is the finding that exposure to WAR materials has a detectable effect on the development of neo-Nazi ideology within the American skinhead movement. Yet, once again, exposure to these materials has a benign effect on both the internal dynamics of skinhead collectives and on terrorism. Indeed, present results contradict the critics' position straightaway. The control variables described in Table 5.2 provide little support for a terrorist personality thesis. Few suffered from failed personal lives: 7 out of 22 terrorists were university students and 10 were recent high school graduates; 17 were gainfully employed at blue-collar jobs and 2 were white-collar workers. All but one terrorist reportedly got along with their parents while growing up. In essence, these individuals had deeply internalized dominant beliefs about American culture. They were not, in any sense, "the walking wounded from broken families" (Merkl, 1986c:367). Rather, they were hyperactive conformists to the prevailing moral opinions about good education, hard work, and traditional family. This commitment comprises the core value of skinheadism. The original London skinheads were described as a "kind of caricature of the model worker" (Cohen, 1972:55), and as a "hard stereotype of the white lumpen male" (Hebdige, 1979: 56). Consistent with the social process perspective on terrorism (e.g., Crenshaw, 1983; O'Sullivan, 1986), my results show that American skinheads—aided by transnational and transgenerational influences—appropriated this value system and converted it into a literal and imaginative form of neo-Nazism. Then, the American skinheads implemented these ideological politics through their terrorist collectives.

Because they dismiss ideology as unimportant, critics argue that the degree of conformity of the individual to the terrorist collective will be dependent on other factors, such as individual motivation, background, and length of service in the collective. In other words, ideology is not the tie that binds groups together; rather, group cohesion—to the extent that it does exist—depends on the individual self-propelled motivations of persons who suffer from seriously flawed personalities. Because there is no intersection between collective purpose (i.e., ideology) and collective dynamics (i.e., style, education, and affiliation) terrorism is viewed as irrational behavior that occurs on the spur-of-the-moment (Laqueur, 1987; Merkl, 1986a; White, 1991). Under this formulation, terrorism is "a strange and explosive mixture of very private and vaguely expressed political motives conducted through a collectivization of loneliness" (Merkl, 1986c:368).

Present results cannot be dismissed by invoking this alternative image offered by critics of the social process perspective. The most important source of information on the dynamics of terrorism are terrorists themselves. Yet critics have never studied the internal dynamics of terrorist groups firsthand. Hence, the information they use to dismiss the social process position (e.g., published biographies of ex-terrorists who have defected from a group) is—once again—strictly hypothetical and cannot be used to support an adequate social scientific test of the social process thesis. Thus, critics offer no plausible alternative hypothesis to dismiss my finding that terrorism is a product of collective dynamics.

Finally, my results coincide with the critics' position on the crime of terrorism. Critics advance arguments of contagion theory, human pathology, and irrationality. I offer explanations related to persuasive communications, ideology, and group dynamics. Yet we arrive at the same conclusion: There is something *sensual* about the act of terrorism. Merkl (1986c:367) describes terrorism as "the politics of heroic ecstasy." Wilkinson (1986) notes that "headstrong youths can become so hooked on the life of terrorist murder that they perform their tasks in a kind of sacrificial ecstasy" (1986:67). And fully recognizing this aspect of terrorism, an exasperated Dror (1983) writes that "social science lacks the frames of appreciation, cognitive maps, concept packages, and methodologies to comprehend such complex phenomena" (1983:67).

In keeping with this position, I have suggested that the act of beserking among American skinheads is an enjoyable and altogether thrilling experience. This finding is consistent with a vast body of ethnographic research conducted on European skinheads (e.g., Hebdige, 1979; Knight, 1982; Seidel-Pielen, 1991). Katz (1988), for example, notes that the skinheads originally carved out their subcultural space in the London underground by searching out provocation with racial minorities. Katz describes skinheads as "street elites" who would drunkenly saunter into racially mixed neighborhoods looking for a fight. "Violence," says Katz "is essential so that membership [in the skinheads] may have a seductively glorious...significance....Being in this world of experience is not simply a matter of detailing posture and using violence to raise the specter of terror. It is also a contingent sensual involvement" (1988:128,139).

CONCLUSIONS

Laqueur (1987) argues that the major question associated with theory of terrorism:

> is not whether great caution should prevail with regard to generalizations; the real issue is to what extent generalizations are at all possible. We shall know the answer once there are more systematic studies of specific terrorist groups, which at present are virtually nonexistent.(1987:162)

I have attempted to fill this void by entering and examining the internal structure of American neo-Nazi skinhead collectives. I have attempted to show that social processes are measurable, and that they are important in the identification of propitious circumstances for a general theory of terrorism. This theory modifies the work of Gibbs (1989) who argues that an explanation of social processes "is needed...; but a theory will not be realized unless social scientists take [social processes] seriously" (1989:338). I have attempted to take them seriously, but mine is by no means the definitive study of the relationship between social processes and terrorism.

My theory is based on logical constructs derived from the personal experiences of terrorists themselves. Yet I have ignored the underlying historical processes that may facilitate or mitigate against terroristic activity among youth. Thus, perhaps the most fruitful work that can be motivated by this study is a continued test of the fifth step of the modified vicarious social control theory. If messages of perceived victimization, ideology, and group dynamics are connected to the emergence of terrorism, it then becomes plausible to conceive of these factors as the crucial point upon which research into social control policy must now turn.

APPENDIX A

Principles and Corresponding Items Used to Derive Occult Religion Measures

Principle 1:   "Satan represents indulgence instead of spiritual abstinence!"

Item: All of us want the good things in life: Money, laughter, sex. We want all kinds of pleasure. Which describes your attitudes about pleasure?

Response Options: I believe "anything goes," I'll do what I have to in order to get my pleasure (coded 3);
I'm not sure (2);
I believe it is more important to control my desire for pleasure, than to take an "anything goes" attitude (1)

Responses: Anything goes=0;
not sure=6;
control desire=30;
mean=1.17;
sd=.38;
item/total correlation=.16

Principle 2:   "Satan represents vital existence, instead of spiritual pipedreams!"

Item: Some people believe only in the here-and-now of life. Others believe that there is something more than here-and-now, and they look forward to a spiritual afterlife. Which best describes your beliefs?

Response Options: There is no afterlife for us (3);

not sure (2);

there is an afterlife (1)

Responses: No afterlife=11;

not sure=5;

afterlife=20;

mean=1.75;

sd=.90;

item/total correlation=.55

Principle 3:   "Satan represents kindness to those who deserve it, instead of love wasted on ingrates!"

Item: Some people believe we should offer kindness to everyone. Others believe we should offer kindness to only those who deserve it. Which describes your belief?

Response Options: We should offer kindness to only those who deserve it (3);

not sure (2);

we should offer kindness to everyone (1)

Responses: Only those who deserve it=24;

not sure=7;

everyone=5;

mean=2.47;

sd=.73;

item/total correlation=.27

Principle 4:   "Satan represents vengeance instead of 'turning the other cheek'!"

Item: All of us have problems with other people. Some believe that vengeance is the best way to solve these problems. Others believe that forgiving is the best way. Which do you believe in?

Response Options: Vengeance (3);

not sure (2);

forgiving (1)

Responses: Vengeance=12;

not sure=14;

forgiving=9;

mean=2.08;

sd=.78;

item/total correlation=.43

Principle 5:   "Satan represents man as just another animal, sometimes better, sometimes
                       worse than those that walk on al fours, who, because of his 'divine spir-
                       itual and intellectual development,' has become the most vicious animal
                       of all!"

Item: Some people believe that man is just another animal who, at times, can be
                       the most vicious animal of all. What do you think of that statement?

Response Options: Agree (3);
                       not sure (2);
                       disagree (1)

Responses: Agree=21;
                       not sure=4;
                       disagree=11;
                       mean=2.38;
                       sd=0.93;
                       item/total correlation=.30

APPENDIX B

Items Used to Derive Neo-Nazi Ideology Measures

1. A person who has bad manners, habits, and breeding can hardly expect to get along with decent people (agree=21; uncertain=7; disagree=8; mean=2.36; sd=.83; item/total correlation=.55).

2. What the youth needs is strict discipline, rugged determination, and the will to work and fight for family and country (agree=31; uncertain=4; disagree=1; mean=2.83; sd=0.44; item/total correlation=.26).

3. An insult to your honor should always be punished (agree=19; uncertain=12; disagree=5; mean=2.38; sd=.72; item/total correlation=.32).

4. Sex crimes, such as rape and attacks on children deserve more than mere imprisonment; such criminals ought to be publicly whipped, or worse (agree=34; uncertain=2; disagree=0; mean=2.94; sd=.23; item/total correlation=.05).

5. There is hardly anything lower than a person who does not feel great love, gratitude, and respect for his parents (agree=5; uncertain=20; disagree=11; mean=1.83; sd=.65; item/total correlation=.12).

6. Most of our social problems would be solved if we could somehow get rid of the immoral, crooked, and feeble minded people (agree=30; uncertain=6; disagree=0; mean=2.83; sd=.37; item/total correlation=.18).

7. Homosexuals are hardly better than criminals and ought to be severely punished (agree=23; uncertain=6; disagree=7; mean=2.44; sd=.80; item/total correlation=.44).

NOTES

1 Here, *social control* is defined as "overt behavior by a human [in the belief that] the behavior increases or decreases the probability of a change in the behavior of another human or humans" (Gibbs, 1989:337).

2 Gibbs' proposition is also reflected in the strategic theories advanced by Crenshaw (1981), Laqueur (1987), and Wilkinson (1986) who argues that "The victim or victims of the actual terrorist violence may not be the primary target" (1986:51).

3 Within the terrorism literature, there is well-established precedent for using a single case study for purposes of illustration (Crenshaw, 1981), as demonstrations of hypotheses (Wilkinson, 1986), and for theory building (Gibbs, 1989).

4 This case study was constructed based on information published by the Anti-Defamation League of B'Nai B'rith (1990), *The New York Times* (Aug. 4, 1990); on a speech made by the U.S. Attorney General (Thornburgh, 1990); and on personal interviews with Terrant's wife conducted during 1991.

5 The limitations of using such reports for social scientific purposes are well-known. These reports are based on information that have been collected for specific governmental and agency purposes; hence, such information may have been deliberately tampered with so as to legitimize the goals of government bureaucracies or civil rights agencies. Furthermore, they are subject to changes not only in recordkeeping procedures, but to the vagaries of state and federal law. However, with these caveats in mind, scholars frequently use government and agency reports to formulate testable hypotheses about terrorism (e.g., Laqueur, 1987; Ross, 1988; White, 1991).

6 Satanism was selected for the analysis because of popular opinion on the subject. The link between American skinheads and the Satanic occult has been incorporated into recent police training programs (e.g., Holmes, 1989; National Information Network, 1989), a textbook on terrorism (White, 1991) and has been alluded to in the literature of criminology (Katz, 1988).

7 To provide a context for the research, I also used the same procedures to locate and informally interview about a dozen male skinheads in Montreal, Vancouver, London, Amsterdam, and Berlin.

8 It is ostensibly arguable that the reliability coefficient and item-to-scale correlations (Appendix A) are below what is normally accepted for social scientific purposes. However, when compared to previous studies examining the intersection between religion and crime, the present measures are above standard for two reasons. First, previous attempts to disentangle the relationship between religion and crime have focused almost exclusively on high school populations as the major ecological unit of analysis (e.g., Burkett & Warren, 1987; Hirschi & Stark, 1969). Rarely have analysts strayed from this tradition, and never has the relationship been examined by gang scholars. Second, rarely has a study employed more than a two-item scale (e.g., Albrecht, Chadwick & Alcorn, 1977), and never has a study measured religious concepts that lie outside traditional Judeo-Christian doctrine. In fact, a recent analysis of 15 criminological studies of religion reveals that internal consistency of measures (Cronbach's alpha and item-to-scale correlations) has never been reported in this entire corpus of literature (Hamm, 1992).

9   The reliability of the Adorno F Scale (or Fascism Scale), upon repeated administrations
to a wide variety of groups, has averaged alpha=.90, with a range of .81 to .97 (Dillehay,
1978). Hence, the present statistics seem, once again, to be below standards. Three explanations account for these modest coefficients. First, the high reliability coefficients
reported by previous researchers were generally based on the entire 38-item F Scale
instrument. My method of administering the questionnaire required that I employ a shorter
version (i.e., the seven-item authoritarian aggression sub-scale) designed to examine the
tendency of skinheads to aggress against third parties. Second, I also adopted an abbre-
viated method of coding responses. Whereas previous researchers have used a six-point
scale, I employed a three-point scale because it (1) facilitated the collection of data, and
(2) was consistent with the procedure recommended for administering Srole's (1956)
well-known alienation scale (see Robinson & Shaver, 1973), to be discussed momentar-
ily. Thus, these procedures—although necessary given the exigencies of the present
study—may have artificially constrained subject responses thereby producing a low reliability coefficient and low item-to-scale correlations.

Third, it is entirely possible that the F Scale tapped support for the wrong concept.
There are important and well-documented differences between fascism and Nazism
(Sternhell, 1976). National Socialism, also referred to as "Hitlerism," assumes love of nation
(*National*) and its people (*Socialism*). Implicit within this definition is a belief in biological determinism or Social Darwinianism. Fascist regimes and fascistic movements, by comparison, are not necessarily committed to this concept (e.g., Mussolini's Italy and Franco's
Spain, though fascistic, did not engage in systematic state-organized genocide against
"inferior races" as did Nazi Germany). In this regard, the subjects in this research resem-
bled a group of neo-Nazis, rather than neo-fascists. Hence, a low reliability coefficient and
low item-to-scale correlations would be logical outcomes.

10   Subjects were administered the entire five-item alienation scale (Srole, 1956). However,
fully 100 percent of the sample agreed that "Most public officials are not really interested
in the problems of the average man," and 97 percent agreed that "... the lot of the average man is getting worse, not better." Conversely, nearly all subject disagreed with the two
items concerning the future. Moreover, these four items produced near-zero variance. In
other words, nearly all subjects were profoundly alienated with respect to politics and economics, and almost none were alienated with respect to bearing children and thoughts about
tomorrow. Thus, such concepts as political and economic alienation appear to be of little value for the study of terrorism—a finding that confirms Dror's (1983) pessimistic notion
that "in-depth causes [of terrorism] are beyond useful knowledge" (1983:70). Yet as
responses indicate, this seems not be the case for social alienation. Nearly equal propor-
tions agreed (n=17) and disagreed (n=16) with the idea that "a person doesn't really
know whom he can count on."

11   It is arguable that Gibbs' definition (*supra*) is so rigorous, in fact, that it defies systematic
application and is suitable only for the analysis of case studies.

12   I also found no evidence of Satanism during the field-study phase of the research, either
in the United States or abroad. None of the skinheads wore the inverted cross, the inverted
pentagram, the Mark of the Beast (666), or the Cross of Nero. No one had reportedly "sold
their souls" to Satan, as is required by neophytes in the religion (LaVey, 1969).

REFERENCES

ADL (1983). *The "Identity Churches:" A Theology of Hate*. New York, NY: ADL.

_____ (1987). *"Shaved for Battle:" Skinheads Target America's Youth:* New York, NY: ADL.

_____ (1988). *Young and Violent: The Growing Menace of America's Neo-Nazi Skinheads*. New York, NY: ADL.

_____ (1989a). *1988 Audit of Anti-Semitic Incidents*. New York, NY: ADL.

_____ (1989b). *Skinheads Target the Schools*. New York, NY: ADL.

_____ (1989c). *Law Enforcement Bulletin*. New York, NY: ADL.

_____ (1990). "Neo-Nazi Skinheads: A 1990 Status Report." *Terrorism*, 13:243-275.

Adorno, T. W., E. Frenkel-Brunwik, D.J. Levinson & R. Nevitt Sanford (1950). *The Authoritarian Personality*. New York, NY: Harper & Brothers.

Albrecht, S.L., B.A. Chadwick & D.S. Alcorn (1977). "Religiosity and Deviance: Application of an Attitude-Behavior Contingent Consistency Model." *Journal for the Scientific Study of Religion*, 16:263-274.

Allport, G.W. (1954). *The Nature of Prejudice*. New York, NY: Doubleday/Anchor Books.

Barrett, P.M. (1989). "Hate Crime Increases and Become More Violent; U.S. Prosecutors Focus on 'Skinhead' Movement." *The Wall Street Journal*, July 14:12.

Bell, J.B. (1975). *Transnational Terror*. Washington, DC: American Enterprise Institute.

Bensinger, G.J. (1991). "Hate Crimes: A New/Old Problem." Paper presented at the annual meeting of the American Society of Criminology, San Francisco.

Ben-Yehuda, N. (1990). *The Politics and Morality of Deviance*. Albany, NY: State University of New York Press.

Berrill, K. (1990). "Anti-Gay Violence: Cause, Consequences, and Responses." Address before the Office of International Criminal Justice, Chicago.

Blumenthal, M.D. (1975). *More About Justifying Violence: Methodological Studies of Attitudes and Behavior*. Ann Arbor, MI: Survey Research Center, Institute for Social Research.

Bowling, B. (1990). "Racist Harassment and the Process of Victimization: Conceptual and Methodological Implications for Crime Surveys." Paper presented at the Realist Criminology Conference, Vancouver, B.C.

Brake, M. (1985). *Comparative Youth Culture*. London: Routledge and Kegan Paul.

Brown, C. (1984). *Black and White Britain: The Third PSI Survey*. London: Heinemann.

Burkett, S. & B. Warren (1987). "Religiosity, Peer Associations, and Adolescent Marijuana Use: A Panel Study of Underlying Causal Structures." *Criminology*, 25:109-131.

Cable Street Beat Review (n.d.). "Blood & Honour." 1-4.

Capitanchik, D. (1986). "Terrorism and Islam." In N. O' Sullivan (ed.) *Terrorism, Ideology, and Revolution*, pp. 115-131. Boulder, CO: Westview Press.

Center for Democratic Renewal (n.d.). *Skinhead Nazis and Youth Information Packet*. Atlanta, GA: CDR.

Coates, J. (1987). *Armed and Dangerous: The Rise of the Survivalist Right*. New York, NY: The Noonday Press.

Cohen, P. (1972). "Sub-Cultural Conflict and Working Class Community." *Working Papers in Cultural Studies 2*. Birmingham, AL: University of Birmingham.

Cooper, M.H. (1989). "The Growing Danger of Hate Groups." *Editorial Research Reports*, 18:262-275.

Coplon, J. (1989). "The Skinhead Reich." *Utne Reader*, May/June: 80-9.

Crenshaw, M. (1981). "The Causes of Terrorism." *Comparative Politics* 13:379-399.

_____ (1983). "Introduction: Reflections on the Effects of Terrorism." In M. Crenshaw (ed.) *Terrorism, Legitimacy, and Power*. Middletown, CT: Wesleyan University Press.

Crozier, B. (1974). *A Theory of Conflict*. New York, NY: Charles Scribner's Sons.

Dees, M. (with S. Fiffer) (1991). *A Season for Justice: The Life and Times of Civil Rights Lawyer Morris Dees*. New York, NY: Charles Scribner's Sons.

Dillehay, R.C. (1978). "Authoritarianism." In H. London & J. Exner, Jr. (eds.) *Dimensions in Personality*, pp. 104-137. New York, NY: John Wiley & Sons.

Douglas, M.C. (1993). "Auslander Raus! Nazi Raus! An Observation of German Skins and Jugendgangen" *International Journal of Comparative and Applied Criminal Justice*, 16:1-15.

Dror, Y. (1983). "Terrorism as a Challenge to the Democratic Capacity to Govern." In M. Crenshaw, (ed.) *Terrorism, Legitimacy, and Power*, pp. 65-90. Middletown, CT: Wesleyan University Press.

Fagan, J. (1990). "Intoxication and Aggression." In M. Tonry & J.Q. Wilson (eds.) *Drugs and Crime*, pp. 241-320. Chicago, IL: University of Chicago Press.

Flynn, K. & G. Gerhardt (1989). *The Silent Brotherhood: Inside America's Racist Underground*. New York, NY: The Free Press.

Freedman, L. (1986). *Terrorism and International Order*. London: Routledge and Kegan Paul.

Fromm, E. (1941). *Escape from Freedom*. New York, NY: Rinehart & Co.

Gibbs, J.P. (1989). "Conceptualization of Terrorism." *American Sociological Review*, 54: 329-340.

Gordon, P. (1990). *Racial Violence and Harassment*. London: Runnymede Trust.

Gross, F. (1987). "Causation of Terror." In W. Laqueur & Y. Alexander (eds.) *The Terrorism Reader,* pp. 231-235. New York, NY: NAL Penguin.

Gurr, T.R. (1971). *Why Men Rebel.* Princeton, NJ: Princeton University Press.

_____ (1989). "Political Terrorism: Historical Antecedents and Contemporary Trends." In T.R. Gurr (ed.) *Violence in America,* (Vol. 2), Newbury Park, CA: Sage.

Hamm, M.S. (1993). *American Skinheads: The Criminology and Control of Hate Crime.* Westport, CT: Praeger.

_____ (1992). "Chaos in the Soul: Neo-Nazi Skinheads and the Morality of Domestic Terrorism." Paper presented at the annual meeting of the Academy of Criminal Justice Sciences, Pittsburgh.

Handler, J.S. (1990). "Socioeconomic Profile of an American Terrorist: 1960s and 1970s." *Terrorism,* 13:195-214.

Hebdige, D. (1979). *Subculture: The Meaning of Style.* London: Methuen and Co.

Hiro, D. (1991). *Black British White British: A History of Race Relations in Britain.* London: Gafton Books.

Hirschi, T. & R. Stark (1969). "Hellfire and Delinquency." *Social Problems,* 17:202-213.

Hofstadter, R. (1967). *The Paranoid Style in American Politics and Other Essays.* New York, NY: Vintage Books.

Holmes, R.M. (1989). "Youths in the Occult: A Model of Satanic Involvement." *The National FOP Journal,* January:20-3.

Horowitz, L.I. (1983). "The Routinization of Terrorism and Its Unanticipated Consequences." In M. Crenshaw (ed.) *Terrorism, Legitimacy, and Power,* pp. 38-51. Middletown, CT: Wesleyan University Press.

Jackson, J.O. (1991). "Unity's Shadow." *Time,* July 1:6-14.

Jankowski, M.S. (1991). *Islands in the Street: Gangs in American Urban Society.* Berkeley, CA: University of California Press.

Katz, J. (1988). *Seductions of Crime.* New York, NY: Basic Books.

Kingsman, C. (n.d.). "High Theory ... No Culture: Decolonizing Canadian Subcultural Studies." Unpublished manuscript. Ottawa, Ontario: Carleton University.

Klanwatch (1991). *The Ku Klux Klan: A History of Racism and Violence.* Montgomery, AL: Southern Poverty Law Center.

Knight, N. (1982). *Skinhead.* London: Omnibus Press.

Kraemer, H.C. & S. Thiemann (1987). *How Many Subjects? Statistical Power Analysis in Research.* Newbury Park, CA: Sage.

Kushnick., L.V. (1981). "Racism and Class Consciousness in Modern Capitalism." In B.P.
Bowser & R.G. Hunt (eds.) *Impacts of Racism on White Americans*, pp. 191-216.
Newbury Park, CA: Sage.

Langer, E. (1990). "The American Neo-Nazi Movement Today." *The Nation*, July 16/23:82-108.

LaVey, A.S. (1969). *The Satanic Bible*. New York, NY: Avon Books.

Laqueur, W. (1987). *The Age of Terrorism*. Boston, MA: Little, Brown and Co.

Lichter, S.R. (1979). "A Psychopolitical Study of West German Male Radical Students."
Comparative Politics, 12:27-48.

Linz, J.J. (1976). "Some Notes Toward a Comparative Study of Fascism in Sociological
Historical Perspective." In W. Laqueur (ed.) *Fascism: A Reader's Guide*, pp. 3-124. Hants:
Wildwood House Limited.

Liska, A.E. (1987). *Perspectives on Deviance*. Englewood Cliffs, NJ: Prentice-Hall.

London Borough of Newham (1986). *The Newham Crime Survey*. London: LBN.

Lupsha, P. (1971). "Explanation of Political Violence: Some Psychological Theories Versus
Indignation." *Politics and Society*, 2:89-104.

Mannheim, K. (1936). *Ideology and Utopia*. London: Routledge and Kegan Paul.

Marcus, G. (1989). *Lipstick Traces: A Secret History of the Twentieth Century*. Cambridge,
MA: Harvard University Press.

Merkl, P.H. (1986a). "Approaches to the Study of Political Violence." In P.H. Merkl (ed.) *Political
Violence and Terror*, pp. 19-59. Berkeley, CA: University of California Press.

_____ (1986b). "Rollerball or Neo-Nazi Violence?" In P.H. Merkl *Political Violence
and Terror*, pp. 229-256. Berkeley, CA: University of California Press.

_____ (1986c). "Conclusion: Collective Purposes and Individual Motives." In P.H. Merkl
(ed.) *Political Violence and Terror*, pp. 335-374. Berkeley, CA: University of California
Press.

Mücke, T. (1991). "Bericht Uber das Projeckt—Miteinander Statt Gegeneiandeer." *Jervental*,
38-47.

Nash, J. (1985). *Social Psychology: Society and Self*. St. Paul, MN: West Publishing Co.

National Gay & Lesbian Task Force Policy Institute (1991). *Anti-Gay/Lesbian Violence,
Victimization & Defamation in 1990*. Washington, DC: NG&LTFPI.

National Information Network (1989). *General Information Manual With Respect to Satanism
And The Occult*. St. Charles, MO: NIN.

O'Brien, C.C. (1983). "Terrorism under Democratic Conditions: The Case of the IRA." In
M. Crenshaw (ed.) *Terrorism, Legitimacy, and Power*, pp. 91-104. Middletown, CT: Wesleyan
University Press.

O'Sullivan, N. (1986). "Terrorism, Ideology and Democracy." In N. O'Sullivan (ed.) *Terrorism, Ideology, and Revolution,* pp. 3-26. Boulder, CO: Westview Press.

Parry, A. (1976). *Terrorism: From Robespierre to Arafat.* New York, NY: Vanguard Press.

Poertner, R. (1971). *The Vikings.* London: St. James Press.

Post, J.M. (1987). "Rewarding Fire with Fire: Effects of Retaliation on Terrorist Group Dynamics. *Terrorism,* 10:23-36.

Prinsky, L.E. & J.L. Rosenbaum (1989). "'Leer-ics' or Lyrics: Teenage Impressions of Rock 'n' Roll." *Youth & Society,* A.S. 18:384-397.

Redlick, A.S. (1979). "The Transnational Flow of Information as a Cause of Terrorism." In Y. Alexander, D. Carlton & P. Wilkinson (eds.) *Terrorism: Theory and Practice,* pp. 73-98. Boulder, CO: Westview Press.

Robinson, J.P. & P.R. Shaver (1973). *Measures of Social Psychological Attitudes.* Ann Arbor, MI: Survey Research Center.

Ross, J.I. (1988). "An Events Database on Political Terrorism in Canada: Some Conceptual and Methodological Problems." *Conflict Quarterly,* 8:47-65.

Seidel-Pielen, E. (1991). *Krieg im den Stadten.* Berlin: Rotbuch, 34.

Schmidt, A.P. (1983). *Political Terrorism.* Amsterdam: North-Holland Publishing Co.

Skrewdriver (1982). "Nigger, Nigger." *Hail the New Dawn.* London: White Noise Records.

Srole, L. (1956). "Social Integration and Certain Corollaries: An Exploratory Study." *American Sociological Review,* 21:709-716.

Stark, R. (1985). *The Future of Religion: Secularization, Revival, and Cult Formation.* Berkeley, CA: University of California Press.

Sternhell, Z. (1976). "Fascist Ideology." In W. Laqueur (ed.) *Fascism: A Reader's Guide,* pp. 315-378. Hants: Wildwood House Limited.

The New York Times (1990). "Five Texans Convicted of Plot Against Rights." August 4:17.

Thornburgh, R. (1990). Address before the Simon Wiesenthal Center, Chicago.

Toy, Jr., E.V. (1989). "Right-Wing Extremism from the Ku Klux Klan to the Order, 1915 to 1988." In T.R. Gurr (ed.) *Violence in America* (Vol. 2), pp. 131-152. Newbury Park, CA: Sage.

U.S. Department of Justice (1988). *Terrorism in the United States 1988.* Washington, DC: U.S. Deptartment of Justice.

_____ (1989). *Terrorism in the United States 1989.* Washington, DC: U.S. Department of Justice.

van Dijk, T.A. (1987). *Communicating Racism: Ethnic Prejudice in Thought and Talk.* Newbury Park, CA: Sage.

Vigil, J.D. (1988). *Barrio Gangs: Street Life and Identity in Southern California.* Austin, TX: University of Texas Press.

Von Maltitz, H. (1973). *The Evolution of Hitler's Germany.* New York, NY: McGraw Hill.

Waldmann, P. (1986). "Guerrilla Movements in Argentina, Guatemala, Nicaragua, and Uruguay." In P.H. Merkl (ed.) *Political Violence and Terror,* pp. 257-282. Berkeley, CA: University of California Press.

Wardlaw, G. (1990). *Political Terrorism.* Cambridge, MA: Cambridge University Press.

Wasmund, K. (1986). "The Political Socialization of West German Terrorists." In P.H. Merkl (ed.) *Political Violence and Terror,* pp. 199-228. Berkeley, CA: University of California Press.

Weinberg, L. (1986). "The Violent Life: Left-and Right-Wing Terrorism in Italy." In *Political Violence and Terror,* pp. 145-168. Berkeley, CA: University of California Press.

Wilkinson, P. (1986). *Terrorism and the Liberal State.* New York, NY: New York University Press.

White, J.R. (1991). *Terrorism: An Introduction.* Pacific Grove, CA: Brooks/Cole.

Yablonsky, L. (1990). *Criminology: Crime and Criminality.* New York, NY: Harper & Row.

6

Hate Crime in Canada:
Growing Pains with
New Legislation

Jeffrey Ian Ross
University of Lethbridge

INTRODUCTION

In Canada hating has never been illegal, but since 1970 acting upon this feeling is illegal. While hate has been part of the cultural, political, and social fabric of this sometimes "peaceable kingdom" (e.g., Friedenberg, 1979), it was only in the 1960s that a strong enough popular and legislative agenda developed to amend the *Criminal Code of Canada*, (hereafter the *Code*), to include a hate crime law. This legislative change was one of many reactions to a rise in right-wing ideology, racial discrimination, and violence in Canada.[1]

The study of hate crime in Canada has been covered under the umbrella terms of anti-Semitism, discrimination, freedom of expression and speech, immigration, prejudice, nationalism, nativism, racism, refugees, and, right-wing activity. Already, a considerable amount of research has been conducted on this subject.[2] This chapter is primarily a historical analysis of the introduction of hate crime legislation in Canada, the situations where charges were filed and well publicized, as well as those cases where hate crime charges were considered by authorities but avoided.

HISTORY BEHIND THE LEGISLATION[3]

While prior to the 1970s section 181 of the *Code* was the only provision dealing with offenses of group defamation, the contemporary origins of hate crime legislation can be traced to January 29, 1965 when Guy Favreau, then Minister of

Justice, appointed a special committee headed by Maxwell Cohen, Dean of McGill University Law School, "to study and report upon the problems related to the dissemination of varieties of 'hate propaganda' in Canada."[4] The formation of the committee was a reaction to the activities of a seemingly increasing number of neo-Nazi organizations in Canada, distributing contentious literature "all of which promoted some variation of anti-Semitic or other racist dogma" (Morgan, 1991:91). Additionally, the reminders of horrors of the Holocaust "generated renewed calls for some criminal sanction for group defamation" (e.g., MacGuigan, 1966). While Canada, like other nation-states, signed "international instruments which denounced... racism" (e.g., International Convention on the Elimination of All Forms of Racism), domestic measures were perceived to be lacking (Elman, 1989:73). Although "[p]rivate members [of parliament] had made initiatives before" the 1960s and by the end of the 1960s Canada had a rich history of group defamation suits (e.g., Fenson, 1964-65), it took the coalescing of the above-mentioned factors to prompt the government to investigate in earnest the problem and initiate a legislative agenda (Pettman, 1982).

The *Report of the Special Committee on Hate Propaganda*, also known as the Cohen Committee Report, presented on November 10, 1965, recommended that the *Code* was inadequate to deal with the problem of hate propaganda. It suggested an amendment to C-24 of the *Code* that would put into Canadian law a scheme of legislative sanctions dealing with hate propaganda and related actions (Elman, 1989; Morgan, 1991).

A bill incorporating most of these recommendations was tabled in Parliament in 1966. Four years later, in May/June 1970, after further debate, these recommendations, with a number of significant amendments, were finally incorporated into the *Code*, as sections 281.1, 281.2, and 281.3 and because of a revision of the entire *Code* during the 1980s as section 319.[5]

The main sections of the law are as follows:

> 281.1(1) Everyone who advocates or promotes genocide is guilty of and indictable offence and is liable to imprisonment for five years...

> 281.2(1) Everyone who, by communicating statements in any public place, incites hatred against any identifiable group where such incitement is likely to lead to a breach of the peace, is guilty...

> 281.2(2) Everyone who, by communicating statements, other than in private conversation, wilfully promotes hatred against any identifiable group...

> 281.3(1) A judge who is satisfied by information upon oath
> that there are reasonable grounds for believing that any publi-
> cation, copies of which are kept for sale or distribution in
> premises within the jurisdiction of the court, is hate propa-
> ganda, shall issue a warrant under his hand authorizing seizure
> of the copies....

In sum, Parliament enacted an amendment to the *Code* making it illegal to espouse racial, religious, and ethnic hatred. In particular, this hate crime law prohibited the advocation of genocide, the public incitement of hatred, and the wilful promotion of hatred.

By no means was this legislation agreeable to all segments of the Canadian public. Many public and private organizations opposed the law claiming that it was either too strict or loose.[6] During the debate over passage of the legislation, and presently minority, racial, religious, and ethnic groups, newspaper editors, observers, and legal experts, developed six arguments against the new legislation.

Arguments Against the New Legislation[7]

C-34 Does Not Need to be Amended Because Other Criminal Sanctions Exist. This argument was based on the premise that the existing *Code* already made it an offense to "mail indecent or scurrilous literature" (Sec. 153); "wilfully publish a statement, news, or tale that he knows is false and that causes or is likely to cause injury or mischief to a public interest" (Sec. 177); engage in sedition (Sec. 60); incite persons to commit offenses (Sec. 407); and, conspire to effect an unlawful purpose (Sec. 408 (2)). In sum, remedies to combat so-called hate crimes were already part of the existing *Code*. Regardless of this argument, it was deemed that:

> the offense of defamatory libel applied only to the vilification
> of individuals and not of groups. Further, the offense of deitious
> libel was interpreted in a very narrow fashion by the Supreme
> Court of Canada....The crime of spreading false news was also
> interpreted in a restrictive manner (Elman, 1989:73).

Amend C-34 in Lieu of Other Sections of the Code. Alternative sections of the *Code* that could have been amended at the time were intimidation (Sec. 316), and threat (Sec. 366) (Pettman, 1982). On the other hand, it was perceived that only changes to the *Code* sent an indisputable message of official concern and "upon the educative as well as the punitive aspects of the problem" (Pettman, 1982:21-22).

Other Sections of the Code Need to be Amended Before Changing C-34. Some critics argued that parts of the *Code*, in particular those dealing with publishing false news (Sec. 166), and counseling an offense (Sec. 407), needed to be amended before a conviction could be obtained under the hate crime legislation (Lefole,

1964). This argument was eventually dismissed though reasons for doing this have not been addressed in the academic or legal literature.

Infringement on Freedom of Expression. Some opponents of the hate crime legislation argued that section 281.2(2) unintentionally infringes on the fundamental freedoms of expression, speech, and press. This point was rearticulated and tested almost one and one-half decades after the *Charter of Rights and Freedoms*, (hereafter the *Charter*), was introduced into Canadian jurisprudence. Observers argued, that "the *Charter*'s right to freedom of expression might take precedence over any law restraining hate literature, as the Alberta Court of Appeal ruled in *R. v. Keegstra*" (Morgan, 1991:91).[8]

According to one informed observer:

> Obviously, the special defenses were incorporated into the law to protect the all-important right of freedom of speech, to make sure that every citizen could express an opinion without fear of prosecution. But these defenses are so all-encompassing, the chances of convicting a propagator of racism are minimal. After all, it is easy for anyone to maintain that he or she believed his or her statements to be true (Sher, 1984:21).

The debate over when a democratic society should determine that a particular action violates others rights without infringing on the right of that individual to freedom of expression merely reignited the anti-hate legislation. As Sher states although there are already at least 15 sections of the *Code* that limit freedom of speech it is still possible for a racist to commit a crime of hate against a group of people (Sher, 1984:21).

The Hate Crime Law is Unworkable. Critics claimed that subsections (2) and (3) of section 281 of the *Code* were unworkable because without the approval of a province's attorney general no charges can be laid. This argument was supported "by many of the attorneys general across the country who were reluctant to commence prosecutions which they believed had little chance of succeeding" (Elman, 1989:74-75). There were efforts to delete the "wilful" requirement and the necessity "that certain prosecutions must have the consent of the attorney general in the affected province" (Borovoy, 1985:143).

The Hate Crime Law is Unenforceable. It was argued that subsection 2 of section 281.2 is unclear about what constitutes a private conversation and how wilfulness is to be established. The word "wilfully" alone had cautioned Crown attorneys against using the law, because it is difficult to establish intent (Bercuson & Wertheimer, 1985). This subsection also allowed four defenses in addition to those normally available (i.e., where the statement is true; said on good faith, relevant and, reasonably believed to be true) (Bercuson & Wertheimer, 1985). In addition, according to Lawlor, there are "difficulties with the 'sincere fanatic' defence of section C, and the 'good faith' of section D...." (Bercuson & Wertheimer, 1985:173).

The Legislative Aftermath

Most of the above-mentioned criticisms were not sufficient to prevent the legislation from being passed. In the interim, a series of events took place lessening the likelihood that authorities will use hate crime laws, and that highlight the use of alternative sanctions against those engaging in the same type of activity for which the act was designed. For example, in 1977, the *Canadian Human Rights Act*, (hereafter the *Act*), was passed, section 13 of which, prohibits people "from using the telephone to expose others repeatedly to hatred or contempt by reason of their race, national or ethnic origin, color, religion, age, sex, marital status or handicap" (Pettman, 1982:21).[9] In addition, each province introduced their own human rights legislation as well as legal bodies for monitoring these kinds of violations. In one of the most thorough reviews of provincial codes, only the codes of Manitoba, Saskatchewan, and British Columbia refer explicitly to incitement to group hatred (Pettman, 1982:22); all codes including these prohibit discriminatory policies, signs, and other modes of expression. Throughout the 1970s and 1980s, however, various individuals and groups lobbied to have the *Code* changed.

In August 1977, Ontario's Attorney General Roy McMurtry proposed changes to the hate legislation that would make it possible for class action suits for defamation to be filed by racial or ethnic groups (Oziewicz, 1977). The *Globe and Mail*, Canada's most influential newspaper, wrote a bitter editorial against the proposed amendments citing among other things that the hate literature bill "has been a bust" and that "Hatred is simply not amenable to legislation" (*Globe and Mail*, 1977a). On August 25, 1979, in what must have appeared as a vote of nonconfidence, "Ontario Government lawyers...rejected as unworkable" McMurtry's proposal to change the hate laws (*Globe and Mail*, 1979b).

Later, when the Ku Klux Klan began organizing in British Columbia, the government initiated a study, and among the conclusions of the 1981 *Report Arising Out of the Activities of the KKK in British Columbia* (McAlpine, 1981) were the strengthening of existing remedies, including improving the criminal offense of wilful promotion of hatred.

The following year, on April 17, 1982, Canada's long-awaited *Constitution Act* was proclaimed by Queen Elizabeth II. It included a number of changes. One of the most important was the constitutional entrenchment of the *Charter* (Gibbins, 1990:248). The *Charter* gives constitutional protection to individual rights and freedoms. This new constitution would prove important when the constitutionality of hate crime laws was later questioned.[10]

In September 1983, for instance, the B'nai Brith League for Human Rights tried "to persuade the federal Minister of Justice to remove loopholes in the law so that provincial attorneys general would be more willing to use it" (Weinman & Winn, 1986:18-19).

In March 1984, the all-party Parliamentary Special Committee on the Participation of Visible Minorities in Canadian Society submitted its report titled *Equality Now*.

In general, it suggested a wider-ranging prohibition. Among the recommendations of this report were: the deletion of the word "wilfully" from the definition of the offense of a hate crime. This change, it was argued, would make it easier for the attorneys general to prove that the accused specifically intended to publicly promote hatred against an identifiable group. "Shift the onus of proof to the accused to defend his or her actions" (Sher, 1984:20). Additionally, it urged the Department of Justice to amend the hate propaganda section of the *Code* to eliminate obtaining consent from the attorney general before prosecution. Furthermore, it advised "giving appropriate powers to the Canadian Human Rights Commission to to deal with hate propaganda" (Berlin, 1985:31).

These amendments, were criticized because:

> they might not go far enough. For one thing they ignore the latest innovation in racist propaganda; high-tech hate via computers. The existing law refers only to statements communicated "in any public place other than in a private conversation, and the Aryan Nations computer network is easily accessed anywhere in Canada public or private (Sher, 1984:20).

> More seriously, the amendments leave intact the special defenses available to the accused hate propagandist—an escape clause which makes the hate law virtually unenforceable. As the law now stands a person can be accused of disseminating hate propaganda if he can prove that his statements were true, if they were expressed as a religious opinion, or if they were made in a discussion on a subject of "public benefit" and on reasonable grounds he believed them to be true (Sher, 1984:21).

Shortly after the publication of that report, in June 1984, the Canadian Civil Liberties Association "made an unsuccessful attempt to convince the Canadian Jewish Congress to join them in having the constitutional matter [over the Hate Crime Laws] referred to a special hearing of the Supreme Court of Canada" (Bercuson & Wertheimer, 1985:183).

On June 1, 1984, then Justice Minister Mark MacGuigan, acting on the recommendations of the all party House of Commons Special Committee's report, *Equality Now* announced new measures against the dissemination of hate propaganda in Canada including amending section 281.2 (2) of the *Code* to remove the word "wilfulness," eliminating the requirement that called for the attorney general's consent prior to prosecution, and clarifying the section "so that the accused would be fully responsible for establishing any defenses to the charges of disseminating hate propaganda" (Berlin, 1985:32).

In July 1984, the Canadian Bar Association's *Report of the Special Committee on Racial and Religious Hatred* (Norman, McAlpine & Weinstein, 1984) found that the hate crime law still had an important role to play, both at the criminal and civil levels, in restricting the dissemination of hate propaganda to curtail racial and religious hatred (1984:12).

In April 1985, hate propaganda was officially barred from entering Canada and Revenue Canada was responsible for monitoring this process. Much of the material was prohibited because it constituted hate propaganda and included books, journals, and newsletters, as well as audiocassettes and videocassettes. In December 1987, Custom's officers were given official guidelines to help them perform this duty (Canadian Press, 1987).

In 1986, as an outgrowth of its earlier working paper titled *Defamatory Libel*, the now defunct Law Reform Commission of Canada made an in-depth study of hate propaganda (Canada, 1986). In addition to analyzing the current hate crime laws, it made seven recommendations including:

- All these crimes should protect those groups identifiable on the basis of race, national or ethnic origin, colour, religion, sex, age or mental or physical disability;

- the definition of identifiable group should be removed from the offence of advocating genocide and put into a separate section;

- these crimes should be placed in our new code in a chapter on offences against society;

- [the crime of genocide should not be placed in the new code] but should be deferred for future consideration;

- the crime of advocating or promoting genocide should be retained;

- and, the crime of publishing false news should be abolished (1986:40-41).

The extent to which these recommendations were acted upon has not been analyzed.

Approximately five years later, on December 13, 1990, the Supreme Court of Canada ruled that the Charter "does not protect the right to promote hatred." The two sections of the *Code* dealing with the promotion of hatred and a section dealing with discrimination under the *Act* were adjudicated constitutional with this court ruling. In this manner, the court asserted its commitment to guarantee freedom of expression and protect ethnic and racial minorities from group defamation (Morgan, 1991:910; Fraser & Certinig, 1990).[11]

Then on June 19, 1991, Bill C-247, designed to amend the hate propaganda section of the *Code* was first read in parliament. This change extended the term "identifiable group" from "any section of the public distinguished by color, race, religion, ethnic origin" to also include sex or sexual orientation (Canada, 1991).

Summary

Despite the original criticisms of the hate crime legislation, attempts to revise it, as well as the arrival of other sanctioning mechanisms, the legislation as it exists today is perceived by law authorities, scholars, and most importantly provincial attorneys general as unworkable. Hence, lawmakers are hesitant to file charges using this particular legislation.

PERPETRATORS OF HATE CRIMES

Introduction

Just because hate-crime legislation was passed in Canada in 1970, it does not mean that this behavior is a phenomenon of the post World War II era. Canada has a history of racism, right-wing violence, and group hatred that predates written history on Canada. Hate crime is generally perpetrated by members of the radical-right. A variety of these individuals and groups have existed throughout the history of Canada (Betcherman, 1975; Barrett, 1987; Robin, 1992; Ross, 1992). Traditionally, hate crime in Canada has been the by-product of racist, anti-Oriental, anti-Catholic, anti-Communist, anti-Semitic, anti-immigrant, and anti-homosexual sentiments. This pattern of right-wing violence, particularly the type connected with economic issues, is a recurrent phenomenon in the history of Canada.

Groups and Individuals

During the 1960s, when there was a strong political agenda to introduce hate crime legislation, a series of radical right groups existed in Canada (e.g., Canadian Nazi Party/Western Guard, Edmund Burke Society, Canadian League of Rights, etc.). In general, these organizations reacted to the increased immigration of visible minorities to Canada; perceived a loss of employment as a result of this immigration influx; and resisted the rise of left-wing political activity. In the 1970s, the radical right-wing agenda was carried out primarily by the Ku Klux Klan which re-entered Canada from the United States and tried to organize in large urban areas, attempting to garner support for many of the same issues that the radical right-wing had organized around during the 1960s.

In the 1980s, several right-wing individuals and groups fomented, organized and, in some cases engaged in violence.[12] Most noticeable of the groups were the skinheads and the Aryan Nations of Canada. The most salient issues around which they organized were trials of hate mongers, war criminals, and doctors and clinics procuring abortions. Publisher Ernest Zundel and high school teacher James Keegstra, with the aid of a sensationalizing media, in particular, attracted national attention not only for the actions they committed, but also for the public debate their cases created. Additionally, the government's detection, loss of citizenship trials, and deportation of former Nazi war criminals living in Canada, including the "Commission of Inquiry on War Criminals" began in 1985.[13] Finally, the unresolved abortion debate, like the one occurring in most advanced industrialized nation-states, led to large-scale protests and some violence surrounding a woman's right to have an abortion. These events provided additional settings for hate mongers to recruit new members, encourage group cohesion, and promote their own ideology.

With the passing of time, skinheads, originally more style than substance, became increasingly prominent in Canadian urban locales. Many joined existing right-wing organizations while others engaged in individual hate crime activities. Finally, a number of Canadian right-wingers attended the Aryan Nation meeting in Hayden Lake, Idaho, and some (e.g., Terry Long) came back to Canada to organize training camps for "Aryan Warriors."

Now that a context has been established for perpetrators, it is wise to examine those situations where the legislation has been utilized.

CASES IN WHICH HATE CRIME CHARGES WERE FILED

Introduction

Like statistics on most criminal behavior, accurate data on hate crime are rare. Incidents of hate crime frequently go unreported, especially when the victims do not want publicity or do not trust authorities (Lavin, 1991:24). Canada, unlike the United States, does not have a federal *Hate Crimes Statistics Act*. Consequently, it is difficult to ascertain whether there is more hate crime in Canada than in other countries. Despite the incidence of radical right-wing violence (Ross, 1992), and the resources devoted to analyzing this particular law, only a handful of individuals have been charged under the hate laws for a number of actions including the distribution of hate propaganda, and teaching Holocaust denial theory to their students. Two of these cases led to acquittals; one because the identity of the accused could not be proven, and the other because the defendant's purpose was determined not to promote hatred. In another case, a conviction was achieved as part of an apparent plea bargain (Elman, 1989:76). But to date, there has only been one successful conviction.

Shriners' Parade

In June 1975, during a Shriners' Parade in Toronto, "the police used the anti-hate law to arrest young people who had been distributing leaflets bearing the words, 'Yankee go Home'" (Borovoy, 1985:141). Although the charge was later dropped by the Crown attorney, these young activists were detained in jail two days. Furthermore it was perceived that their free-speech rights were violated.

Buzzanga and Derocher

In January 1977, Robert Buzzanga and Jean Derocher, both French Canadians, were charged under section 281.2(2) for wilfully promoting hatred against an identifiable group. The two had distributed satirical anti-French leaflets at the University of Windsor, as well as homes and businesses in the Ontario counties of LaSalle and Essex to create pro-French sympathy (Canadian Press, 1977). Buzzanga and Derocher sought an official reaction, to gather French Canadian support for the building of a local French-language secondary school (Pettman, 1982:20). In December 1977, despite pleading not guilty, they were convicted of hate crime charges, but received suspended sentences in January, 1978 (Canadian Press, 1978). The conviction was eventually overturned on appeal. Both the Shriners case and the Buzzanga and Durocher case were unusual because they involved "harassment against people quite different from the anti-Semites and racists for whom the law was designed" (Borovoy, 1985:141).

Andrews and Smith

In 1985, Donald Clarke Andrews, leader of the white supremist Nationalist Party and publisher of the *Nationalist Reporter*, a racist newsletter, and Robert Wayne Smith, party-secretary and editor of the publication, "were charged with the wilful promotion of hatred of Blacks and Jews as a result of their having published white supremist anti-Semitic material" (Elman, 1989:80). In December 1985, the two were convicted of wilfully promoting hatred through publication of the bimonthly newsletter. Although the Ontario Court of Appeals dismissed the men's challenge, it reduced their jail sentences from 12 to three months given to Andrews, and from seven to one month meted out to Smith. This decision "left the Ontario court at odds with the Alberta Court of Appeal, which ruled on June 6 that the prohibition is an unlawful infringement of free speech as guaranteed by the Charter of Rights and Freedoms" (Claridge, 1988).

In August 1988, the two men again appealed their charges "on the contention that section 281.2(2) of the ... *Code* was an infringement of freedom of speech as guaranteed by the *Charter*. In a judgment delivered July 29, 1988, the Ontario Court of Appeal affirmed the convictions" (Elman, 1989:80). Judge Corry's decision to allow the appeals against the sentence, was based on his understanding that while both men had been free pending the challenge they had complied with the judge's orders not to continue publishing the *Reporter*. In addition to the reduced jail sentences, both men were placed on three years probation. As part of their probation, they were ordered to refrain from resuming publication of the journal or one like it "or having anything to do with the writing, publication, distribution or financing of it or a similar publication" (Claridge, 1988).

In December 1990, after the Alberta Court of Appeal set aside the conviction of Keegstra, the Supreme Court of Canada was asked to decide on the constitutionality of the hate crime legislation. The Supreme Court upheld the laws against hate propaganda committed by Andrews and Smith (Downey, 1990). They are the only Canadians to be jailed under the hate-propaganda section of the *Code*.

Keegstra[14]

On January 11, 1984, James Keegstra, a high school teacher from Eckville, Alberta was charged with wilfully promoting hatred which is contrary to section 281.2(2) of the *Code*. The subject of the charge was statements made by Keegstra while teaching students at Eckville Junior and Senior High in Alberta between September 1, 1978 and December 31, 1982. "For twelve years, he indoctrinated his students with Jewish conspiracy explanations of history ... biased statements principally about Jews, but also about Catholics, Blacks, and others" (Bercuson & Wertheimer, 1985:xi). His teaching included a denial of the historical facts of the Holocaust and he penalized students with lower grades if they did not repeat what he wanted.

The decision of the Alberta Attorney General to prosecute Keegstra was a cause for celebration for major national Jewish organizations. Despite this success, many Jews and non-Jews felt the hate crime legislation was "virtually impossible to enforce and that it ought to be changed" (Bercuson & Wertheimer, 1985:xiii).

Prior to his trial, in October 1984, Keegstra applied to the Court of Queen's Bench to challenge section 281.2(2) of the *Code*. The application was based on the argument that this section of the hate crime law was inconsistent with section 2(b) of the Charter and therefore section 281.2(2) "of no force or effect" (Elman, 1989:78). Justice Quigley rejected Keegstra's application. on the grounds that section 281.2(2) was not an infringement on his freedom of speech (Elman, 1989:78).

Keegstra's trial began on April 9, 1985 and lasted three-and-one-half months, providing extra publicity for a whole host of constituencies operating in Canada. On July 20, 1985, following three-and-one-half days of deliberation, the jury found Keegstra guilty (Bercuson & Wertheimer, 1985:187). The judge sentenced him to five months in jail and fined him $5,000 (Weinman & Winn, 1986).

In April 1987, as part of Keegstra's overall appeal from conviction, he challenged Quigley's decision. While several governmental and nongovernmental parties[15] intervened in the appeal on the side of the Crown, this time Keegstra was successful and on June 6, 1988, the Alberta Court of Appeal ruled that section 281.2(2) was of "no force or effect," thereby reversing Quigley's decision. Consequently, the Court registered an acquittal against Keegstra (Elman, 1989:79).

The Court of Appeals' decision that the law was constitutional proved to be a serious setback to those concerned with protecting minority groups from the harmful consequences of hate propaganda (Elman, 1989:72). However, in December 1990, the Supreme Court of Canada ruled that the provisions against hatred in the *Code* were justifiable in a democracy, but directed the Alberta Court of Appeal to rule on whether the jury in Keegstra's trial was impartial (Certinig, 1991). In March 1991, the Appeal Court of Alberta ruled "that the trial had been unfair, because Mr.

Keegstra had no chance to challenge the impartiality of his jurors. It quashed the conviction yet again, and ordered a new trial" (*Globe and Mail*, 1991). The case is currently being reviewed by the Alberta Attorney General's office.

Summary

By 1989, the conviction in the Ontario case and the appeal in the Alberta case set up a battle at the Supreme Court of Canada to decide the constitutionality of the hate legislation. The law was held to be constitutional, but the partiality of the jury in Keegstra's case helped his judicial proceedings. This process was both a shot in the arm to victims of hate crime and a blow to civil libertarians who felt the hate crime legislation was overinclusive. Far more important perhaps were the situations where hate crime laws could have been applied but were not.

SITUATIONS WHERE THE HATE CRIME LAWS COULD HAVE BEEN APPLIED BUT WERE NOT

Introduction

While hate crimes take place everyday in Canada, charges are rarely filed. In particular, a series of incidents occurred that garnered considerable media attention, which might have resulted in hate crime charges being filed, but other charges were used instead. The three situations that garnered the greatest media response were those where alternative types of charges against John Ross Taylor, Ernest Zundel, and Malcolm Ross were filed.[16] These individuals' actions were sanctioned by section 177 of the *Code*, "Spreading False News," which was a lot easier to investigate, charge, and get a conviction from, under provincial or federal human rights legislation, than would have been under the hate crime law. In contrast those cases that do not receive a considerable amount of media attention are typically charged with mischief and assault, and under the *Customs Act* and Human Rights *Act*. Finally, infamous visitors to Canada, espousing racist views and distributing racist propaganda are commonly expelled from the country.[17]

Taylor

Between 1973 and 1979, the Toronto-based Western Guard, a neo-fascist group, played racist telephone recorded messages to those who called in. John Ross Taylor, leader of the Guard, was brought up between June 12-15, 1979 before "a special tribunal, the first of its kind set up by the federal Human Rights Commission," which had the power of a Federal Court of Canada, "to investigate the taped messages" (*Globe and Mail*, 1979a).[18] "It did not have the power to levy fines or impose a prison sentence, but it could issue a cease-and-desist order, which is precisely what it did on 22 August 1979" (Barrett, 1987:99).

The group was ordered to stop playing the messages which contravened the section of the *Act* prohibiting the repeated communication of hate messages by telephone (*Globe and Mail*, 1979). Taylor "apparently had indicated that he would change the messages" but they were only done slightly (Barrett, 1987:99). In February 1980, Taylor was "sentenced to one year in jail and his movement...fined $5,000 for contempt of court for continuing to disseminate anti-Jewish propaganda. The dissemination was in violation of a decision by the previous human rights tribunal." But in the same month, the sentence and fine were "suspended on condition that...Taylor and his associates respect the order" (*Globe and Mail*, 1980a). Then in June 1980, when Taylor and his members continued to spread racist telephone messages, thereby failing to comply with the February court order, he was given a jail sentence (*Globe and Mail*, 1980c). Later that month (June), the court "agreed to delay his jailing until an appeal of the original contempt charge is heard...." This decision was based on two conditions: post a $5,000 bond with two sureties and submit to the court a written promise to discontinue playing the recorded messages (*Globe and Mail*, 1980d). In June 1980, "a warrant for his arrest and for the Western Guard to pay the $5,000 fine was issued by a federal court judge because the taped messages, with little modification, continued. Taylor initially went into hiding, but finally turned himself in to the authorities in April 1981. He spent eight days in jail before bail was arranged pending his appeal of the sentence, which he lost. After 243 days behind bars, he was released in March 1982. On June 21,1982 the Western Guard's white-power message resumed" (Barrett, 1987:99). Taylor complied with these requirements.

Zundel

During the 1970s and 1980s, Ernest Zundel became Canada's most famous publisher of hate propaganda. By the end of the 1970s his message of hatred had reached many countries. Ironically, in March 1981 when West German police raided the headquarters of neo-Nazi organizations, they discovered that "the bulk of the hate materials" found in these premises were published by Zundel in Toronto (Abella, 1986:13; Barrett, 1987:156).

In November 1981, the Canadian post office's Board of Review "prompted by a complaint lodged by the Canadian Holocaust Remembrance Association, issued an interim prohibitory order against Samisdat Publishers Ltd. [Zundel's publishing company]" (Barrett, 1987:160). The Board, however, reversed its decision because of the partiality of the specialist who did a content analysis:

> But the Board's decision to find Zundel not guilty and restore his mail privileges ... on the basis that the whole matter was essentially an ethnic quarrel ... is more difficult to understand. Perhaps the Board was influenced by the Canadian Civil Liberties Association whose representatives defended Zundel on the grounds that postal services should not be denied to anyone not convicted of a crime ... (Barrett, 1987:166-161).

In response the members of the Canadian Jewish community, especially the Canadian Holocaust Remembrance Association charged Zundel "in court with two counts of knowingly publishing false news that caused or was likely to cause damage to social or racial tolerance" (Barrett, 1987:16).

Zundel, however, was not charged under the hate crime legislation, but with "spreading false news," section 177 of the *Code*. Unlike prosecution under the hate propaganda legislation, charges under section 177 do not need the attorney general's consent. In this case, Ontario's Attorney General would not give his approval for launching hate crime charges because he believed the federal hate law was so unworkable that a guilty conviction would have been impossible to achieve. Consequently, in September 1983, the League for Human Rights lobbied the federal Minister of Justice to remove loopholes in the hate law to make it easier for provincial attorneys general to use it (Weinman & Winn, 1986:18-19).

In September 1984, a pipe bomb had damaged Zundel's car and threats had been made on his life. His house was turned into a "virtual fortress" (Barrett, 1987:162). In the trial it was discovered that "Zundel was not a Canadian citizen." This prompted cries for "his deportation to West Germany." But "in 1982 the West German government had refused to renew his passport. Shortly after, Zundel was, in fact, ordered to be deported by an immigration commission adjudicator, but that was a regular formality in such cases, and no action could be taken until his criminal appeal was heard" (Barrett, 1987:163).

Regardless of these private citizen actions, on February 28, 1975 Zundel was convicted of his charges under the "spreading false news" section. On March 25, "Zundel was sentenced to 15 months in prison. After a hearing in May, Zundel was ordered deported. By autumn, his deportation order was in the process of being carried out" (Weinman & Winn, 1986:17). Zundel, however, remains in Canada and has appealed his deportation. "Zundel's conviction was reversed by the Canadian appellate court and a new trial was ordered. The defendant emerged as a victim, if not a hero, in the eyes of many Canadians. In his second trial, Zundel was once again convicted, and sentenced to nine months in prison." On appeal, "his principal argument is that the trial judge had erred in ordering the jury to regard the Holocaust as a historical fact" (Dershowitz, 1991:172).

Ross

During the 1970s, Malcolm Ross, a junior high school teacher in Moncton, New Brunswick wrote a series of books, the most controversial being *Web of Deceit*. In this book, Ross denies the existence of the Holocaust and suggests that a Zionist plot is trying to undermine Christianity. During the mid 1970s, he was investigated and defended by his school board on the grounds that he "did not teach what he wrote" (Martin, 1987). In 1978, retired chemistry professor Julius Israeli of Newcastle, N.B. "started a campaign to have him charged under hate-literature laws" (Martin, 1987).

Adding insult to injury, a Progressive Conservative and Liberal provincial attorneys general successively refused to prosecute Ross. The Liberal Attorney General erroneously argued that since that *Web of Deceit* was out of print and unavailable, charges were unnecessary (Martin, 1987). And like so many others before him, both attorneys general declared that Canada's hate crime laws were "too vague to ensure a conviction" (Canadian Press, 1988).

In November 1988, a New Brunswick Human Rights Commission board of inquiry was formed to investigate whether Ross "should be fired by his school board" (Jones, 1988). And in September 1990, the New Brunswick Court of Appeal rejected a bid by Ross to block an inquiry into complaints against him (Canadian Press, 1990). The Labour Minister ordered an inquiry after the provincial Human Rights Commission "was unable to resolve a complaint" against Ross. The inquiry concluded that "[a]lthough there was no evidence that Mr. Ross taught his views in the classroom," they felt that the school board's inaction over Ross's views encouraged students to express anti-Semitic comments, while "depriving minority students of equal opportunity within the school system" (Platiel, 1992). Finally, a New Brunswick judge upheld a board of inquiry's order to remove Ross from the classroom because of his anti-Semitic writings. The Court of Queen's Bench upheld the inquiry's order to place Ross on unpaid leave for 18 months; the School Board was ordered to offer him any qualified non-teaching position that became available, during this period. But if Ross did not accept a job or one was not available, then he would be dismissed at the end of the 18-month period (Platiel, 1992).

Summary

In general, as the public record indicates, it is much easier to impose sanctions against individuals who engage in hate crime actions under Canadian non-hate crime statutes than it is under the hate crime laws. The only way researchers could accurately identify the reasons that attorneys general, and by extension police departments do not charge these individuals with hate crimes is to speak to the individual police departments and/or provincial attorneys general, directly, something beyond the scope of this paper. Additionally, sources consulted in this paper could be extended to include interviews with hate crime sections of major police departments, crown prosecutors, and members of activist organizations who lobbied for changes in the hate crime laws.

CONCLUSION

What does the future hold for the existence and use of hate crime legislation in Canada? Certainly, a number of domestic and international issues[19] will prompt hate mongers to act on their beliefs, increasing the likelihood that a variety of groups will engage in hate crimes. While traditional concerns such as anti-Communism may be neutralized with the fall of the Soviet Union and its satellite states, the emergence of neo-Nazi and right-wing groups in Western and Eastern Europe has the potential to ignite anti-Semitism, anti-Catholicism, anti-Oriental, anti-immigration, anti-homosexual, and anti-abortion sentiment in Canada and hence pave the way for an increase in hate crimes.

Other factors fueling hate crime in Canada are hard economic times with consequential loss of jobs and inflation. This no doubt has been exacerbated by the North America Free Trade Agreement, and blamed by radical right-wing individuals and groups on Jews. Similarly, Francophone, especially Catholics, and Anglophone discrimination in Quebec could rise in the wake of the failed 1992 referendum to amend the constitution. And French- or English-only language militants, who have had some success in the United States are slowly making their way into Canada to engage in hate crimes (Goldenthal & Roberts, 1990).

Growing intolerance and discrimination are also being directed toward immigrants. Most predictions about the future of Canada involve an increase in the number of immigrants, particularly visible minorities, to the major cities. These new émigrés are available targets for promoters and practitioners of violence. Other targets of hate crime are abortion clinics and homosexuals. Changes in the abortion laws are already making some anti-abortionists increasingly militant, as was demonstrated by the recent bomb attack at the Morgentaler clinic in Toronto (May, 1992). And as the United States attempts to introduce legislation concerning the entrance of homosexuals into the military, Canada will experiment with the same type of laws, which is certain to promote hate crimes.

Perhaps the greatest threat of hate crimes these days is from skinheads. Canadian skinheads are anti-American, anti-black, anti-free trade, anti-homosexual, anti-immigrant, and pro-death penalty, among other things. Their membership is increasing, particularly by recruiting young people who more often than not are school dropouts, economically depressed, angry about their present condition and disillusioned about their future.

Finally, the police and national security agencies have been relatively successful at discovering and bringing to trial members of the radical right in a number of conspiracy cases (e.g., bombings and murders). These cases have led to the conviction and incarceration of several prominent members of the radical right and have helped to cripple the efforts and finances of individuals and groups engaging in hate crimes.

Given all these intricacies, one can conclude that hate crimes will continue, and that authorities will use current hate laws as a last resort if they cannot secure a conviction through other types of charges.

NOTES

1 The introduction of hate crime laws may simply be a reflection of the general increase in:

> the passage of more and more laws [which] may indicate that social solidarity and more effective informal modes of control in the society are weakening ... increased crime levels may be latent functions of increased freedom, affluence, competition, and otherwise desirable manifest functions in society (Hagan, 1990:11).

See, for example, Ross (1992) for a review of "Radical Right-Wing Violence in Canada A Quantitative Analysis."

2 The researcher examined government documents, the *Social Sciences Citation Index, the Canadian News Index* for articles listed in the *Globe and Mail,* the *Canadian Periodical Index* and cases cited in legal decisions, under these umbrella terms for appropriate literature. He was greatly aided by Morgan's (1991) excellent bibliography on hate crime in Canada.

3 For a history of the introduction of the legislation see, for example, Kayfetz (1970); Cohen (1971); Canada (1986).

4 "Requests for legislation against religious and racial hate propaganda" can be traced to "March 1953, when representations were made by the Canadian Jewish Congress and other interested and classically "vulnerable" minority groups to a Joint Committee of the House of Commons and Senate dealing with revisions of the Criminal Code" (Cohen, 1971:61). "In Canada, the post-war mood saw an attempt to include anti-hate propaganda provisions in the 1953 revision of CCSS 1953-1954. c. 51, but the most influential (was the special committee)" *(R. v. Keegstra,* 1991. 1 C.R. 4th, p. 152).

5 This legislation "can also be found in regulations of the *Post Office Act* and the *Customs Act"* (Morgan, 1991:91). For examples of this legislations' use in customs matters see, for example, *R. v. Keegstra,* 1991. 1 C.R. 4th, p. 258.

6 See Hage (1970:62) for a list. Also included were the Canadian Human Rights Commission, the Canadian Jewish Congress, League for Human Rights of B'nai Brith, the Canadian Holocaust Remembrance Association, the Canadian Civil Liberties Association, and the individual provincial Civil Liberties and Human Rights Associations. According to Borovoy (1985), the demand for changes mainly "came from Jews who had survived the horrors of Nazi concentration camps, Blacks whose memories embraced lynch mobs of the Ku Klux Klan, veterans of World War II, and many many others who sought simply to maintain racial and inter-group harmony in their communities" (19985:140).

7 See Gropper (1965:194-197) for similar arguments.

8 This has not been the first time that the federal government has tried to limit free speech. For example, in 1984 the federal government tabled Bill C-169 which would effectively limit freedom of speech during elections. See Elman (1984:73); and Regel (1983/84) for further discussion.

9 "That section has also seen only one case though—that brought by the Canadian Human Rights Commission (and others) against the Western Guard Party and John Ross Taylor" (Pettman, 1982:22).

[10] Gibbins (1990) writes,

> However, the Charter enumerates those rights and freedoms, entrenches them within the written constitution, and transfers the power to determine the practical limits of their application from a political process that is federally divided to a judicial process which is not. The courts have now been placed in position where they can judge acts of either Parliament or provincial legislatures to be unconstitutional on grounds other than contravention of the federal division of powers (1990:248).

[11] In June 1991 the U.S. Supreme Court "clouded the issue for state and local authorities when it agreed to decide whether states and communities violate constitutional free-speech protections by adopting laws against such hate crimes as cross-burning and the display of swastikas" (Lavin, 1991:24). In June 1992 the Supreme Court ruled "that hate crime laws that ban cross-burning and similar expressions of racial bias violate free-speech rights. Voting 9-0 the justices struck down a St. Paul, Minnesota ordinance that banned cross-burning, swastika displays, and other expressions of racial supremacy and bias" (Associated Press, 1992).

[12] In recent years, several publications have addressed either incidents of anti-Semitism (e.g., Levitt & Shaffir, 1987) or the presence of Nazism and fascism in Canada (e.g., Betcherman, 1975). Broad treatments (e.g., Barrett, 1987; Robins, 1992) are rare.

[13] Also known as the Deschenes Commission Report (Canada, 1989). There were allegations that an international network of Rumanian Nazi's and so-called war criminals was operating in Canada (Tompson, 1983; *Globe and Mail*, 1983).

[14] For a more detailed explanation, see, *R. v. Keegstra* and the Attorney General of Canada Criminal Reports; Bercuson & Wertheimer (1985); Mertl & Ward (1985).

[15] The list includes "The Attorney's General of Canada, Quebec, Ontario, Manitoba, and New Brunswick, the Canadian Jewish Congress, Interamicus, the League for Human Rights of B'nai Brith Canada, and the Women's Legal Education and Action Fund (LEAF)" (Criminal Reports 1 C.R. p. 144).

[16] The selection of these incidents is based on the number of citations of *Globe and Mail* articles listed in the *Canadian News Index*, of hate crime related incidents. Only those events that garnered greater than five articles were reviewed.

[17] A series of white supremists have entered the country but were quickly detained and then deported. First, in April 1980, David Duke, the Imperial Grand Wizard of the Ku Klux Klan was "arrested by Canadian immigration officials ... on a charge of entering the country illegally" (*Globe and Mail*, 1980b).

Second, in April 1989, Howard Pursley, a member of the Aryan Nations group, seeking refugee status in Canada was ordered deported April 4, 1989. (Canadian Press, 1989a). Third, in May 1992, Tom Metzger and his son, actively recruiting for White Aryan Resistance, were arrested shortly after a skinhead rally and charged with unlawful entry into Canada on the grounds that they were "likely to commit an indictable offence" (*Toronto Star*, 1992).

Fourth, David Irving, in November 1992, "A British author who says the Holocaust was exaggerated was ordered deported from Canada at an immigration hearing." "Mr.

Irving, 56, had been free on $20,000 bail while hearings were held over the past two weeks to determine whether he had violated an order to leave Canada." He "ran afoul of Canadian immigration authorities (in October 1992) when they arrested him in British Columbia and he pleaded guilty to misrepresenting himself" (*Globe and Mail*, 1992). These individuals were deported before they could engage in further activities.

[18] This action was prompted by "complaints from the Canadian Holocaust Remembrance Association and other concerned parties" (Barrett, 1987:98). During the past three decades a series of individuals and organizations established telephone lines where callers could receive some racist message or slogan. Most of the individuals who operated those hate lines were investigated by human rights organizations. In fact a human rights tribunal ordered Terry Long, leader of the Church of Jesus Christ Christian-Aryan Nations in Caroline Alberta 1987-1988, to stop playing hate messages over the phone (Canadian Press, 1989b).

In January 1992 Canadian Liberty Net in Vancouver, B.C., "a telephone message service that provides callers with recorded messages that condemn nonwhite immigration and suggest Jewish conspiracies behind everything from the entertainment industry to grocery prices" was investigated by the Alberta Human Rights Organization (Wilson, 1992).

[19] Shortly after the cemetery desecrations in France similar vandalizations took place in Quebec City and in Glouchester, Ontario.

REFERENCES

Abella, I. (1986). "Introduction." In G. Weinman & C. Winn. *Hate on Trial*, pp. 13-15. Oakville, Ontario: Mosaic Press Associated Press (1992). "Cross-Burning Ban Overturned," *Globe and Mail*, June 23, p. A10.

Barrett, S.R. (1987). *Is God a Racist?: The Right Wing in Canada.* Toronto: University of Toronto Press.

Bercuson, D. & D. Wertheimer (1985). *A Trust Betrayed, The Keegstra Affair.* Toronto: Doubleday Canada Ltd.

Berlin, M. (1985). "Hate Unbridled." *Policy Options Politiques,* July, pp. 31-32.

Betcherman, L.R. (1975). *The Swastika and the Maple Leaf.* Toronto: Fitzhenry & Whiteside.

Borovoy, A.A. (1985). "Freedom of Expression: Some Recurring Impediments." In R. Abella & M.L. Rothman (eds.) *Justice Beyond Orwell*, pp. 125-160. Montreal: Les Editions Yvon Blais, Inc.

Canada (1986). *Hate Propaganda.* Working Paper 50. Ottawa: Law Reform Commission of Canada.

_____ (1989). *War Criminals: The Deschenes Commission.* Ottawa: Library of Parliament Research Branch.

_____ (1991). *Bill C-247.* Ottawa: Supply and Services.

Canadian Criminal Reports 1 C.R., p. 144.

Canadian Press (1977). "Anti-French Literature Brings Two Convictions," *Globe and Mail,* December 26, p. 9.

_____ (1978). "Two Get Suspended Sentences for Anti-Francaphone Handbills," *Globe and Mail,* January 7, p. 11.

_____ (1987). "Guide Drawn Up On Propaganda," *Globe and Mail,* December 24, p. A5.

_____ (1988). "Anti-Jewish Teacher Perplexes McKenna," *Globe and Mail,* March 11, p. A3.

_____ (1989a). "White Supremist Ordered Deported," *Globe and Mail,* April 5, p. A5.

_____ (1989b). "Stop Hate Calls, Tribunal Orders," *Globe and Mail,* July 26, p. A4.

_____ (1990). "N.B. Court Rejects Author's Bid to Stop Rights Panel Inquiry," *Globe and Mail,* September 7, p. A6.

Certinig, M. (1991). "Keegstra Given Home-Town Support," *Globe and Mail,* March 18, p. A3.

Claridge, T. (1988). "Ontario, Alberta Courts at Odds Over Hate Law," *Globe and Mail,* August 3, p. A1, 11.

Cohen, M. (1971). "Human Rights and Hate Propaganda: A Controversial Canadian Experiment." In S. Shlomo (ed.) *Of Law and Man: Essays in Honor of Haim H. Cohn,* pp. 59-78. New York: Sabra Books.

Dershowitz, A.M. (1991). *Chutzpah.* Toronto: Simon & Schuster.

Downey, D. (1990). "Nationalist Party Leaders Jailed," *Globe and Mail,* December 15, p. A8.

Elman, B. (1989). "Review Article: The Promotion of Hatred and the Canadian Charter of Rights and Freedoms: A Review of Keegstra v. The Queen." *Canadian Public Policy,* Vol. 15, No. 1, pp. 72-83.

Fenson, M. (1964-65). "Group Defamation: Is the Cure Too Costly?" *Manitoba Law School Journal,* Vol. 1, pp. 255-281.

Fraser, G. & M. Certinig (1990). "Supreme Court Upholds Curbs on Free Expression," *Globe and Mail,* December 14, p. A1, A8.

Friedenberg, E. (1979). *Deference to Authority,* Armonk: M.E. Sharpe.

Gibbins, R. (1990). *Conflict & Unity: An Introduction to Canadian Political Life.* Scarborough, Ontario: Nelson Canada.

Globe and Mail, (1977a). Editorial, "In Pursuit of Hatred," August 9, p. 6.

_____ (1977b). "Group Defamations Actions Rejected," August 25, p. 5.

_____ (1979a). "Won't Halt Phone Message, Guard Says," June 16, p. 15.

_____ (1979b)."Stop Hate Message, Guard Ordered," August 23, p. 5.

_____ (1980a). "Western Guard Fine, Sentence Suspended," February 23, p. 5.

_____ (1980b). "Leader of Klan Held for Entering Canada Illegally," April 2, p. 9.

_____ (1980c). "Western Guard Leader Ordered to Jail for Continuing Racist Phone Messages," June 13, p. 5.

_____ (1980d). "Despite 'Flagrant Contempt,' Racist Leader Won't Be Jailed," June 25, p. 4.

_____ (1983). "Trial Presents Spectre of World-Wide Nazism," February 8, p. 22.

_____ (1991). "The Case of Mr. Keegstra," March 20, p. A12.

_____ (1992). "Anti-Holocaust Author Deported from Canada: Briton Accused of Concocting Story to Prolong Stay, Gain Publicity," November 14, p. A10.

Goldenthal, H. & W. Roberts (1990). "Franco-Phobia," *Now* Vol. 17, March, p. 10.

Gropper, M. (1965). "Hate Literature—The Problem of Control," *Saskatchewan Bar Review*, Vol. 30, No. 3, pp. 181-202.

Hagan, F. (1990). *Introduction to Criminology*. Chicago, IL: Nelson-Hall.

Hage, R. (1970). "The Hate Propaganda Amendment to the Criminal Code," *University of Toronto Faculty of Law Review*, Vol. 28, pp. 63-73.

Jones, R. (1988). "N.B. Judge Stays Inquiry on Teacher," *Globe and Mail*, November 18, p. A9.

Kayfetz, B.G. (1970). "The Story Behind Canada's New Anti-Hate Law," *Patterns of Prejudice*, Vol. 4, No. 3, pp. 5-8.

Lavin, C. (1991). "The People Next Door: A Real-Life Horror Story of Bigotry and Torment," *Chicago Tribune Magazine*, August 4, pp. 14-17, 24.

Lefole, K. (1964). "Editorial." *Maclean's*, Vol. 77, No. 7, April 4, p. 4.

Levitt, C.H. & W. Shaffir (1987). *The Riot at Christie Pits*. Toronto: Lester & Orphen Dennys.

MacGuigan, M. (1966). "Hate Control and Freedom of Assembly," *Saskatchewan Bar Review*, Vol. 31, pp. 232-250.

McAlpine, J. (1981). *Report Arising Out of the Activities of the KKK in British Columbia*. Presented to the Honourable Minister of Labour for the Province of British Columbia.

Makin, K. (1985). "Covering the Zundel Trial: A Reporter's Notebook," *T.O. Magazine*, May/June, pp. 20-28.

Martin, R. (1987). "N.B. Teacher Investigated After Anti-Semitism Alleged," *Globe and Mail,* January 30, p. A5.

Mertl, S. & J. Ward (1985). *Keegstra: The Trial, the Issues, the Consequences.* Saskatoon: Western Producer Prairies Books.

Morgan, K. (1991). "Hate Literature and Freedom of Expression in Canada: An Annotated Bibliography, 1964-1990," *Canadian Law Libraries,* Vol. 16, No. 3, pp. 91-96.

Norman, K., J.D. McAlpine & H. Weinstein (1984). *Report of the Special Committee on Racial and Religious Hatred.* Ottawa: Canadian Bar Association.

Oziewicz, S. (1977). "Ontario Considers Class Actions for Ethnics in Defamation Suits," *Globe and Mail,* August 6, p. 6.

Pettman, R. (1982). "Incitement to Racial Hatred: The International Experience," Occasional Paper No. 2. Australian Government Publishing Service.

Platiel, R. (1992). "N.B. Judge Upholds Removal of Teacher over Anti-Semitism," *Globe and Mail,* January 3, p. A5.

Regel, A.R. (1983/84). "Hate Propaganda: A Reason to Limit Freedom of Speech," *Saskatchewan Law Review,* Vol. 49, pp. 303-318.

Robin, M. (1992). *Shades of Right.* Toronto: University of Toronto Press.

R. v. Keegstra, 1991 1 C.R. (4th).

Ross, J.I. (1992). "Radical Right-Wing Violence in Canada: A Quantitative Analysis," *Terrorism and Political Violence,* Vol. 4, No. 3, Autumn, pp. 72-101.

Sher, J. (1983). *White Hoods: Canada's Ku Klux Klan.* Vancouver: New Star Books.

_____ (1984). "The Propaganda of Hatred," *Canadian Forum,* Vol. 64, No. 744, December, pp. 20-21.

Tompson, B. (1983). "Nazi Group Operating Here," *Toronto Sun,* July 5, p. 36.

Toronto Star (1992). "Canada Ejects 2 Men for Inciting Hatred," July 3, p. A24.

Weinman, G. & C. Winn (1986). *Hate on Trial: The Zundel Affair: The Media, Public Opinion in Canada.* Oakville, Ontario: Mosaic Press.

Wilson, D. (1992). "Panel Seeks Injunction on 'Hate Line'," Globe and Mail, January 18, p. A4.

7

Conceptualizing Hate Crime
in a Global Context

Mark S. Hamm
Indiana State University

Look at the liars and the propagandists among us, the skinheads...here at home, the Afrikaners Resistance Movement in
South Africa, the radical party of Serbia, the Russian Black
Shirts.... We must stop the fabricators of history and the bullies
as well. Left unchallenged, they would still prey upon the pow-
erless, and we must not permit that to happen again.

—U.S. President Bill Clinton
Upon Dedication of the United States Holocaust Museum
Washington, D.C.
April 22, 1993

Since the collapse of the Soviet empire and the destruction of the Berlin Wall,
more than two million poor immigrants from Eastern Europe have crossed borders to the countries of Western Europe. Another one million immigrants, truly
disadvantaged men and women from third-world nations, have also crossed these
borders seeking political and economic asylum.

This migration has been tragic for many émigrés; especially in Germany—the
birthplace (let us never forget) of national socialism. Since 1990, an estimated
4,000 immigrants from Albania, Bosnia-Herzegovina, Bulgaria, Croatia, Romania,
Turkey, Algeria, Morocco, Pakistan, Nigeria, Uganda, Mozambique, and Vietnam
became victims of violence committed by German neo-Nazi skinheads and other
young extremists. Yet this is an official statistic; it is estimated that the frequency
of violent attacks against foreigners may actually be closer to 80,000. This violence

has been wretchedly brutal, ranging from gang beatings to firebombings and murder. Currently, an average of 60 immigrants are harassed, beaten, or firebombed each day by highly organized groups of young males who often revere the memory of Adolf Hitler and Nazism. Forty-seven years after the allied liberation of Nazi Germany, this youthful convolution of violence also includes a distinct anti-Semitic dimension: Skinheads have recently desecrated dozens of Jewish cemeteries and attacked concentration camp memorials at Satchsenhausen, Ravensbrueck, and Dachau. Among German government officials, police, and researchers, this catastrophic social problem is referred to as *right-wing violence*.[1]

But Germany is not the only country to suffer from political violence in the post-communist era. Racist skinheads and other neo-Nazi youth collectives also exist in Belgium, Britain, Denmark, France, the Netherlands, Norway, Sweden, Switzerland, and in former Eastern bloc countries such as Hungary and Poland. These groups have committed some 4,000 violent attacks against Eastern European, Pakistani, East Asian, and third-world immigrants—including more than 25 murders, and dozens of firebombings and desecrations of Jewish and Muslim religious institutions. In Belgium, the Netherlands, and Norway this crime is defined by government officials and researchers as *racist violence*. In Britain and France, it is called *racial violence*.[2]

In North America, skinhead youth gangs have been implicated in the murder of more than 100 young African-Americans and third-world immigrants; at least four homicides against gay men; nearly 400 assaults against black males; more than 300 cross-burnings; 14 firebombings of African American churches; more than 200 assaults against gays and lesbians; some 40 desecrations of Jewish cemeteries; and nine acts of violence perpetrated against worshipers at Jewish synagogues, including one attempted mass murder in Dallas, Texas (Hamm, 1993; Klanwatch, 1991; Thornburgh, 1990). Because Canada's share of the problem is so small, government officials and researchers have yet to reach a consensual definition for this type of crime (Ross, Chapter 6). But not so in the United States. Here, we suffer from an excess of definitions.

In the United States, attacks by white neo-Nazi youth against African-Americans, immigrants, gays, and religious institutions have been referred to with such diverse terms as *hate crime, hate-motivated crime, bias crime, bias-motivated crime* and *ethno-violence* (e.g., Berk, 1990; Bensinger, 1991; Garofalo & Martin, 1991; Weiss, 1991). Because the use of these various terms often feeds community divisiveness, especially in racially charged times, several urban police departments have even created the label *possible bias crime* in an effort to contain media attention and hostile reactions from special interest groups (Fritsch, 1992). Finally, politicians and feminist scholars from all points on the ideological spectrum have argued that rape should also be included in the hate crime category (Buchanan, 1990; Miller, 1992; Renzetti, 1993).

In summary, crimes motivated by a victim's race, ethnicity, or religion are defined at least nine different ways in seven different nations around the world.[3] These diverse definitions of a common criminal event suggest the need for a global definition of the social problem at hand. Such a definition would serve two important functions. First, it would create a common language for social scientists with an interest in the problem. The failure of doctrines associated with the teachings of Engels, Marx, and Lenin has taught us that "human imagination driven by an improper use of language is vulnerable to extreme errors" (Ostrom, 1990:245). In the same way, erroneous cognition of a criminal phenomenon can produce social control doctrines that yield greater errors in magnitude than the problems they are meant to solve. In Germany, this would likely exacerbate a social problem that is already catastrophic.

Second, a global definition is necessary because the crime is a global problem. The fall of communism has brought with it "a growing interdependence of nations for their economic progress and political stability" (Chambliss, 1992:1). A global definition promises to help scholars and policymakers better understand how the emergence of a global economic and political system effects the emergence of a particularly insidious social problem.

TOWARD A GLOBAL CONCEPTUALIZATION

Globally, hate crime (alternatively referred to as right-wing violence, racist violence, etc.) must be conceptualized as an international youth movement toward racism. This is so because it is *racism* (not homophobia, and certainly not misogyny) that fuels the fires of neo-Nazi skinhead violence from Rostock to London, from Amsterdam to Paris, and from Stockholm to Dallas. Across international contexts, three features remain constant. According to the overwhelming body of evidence gathered since the fall of the Berlin Wall:

1. Eastern European, Asian, Pakistani, and third-world immigrants are the most frequent victims of hate crime;

2. Groups of young white males are most often the aggressors; and

3. Among these aggressors, neo-Nazi skinheads are responsible for the most egregious acts of violence in the world today.[4]

Therefore, the neo-Nazi skinheads present a worst-case scenario. Yet this also makes them an identifiable target for social scientists who wish to understand the criminology and control of hate crime in the post-communist era.

Neo-Nazi Skinheads

The study of hate crime begins like any other problem in criminology: With an examination of the motives that lead certain individuals, under certain circumstances, to commit crime. Yet with the neo-Nazi skinheads we are not interested in all crime. We have no interest, for example, in the number of robberies, extortions, or larcenies committed by skinheads because skinheads do not commit these crimes (Anti-Defamation League of B'nai B'rith, 1989; Hamm, 1993; Seidel-Pielen, 1991). Globally, we are only interested in their violence against racial and ethnic minorities.

I argue that if we want to make better social policies to control hate crime, we should pay less attention to broad generalities, and more attention to the growing volume of specific examples of hate crime being committed around the world. Instead of constructing macro-level sociological treatises on hate crime, generalizing hate crime to other victims, or devising more elaborate definitions of hate crime, we must focus on patterns that lead certain white neo-Nazi youths, under certain conditions, to commit violence against social outgroups. It is only through an understanding of these patterns that we can achieve a global definition for the hate crime phenomenon. I am suggesting that a criminology of hate crime—based on facts about the most extreme and essential cases—must be articulated before any global definition can be reached; and long before any social policy is justified.

THE CRIMINOLOGY OF HATE CRIME

I begin with the meditations of Holocaust scholar Hannah Arendt:

> Racism, as distinguished from race, is not a fact of life, but an ideology, and the deeds it leads to are not reflexive actions, but deliberate acts based on pseudo-scientific theories. Violence in interracial struggle is always murderous, but it is not "irrational," it is the logical and rational consequence of racism (1963:42).

Following this insight, we may assume two theoretical tenets concerning the most violent form of hate crime as it exists in the world today (i.e., the brutal victimization of thousands of immigrants by German neo-Nazi youths). First, this form of crime is grounded in an ideology of racism. The motivation toward hate crime does not exist in the abstract world where randomness and chaos prevail; rather, it lies in a structured philosophical system of simple, traditional beliefs called *neo-Nazism* that features racism as its defining characteristic (Hamm, 1993; Mücke, 1991; Protzman, 1992a). From this perspective hate crime can be considered globally. By conceptualizing the phenomenon in terms of a circumspect yet international youth movement toward lunatic extremism, it becomes isolated. Thus, it forms a concept package for researchers (right-wing extremism) and a target set of subjects to investigate: neo-Nazi youth—wherever they exist around the globe. To reemphasize, in its most violent form, hate crime is always ideological.

Second, because it is ideologically motivated, hate crime is rational. In the minds of neo-Nazi skinheads, hate crime is not irrational nor is it "magical." To the contrary, hate crime is premeditated violence carried out in heroic ecstasy. Inspired by the social and political brio of skinhead "Oi" music, this *sensuality of violence* is used by youths as a tool to advance group goals, to maintain order within their community, and to punish those who threaten the well-being of each tiny neo-Nazi skinhead cell from Munich to El Paso. This organized use of sensual violence continues to draw a growing number of youths into a thrill-seeking cult of right-wing lunatics throughout Europe and the United States (Hamm, 1993). Today, the heartbeat of this lunacy can be heard most loudly in Germany (Protzman, 1992a-d).

THE ATTEMPTED SOCIAL CONTROL OF HATE CRIME

"The skinheads," writes William Chambliss, "are a world unto themselves. The more they are attacked, the stronger grow the internal ties" (1993:xiv). Until recently, state responses to neo-Nazi skinhead violence have been fairly tame. Throughout Europe and the United States, federal prosecutors have kept clear of cases involving skinhead attacks; preferring instead to let these cases be handled by local jurisdictions where violent skinheads have typically been charged with no offense more serious than disturbing the peace (see Benjamin, 1992; *The Economist,* 1992; Witte, 1992). Even in murder cases, light sentences have been handed down to the German skinheads (Kinzer, 1992d). Yet this approach seems to be changing.

In December of 1992, the German Ministry of Justice made two broadsweeping changes in the nation's criminal justice system to deal with the rising tide of violence against foreigners. First, it is now illegal for youths to join organizations that question the democratic principles of the German republic. Recently, for example, memberships in the Nationalistic Front and the German Alternative Party—both dominated by young skinheads—have been banned (Kinzer, 1992c; Lane & Breslau, 1992). German Interior Minister Rudolf Seiters has charged that the Nationalistic Front is "an active fighting organization aimed at disposing our democratic order" (quoted in Fisher, 1992:2a); about the German Alternative Party, he proclaimed that "the disgusting work of these rabble-rousers must be stopped" (quoted in Toomey, 1992:21). Second, it is now a crime to sell, manufacture, and distribute skinhead Oi music in Germany. It is also a crime for Oi bands to perform in public. The German Parliament has declared that "there is a direct connection between the texts of their songs, which glorify Hitler and call for the murder of foreigners and Jews" (quoted in Protzman, 1992b:A16). Similar attempted control policies have been advanced in Poland, Britain, France, Canada, and the United States (see Protzman, 1992c; Hamm, 1993; Ross, Chapter 6; Witte, 1992). Like the German approach, these attempted control policies feature an immeasurable amount of censorship and suppression of freedom of expression.

The more skinheads are attacked, the stronger grow their internal ties. The stronger the internal ties, the more skinheads attack. Since the Ministry of Justice outlawed skinhead Oi music, it is now available only through clandestine channels. Within German society, these channels lead straight to Nazism and violence. Oi records, cassettes, and compact discs are now available only on the black market. The first group of entrepreneurs to fill this demand were the owners of army and weapons stores (Protzman, 1992b). Hence, Oi music—recently described by *Newsweek* as "the emblem of an international underground of haters"—has become aligned with German militarism and weaponry. *Newsweek* warned that a "a head-on attack [against Oi music] could backfire" (Masland, 1992:53). Perhaps it is for this very reason that the Ministry of Justice recently announced to the 80 million people of Germany that "the right-wing trail of death has just begun" (quoted in Kelly, 1992:2A).

Shortly following this extraordinary statement, *The Economist* observed the tragic fact that:

> Violence against foreigners ... is not unique to Germany. Britain,
> Sweden, France, Italy and now Spain have all seen it. No gov-
> ernment seems to know what to do (1992:55).

A GLOBAL DEFINITION: DOMESTIC TERRORISM

The definition of any crime must clearly delineate the individual and social nature of the phenomenon at hand. This exercise serves an important purpose far beyond the concerns of academic theorizing. If clearly defined, a crime becomes comprehensible to social control agents and implicates the state institutions that should deal with the problem. A clearly defined crime also identifies the social importance of the problem and the potential public resources that can be marshaled to enhance problem-solving capabilities. More than simply reflecting the individual and social nature of a crime, a clear definition also attracts attention to its causes and control.

Because hate crime is ideological and rational, it satisfies the criterion for most definitions of *domestic terrorism*. Between 1941 and 1989, government officials and researchers in Europe and the United States published more than 100 definitions of domestic terrorism (Gurr, 1989; Laqueur, 1987). Domestic terrorism is, on balance, one of the most thoroughly defined crimes in all of international criminology. Ironically, it is also one of the least understood because international criminology is altogether void of original research on the subject (Laqueur, 1987; Ross, 1992; Wilkinson, 1986).

Definition of Domestic Terrorism

Perhaps the most global and rigorous definition of nonstate domestic terrorism has been advanced by Jack Gibbs who stipulates that "in all instances [i.e., in all settings and across all social contexts] ... terrorism is illegal violence or threatened violence directed against human or nonhuman objects" (1989:330, 337) provided that such violence or attempted violence meet five criteria.

> 1. It was undertaken with a view to maintaining a putative norm
> in at least one particular territorial unit.

2. It had secretive, furtive, and/or clandestine features that were expected by the participant to conceal their personal identity.

3. It was not undertaken to further the permanent defense of some area.

4. It was not conventional warfare.

5. It was perceived by the participant as contributing to the normative putative goal (described in point "1") by inculcating fear of violence in persons other than the immediate target of the actual or threatened violence and/or by publicizing some cause.

Globally, there are now tens of thousands of examples of neo-Nazi skinhead violence, which if examined under a sociological microscope, would meet Gibbs' rigorous definition of domestic terrorism. If only they were examined. The data are not hard to come by. They can be gathered from interviews with neo-Nazi skinheads themselves; from their living victims; and from court transcripts, police files, and the international print media. Yet given these diverse data sources, we would expect the applicability of Gibbs' definition to vary because of differences in research methodology, the accuracy and completeness of available evidence, geographical variation in the crime, and variations in the seriousness of the crime across samples and time frames. With these caveats firmly in mind, below I offer four brief case studies—drawn from such data sources—that demonstrate the usefulness of Gibbs' global definition.[5]

THE PORTLAND CASE STUDY

At about 1:30 a.m., November 13, 1988, three teenage skinheads—heavily intoxicated with beer—encountered three Ethiopian immigrants on a rainy backstreet in Portland, Oregon. The skinheads had never met the immigrants before and vice-versa. Unprovoked, the skinheads singled out one immigrant named Mulugeta Seraw, a slightly-built 27-year-old employee of Avis Rent a Car and father of one son. They set upon Seraw with a baseball bat and steel-toed boots, beating him savagely and shouting, "Die nigger, die!" When they were finished, the skinheads had fractured Seraw's skull in two places, killing him. Twenty-four-hours later, Portland police searched the three-room apartment shared by the skinheads. In the first room, they found baseball bats and clubs wrapped in barbed wire. In the second room, they found racist propaganda published by a Southern California organization known as the White Aryan Resistance. And in the third room, they found a small library on the rise and fall of Nazi Germany (Hamm, 1993).

THE WUPPERTAL CASE STUDY

On the evening of November 14, 1992, five skinheads, aged 14 to 18, entered a pub in Wuppertal, Germany—a tiny western village near the Dutch border. Intoxicated with beer, they began a heated argument with a 53-year-old butcher named Karl-Heinz Rohn about immigration policy in unified Germany. At the end of the argument, Rohn called the skinheads a gang of "Nazi swine."

One hour later, the five skinheads met Rohn several blocks away from the pub. They brutally beat Rohn with baseball bats and steel-toed boots, killing him. Then they doused his body with schnapps and set him afire. Assisted by the owner of the pub where the argument originated, the skinheads then loaded the burned corpse into a car trunk and crossed into the Netherlands where they dumped Rohn's body in a canal outside the village of Venlo.

On arrest and interrogation, one of the skinheads said he thought Rohn was Jewish. He was not. Rohn died for another reason: Because of his support for German immigrants (*Chicago Tribune*, 1992; Meyer, 1992; *The Economist*, 1992).

THE MÖLLN CASE STUDY

At about 1:00 a.m., November 23, 1992, two skinheads approached the home of a 51-year-old woman named Bahide Arslan in Mölln—one of western Germany's most prosperous cities located near Hamburg in the state of Schleswig-Holstein. Arslan was a Turkish immigrant who owned a successful grocery business and lived with her 10 children and four grandchildren in a modest three-story house in Mühlen Street—a home she had occupied for the past 25 years. At 1:00 a.m., November 23, the Arslan family was asleep.

The two skinheads were Michael Peters, a 25-year-old unemployed high school dropout, and Lars Christiansen, a hard-working 19-year-old grocery store clerk. Both were members of the Free German Workers' Party, a newly organized grouping of neo-Nazi skinheads and other violence-prone rightists. Both carried firebombs made out of rags stuffed into a canister of gasoline (known in the United States as a Molotov cocktail). They lit their firebombs and smashed them through the windows of the Arslan home. Then they fled in Peters' Volkswagen.

In the ensuing fire, Bahide Arslan was burned to death as she lay atop her grandson, protecting him from the smoke and flames. Another child, Arslan's granddaughter Yelitz Arslan, age 10, also burned to death in the blaze along with her cousin, 14-year-old Ayse Tuknaz, who was visiting from Carsamba, Turkey. Six other family members were hospitalized for severe burns and smoke inhalation.

Just after the firebombs were thrown, Peters anonymously telephoned the Mölln fire department and shouted: "It's burning in Mühlen Street! Heil Hitler!" This was followed by a series of extraordinary events.

Later that morning (November 23), the German Parliament began its daily session with a moment of silence for the Arslan family. Chancellor Helmut Kohl then issued his most forceful and genuine denunciation of right-wing violence since the fall of the Berlin Wall.

> What has appeared here is an act of brutality that for every humane sensibility is incomprehensible. The German government [will invoke] every legal step to combat violence and political extremism (quoted in Benjamin, 1992:44; Masland, 1992:53).

By noon, Chancellor Kohl's office was flooded with faxed condemnations of the killings from international civil rights groups; and from the heads of states of Israel, Turkey, and Italy who threatened to pull economic interests from Germany unless the government got a grip on its catastrophic social problem. Meanwhile, some 10,000 protesters gathered on the streets of Hamburg in silent mourning for the Arslan family. Then the most significant events transpired.

For the first time in the history of unified Germany, a federal prosecutor from the Ministry of Justice took jurisdiction of a case involving right-wing violence. Because of the Holocaust, Germany has an arsenal of federal law for use against political extremism. The strongest laws cover terrorism. On the same day, the president of the Opel car company offered the Ministry of Justice 100,000 deutsche marks ($62,000) towards an award for help in finding the Mölln killers. Opel, like the German government, was interested in protecting its export-based economy.

And so, the German government—in collaboration with the private sector—mounted an aggressive manhunt for Peters and Christiansen. Using the full force of the mighty German law and economy, these powerful interests were not looking for delinquents who were guilty of disturbing the peace. Now they were after a couple of terrorists. "Brutally put," reported the London *Observer*, "a neo-Nazi murder was useful to galvanize the country" (Catterall, 1992:13).

For the next two days, police throughout Schleswig-Holstein conducted an aggressive investigation of the far-right. Focusing on skinheads, they raided more than 100 houses—uncovering caches of weapons, neo-Nazi propaganda, and Oi music. This intense response resulted in the arrest of Peters and Christiansen on November 26. They were officially described as members of a "terrorist organization formed to pursue rightist extremist and xenophobic aims through violent action on foreigners living in Germany" (quoted in Catterall, 1992:13) and were charged with three counts of murder, nine counts of attempted murder, arson, and breach of the peace. (They *were not* charged with terrorism.) Peters and Christiansen were immediately taken to Lübeck prison, 30 miles north of Mölln. After being placed in his cell, Christiansen slashed his wrists with broken glass in a suicide attempt (Benjamin, 1992; Kinzer, 1992e, 1992f, 1992g; Protzman, 1992c; *The Economist,* 1992; *The New York Times,* 1992).

THE HEREFORD CASE STUDY

On the night of February 18, 1991—at the height of the Persian Gulf War—four skinheads approached a Lebanese refugee camp near Hereford, England. They were all members of a London-based neo-Nazi group called the Anti-Pakki League, and they were intoxicated with beer. Each youth carried a homemade bomb made out of rags stuffed into a bottle of gasoline. The skinheads jumped a security fence and firebombed the camp barracks, injuring more than 20 immigrants. Among these victims was a 12-old-girl; one bomb struck her bed as she lay sleeping. As a result, most of the skin was burned from her body. Three days later she died a horrible and agonizing death (Bauerlein, 1992; field notes).

APPLYING GIBBS'S GLOBAL DEFINITION
OF DOMESTIC TERRORISM

In summary, each skinhead gang committed its homicide as an expression of intolerance and contempt for immigrants. Because the United States , Germany, and Britain all assume tolerance and respect for immigrants through liberal or moderate immigration laws (and because laws reflect dominant norms of democratic societies), then the murder of immigrants and their supporters can be viewed as a violent act *undertaken with a view to maintaining a putative norm* of the neo-Nazi skinhead movement. And because four different skinhead groups committed four separate homicides in four different geographical locations, each crime was committed in *one particular territorial unit.* Moreover, the available evidence surrounding each case study satisfies Gibbs's first criteria for domestic terrorism.

Each case also satisfies Gibbs's second criteria: the four homicides had *secretive, furtive, and/or clandestine features that were expected by the participants to conceal their personal identities.* Each murder was carried out in the dead of night by individuals who were affiliated with a group, thus concealing their personal identities. In Portland, these individuals were members of the East Side White Pride, a hybrid neo-Nazi cell created by the White Aryan Resistance. Each skinhead was known by a street name. (For example, the skinhead who wielded the baseball bat, Kenneth Murray Meiske, was known as "Ken Death".) Though we know little about the skinheads who murdered Rohn in Wuppertal, the facts that they immolated his body, transported it across international borders, and then disposed of it in a canal strongly suggest that these secretive and clandestine features of the crime were intended to conceal their personal identities. Furthermore, the Wuppertal skinheads, like Meiske and his accomplices, did not publicly claim responsibility for their murder. Likewise, the Free German Workers' Party skinheads of Mölln—who fled the murder scene immediately—used an anonymous phone call to conceal their personal identities; and the Hereford skinheads, all members of the clandestine Anti-Pakki League, did not publicly claim responsibility for their deadly firebombing.

Gibbs' third criteria is also satisfied. The Wuppertal and Heresford homicides were the first and only crimes committed by these particular skinhead groups against immigrants (or their supporters) in their respective areas. Although the East Side White Pride had been involved in several other beatings of minorities in the Portland area prior to the Seraw murder, and although the Mölln skinheads were involved in the firebombing of an asylum hostel in nearby Kollow, these groups *were not seeking a permanent defense of their areas.* At the time of the Seraw murder, the East Side White Pride had been in existence for less than six months; Peters and Christiansen had known each other for only a few months when they killed Arslan and her children. Accordingly, these skinhead collectives had little time to even prepare for a permanent defense of their areas.

Gibbs' fourth criteria is quickly satisfied across all four cases: baseball bats, steel-toed boots, schnapps, and gasoline firebombs *are not conventional weapons of war.*

With respect to Gibbs' fifth criteria, available evidence suggests that the motive for each crime was to strike out against immigrants and their supporters—the enemy *(contributing to the putative norm)*—thereby *inculcating fear of violence in persons other than the immediate target of the actual violence.* In each case, anti-immigrant prejudice motivated specific acts of violence designed to capture the attention of a larger human audience—the Governments of the United States, Germany, and Great Britain. In other words, these acts of violence were exercises in what Gibbs refers to as *attempted deterrent vicarious social control.* I shall refer to this notion with the shorter, "vicarious social control."

Vicarious Social Control

Gibbs defines domestic terrorism as a case where:

> the first party [i.e., the terrorist group] attempts to punish the third party [i.e., victims of terroristic violence] ... always presuming that such action will influence the second party's [i.e., the government's] behavior [e.g., by attempting to control the third party] (Gibbs, 1989:337).

Figure 7.1: The Global Application of Gibbs' Theory

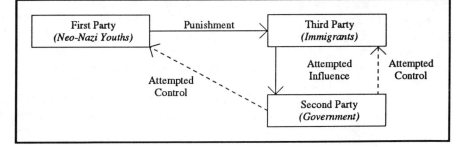

Figure 7.1 presents the notion of vicarious social control. As applied to the evidence reviewed here, the motives of the "first party" were grounded in neo-Nazism. From Kenneth Meiske's portentous library in Portland to Michael Peters' refrain of "Heil Hitler" recited to the Mölln fire department, a belief in modern Nazism served as the common denominator for these four acts of domestic terrorism. And as history tragically reminds us, Nazism represents a *sustained and violent campaign* against certain segments of the civilian population in the pursuit of political and social objectives that defile human morality. This is the first party's ultimate blackmail vicariously posed to Gibbs's "second party"—the governmental structures of the world today. Following the massacre of Turkish immigrants in Mölln, for example, the Minister of Justice charged that the skinheads were attempting "to re-establish a National Socialist dictatorship in Germany" (quoted in Lane & Breslau, 1992:30).

Figure 7.1 shows how the first party (neo-Nazi youths) punishes the third party (immigrants) in an attempt to influence the second party's (the government's) behavior, *presuming that such violence will lead to increased control of the third party through laws enacted by the second party to deter immigration.* Hence, the skinhead slogan "Foreigners Out!" is not only a battle cry for terrorism, it is also a literal and imaginative expression of vicarious social control over the state. The skinheads exert this control by threatening government with a harsh return to national socialism; with lunatic extremism.

Finally, Figure 7.1 outlines the role of the state in responding to domestic terrorism. "Because nonstate terrorists resort to violence," argues Gibbs, "they are certain to be targets of attempted control by the police and/or *the military*" (1989:338, emphasis added).

DISCUSSION

Although neo-Nazi skinheads are not responsible for all hate-motivated crime in the world today, they are responsible for the most violent attacks against racial and ethnic minorities. Globally, however, these attacks are defined more than half a dozen ways. There is, then, no coherent sociological definition for a global phenomenon which has been referred to as "potentially the major social problem of the next century" (Chambliss, 1993:xiii).

I have attempted to fill this void by invoking what Paul Wilkinson refers to as the "mental reenactment of terrorist thought in each tiny terrorist group" (1986:97). Through my brief reenactment of skinhead violence, I have endeavored to show that this international social problem can be defined through reference to Gibbs's (1989) global definition of the phenomenon: Wherever in the world neo-Nazi youths use violence or the threat of violence against persons because of their race or ethnicity, this crime is properly defined as *domestic terrorism.*

Thus, terms such as right-wing violence, racist violence, racial violence, hate crime, hate-motivated crime, bias crime, bias-motivated crime, possible bias crime, and ethnoviolence are all irrelevant sociological abstractions because they do not adequately capture the true meaning of the individual and social content of the crime at hand. Accordingly, the social scientific use of these terms are counterproductive to enhancing problem-solving capabilities in the area. "There is a danger," warns Vincent Ostrom, "that names (symbols, words) may be incorrectly associated with referents." If so, erroneous definitions of a social problem "can yield greater errors in magnitude than simple ignorance" (Ostrom, 1990:244).

A Biomedical Analogy

The international attempt on the part of social scientists to arrive at a consensual definition of violence against racial and ethnic minorities has an instructive analog in biomedical research. I am referring here to that other disastrous global problem—AIDS.

During the early 1980s, as medical professionals became introduced to the pandemic, researchers scrambled desperately to define the disease. In Africa, Europe, and North America, it was initially diagnosed as a form of Kaposi's sarcoma—a terminal illness originating in Southern Africa during the fifteenth century. Yet others defined the disease as *Pneumocystis carinii pneumonia*, a rare form of pneumonia originating in fourteenth-century Central Europe. Both research groups, of course, were wrong. Kaposi's sarcoma and *Pneumocystis* were simply the final symptoms of a far more complicated disease—an unknown disease that destroyed the immune system.

Biomedical researchers in Europe and North America began major and energetic efforts to define the unknown disease. Because it was found in gay men, a plethora of definitions were advanced that located the sickness in the gay lifestyle. In the United States, the disease was originally defined as *gay syndrome* because it was thought to be transmitted in "poppers" (amyl nitrite or butyl nitrite), a highly euphoric drug popularly used as an aphrodisiac in the gay subculture. Because the disease produced *Pneumocystis*, it was also called *gay pneumonia* until early 1982. Then in June of 1982, scientists at the Centers for Disease Control discovered that the sickness was transmitted through blood by a virus that destroyed the immune system of gay men. These scientists then coined the term *Gay-Related Immune Deficiency Syndrome*, or GRIDS.

Through a sort of scientific imperialism, U.S. researchers then began to promote their findings to the European biomedical community—drawing worldwide attention to the fact that the virus was a homosexual disease. Unlike other viruses, U.S. scientists argued that GRIDS tended to respect an artificial division among humans: It only killed gay men. In Denmark and the Netherlands, the virus was subsequently defined as *gay disease*. In Belgium and West Germany, it was called *mystery disease*. And in France, it was originally defined as *charter disease* because so many of the early European cases of the virus were among young gay men who had taken chartered airplane flights from Paris to New York City and San Francisco.

On November 22, 1983, 38 experts from around the globe gathered at the World Health Organization (WHO) headquarters in Geneva for the WHO's first international meeting on the worldwide implications of the virus. For the first time, biomedical researchers adopted a common definition for the pandemic: *Acquired Immune Deficiency Syndrome*, or AIDS.

Meanwhile, the virus had spread to 163 nations on five continents where it would eventually infect an estimated 15 million people. But gay men were not the only ones to become victims of the virus. Soon, millions of heterosexuals began dying from the same virus. Intravenous drug users began dying. Newborn babies were dying. And tens of thousands of hemophiliacs were dying from blood transfusions contaminated by the virus. These people were unrelated to the gay subculture.

In the final analysis, AIDS did not respect any artificial division among humans. It is now clear that AIDS has the ability to spread across all social, cultural, economic, and political boundaries. Eventually, the virus will reach all human communities on earth.

In a word, original attempts to define the disease were wrongheaded. This major *lapsus* in biomedical research between 1981 and 1983 resulted in social control efforts aimed solely at the gay community. This narrow policy focus eventually cost the lives of nearly 12 million "innocent" people around the globe. Erroneous doctrines can yield greater errors in magnitude than simple ignorance.[6]

CONCLUSIONS

The world is currently linked together by the malaise of change. In Europe, the heart of this change is in Germany; where there also beats the heart of a catastrophic social problem. Each day, scores of foreigners are harassed, beaten, or firebombed by young German males who strive to fulfill the hidebound dreams of Nazism. This violence is carried out heroically with baseball bats, brass knuckles, knives, and beer bottles; with gasoline, Oriental throwing stars, starter pistols, steel-toed boots, and schnapps. Such wildcat Aryanization of the general populace has gone on before in Germany's history—bringing with it catastrophic impacts on the moral sensibilities of the Western world.

This same social entropy is now at work in the form of skinhead youth gangs who loiter around subway stations, housing projects, pubs, and public parks in German cities and villages. The post-communist rise of such vitriolic neo-Nazism (at a time when most thought it a remote possibility) has been described as nothing less than "a ball and chain dragging down Germany and all Europe with it" (Lewis, 1992:15A).

The analogy between AIDS and domestic terrorism is more than a literary metaphor for scientific struggles to define catastrophic social problems. Like AIDS, the entrophy that supports domestic terrorism is also contagious. For the first time since Spain's democratic rebirth, swastikas have recently appeared on walls in Madrid. The tolerant Canadian and Dutch Parliaments have begun to complain about immigrants and refugees seeking asylum in their countries.

Mainstream politics begins to walk lockstep with the bloody boots of Nazism. Swastikas begin to appear on sidewalks around the Holocaust Museum in Amsterdam, and near the synagogues of Old Montreal. In Austria, the far-right populist Jörg Haider becomes a candidate for the nation's presidency, advocating a referendum against foreigners; and soon, swastikas appear in the streets of Vienna. In the United States, Republican Presidential candidates Patrick Buchanan and David Duke make nativism a key element of their campaigns, charging that new immigrants would "dilute" the nation's European character. In their 1992 Convention, the Republican Party introduces a plank calling for "a barrier—a wall or trench—along the border with Mexico." And as President Bush signs an executive order forcing the repatriation of Haitians fleeing their country by boat, immigrants across the land begin to feel the brunt of a growing hostility.

Attacks on newly arrived immigrants become a routine occurrence in New York City public schools; as skinheads in the South Bronx start to accost Asian immigrants, spray-painting their faces black. In Houston, two skinheads stomp a 15 year-old Vietnamese boy to death. In Carbondale, Illinois, police begin an investigation of skinhead links to a mass murder of five Asian students. In Great Barrington, Massachusetts, a teenage skinhead goes on a killing rampage with an automatic assault rifle, leaving two dead and four seriously wounded. And in Patterson, New Jersey, a skinhead gang called the "Dotbusters"—named for the dot, or bindi, that some Indian women wear on their foreheads—emerges to terrorize a growing population of East Indian women (see DePalma, 1992; Sontag, 1992).

Meanwhile, the human ravages of "ethnic cleansing" continue in Bosnia-Herzegovina and threaten to spread north through the Baltics, perhaps to Central Europe and south through Albania, perhaps to Greece.

Highly consistent with this global trend toward xenophobia, the ruling conservatives in the German Parliament recently led the way for a wide-bodied capitulation to the demands of the terroristic neo-Nazi youth gangs of their country. On December 18, 1992, the Parliament passed a law making it harder for asylum-seekers and refugees to enter Germany. In effect, the new law bars immigrants from most nations of Eastern Europe, and calls for the repatriation of thousands of immigrants from Vietnam and Romania. Moreover, the skinhead battle cry of "Foreigners Out" has been incorporated into public policy.

This new law has been criticized by left and right alike as the most serious threat to European democracy and peace since the fall of the Berlin Wall. "It must be a matter for the gravest reflection, that for violence in the streets, [Germany's immigration problem] would have continued to mount," wrote conservative analyst William Buckley shortly after its passage (1992:12). Members of Germany's liberal Green Party have described the new immigration law as "a surrender to street fighters who have attacked refugees and the homes where they live" (quoted in Kinzer, 1992h:A6). In sociological terms, the first party vicariously controlled the second party through a sustained campaign of violence against the third party.

This terroristic strategy, therefore, has now proven effective in changing the course of public policy on immigration in Germany; the heart of Europe, if not the world. If domestic terrorists can effectively change immigration policy, then they can also change policies in criminal justice, health, education, welfare, and most importantly—in the military direction of nation-states.

The Global Control of Domestic Terrorism

All of this can change through democratic leadership provided by men and women of goodwill and courage who have the resolve to get control of Gibbs's first party—neo-Nazi youth wherever they exist around the world today. The social institutions exist to effect such change. On this point, history is extremely clear.

During the 1970s and early 1980s, the German Federal Republic showed their ability to impose harsh social control against the violence of such leftist groups as the Baader-Meinhof Red Army Faction. Beginning in the early 1970s and extending up to 1992, the British have employed draconian measures to control the anarchist terrorism of the Angry Brigade and the leftist terrorism of the Irish Republican Army. To this day, the British government combats IRA guerrillas with an elite cadre of anti-terrorist commandos. These agents wear suits of full body armor and are specialists in firearms, explosives, and dog handling; their tactics include state-of-the-art electronic surveillance and routine stop and checks of any vehicle traveling in the Greater London area which might be linked to the IRA. Similarly, American police and federal law enforcement officials moved swiftly and decisively to bring down such leftist groups as the Black Panthers, the Symbanese Liberation Army, and the Weathermen.

This same measure of public energy must now be brought against the far-right. More than simply taking away their rock music and forbidding them to join clandestine groups (thus causing new problems), public officials can begin to view the young neo-Nazis for what they truly are. Since these youths are known to commit violence against persons because of race or ethnicity, they are *terrorists*. They are much more than delinquents involved in boys' pranks. According to Gibbs, these terrorists can only be controlled by throwing the full weight of the state against them.

In Germany—at the epicenter of the international youth movement toward racism—this calls for the use of such law enforcement and military tactics as saturation patrol, stakeouts, electronic surveillance, follow-up investigations, improved crime reporting, and permanent international intelligence machinery designed to remove these youths from the public sector and incarcerate them in prison where they belong. Under any normative definition of democracy, terrorists ought not be entrusted with the power and privilege to shape public policy.

Immediate legal remedies for prosecuting domestic terrorists are available under the federal civil rights laws of all nations (Dees, 1991; Padgett, 1984; *The Economist*, 1992), and methods for their treatment and rehabilitation are described in the international literature of correctional education (Hamm, 1991). In the emerging European community, the alternative to a domestic terrorism approach is simply more of the same: A dangerous social entropy of assaultive violence, profound fear, anxiety, isolation, restricted mobility and, especially among the poor immigrants of Western Europe and Africa, fatalistic despair—the feeling that prudent behavior is unavailing because criminal justice systems are inadequate to the task of providing law and order.

To be reversed, this condition demands the wisdom to change. This process can begin with a global definition that attracts attention to the real causes and control of the problem.

NOTES

1 Official statistics on right-wing violence come from Germany's Federal Office for Protection of the Constitution reported in Fisher (1992), Jackson (1991), Kelly (1992), Kinzer (1992a; 1992b), Marshall (1992), Protzman (1992a), and Whitney (1992a). The estimate of 80,000 attacks since 1990 is based on calculations contained in British Home Office studies that show an overall reporting rate of between only two and five percent among victims of racial harassment and assault (see Bowling, Chapter 1; Brown, 1984; London Borough of Newham, 1986). The organization of German neo-Nazi skinhead groups and their allegiance to the memory of Hitler is reported in Douglas (1993), Jackson (1991), Kinzer (1992b, 1992c), Lane and Breslau (1992), Mücke (1991), Protzman (1992a, 1992b), and Seidel-Pielen (1991). The "catastrophic" nature of this violence was voiced by Chancellor Helmut Kohl's government and reported by the Associated Press in the *Bloomington Herald-Times* (1992a, 1992b). The definition of the crime phenomenon is reported in Cartner (1992), Haberman (1992), Kinzer (1992a, 1992b), Protzman (1992a), Seidel-Pielen (1991), and Whitney (1992a, 1992b).

2 The dimensions and definitions of these problems are reported in Bauerlein (1992), Björgo Chapter 3, Bowling (1990; Chapter 1), Brown (1984), Cooper (1989), Coplon (1989), Gordon (1990), Hamm (1993), Hunt (1992), Hiro (1991), Lane and Breslau (1992), Saulsbury and Bowling (1991), *The Economist* (1992) and Witte (1992).

3 Only in the United States are crimes motivated by a victim's sexual orientation included in the crime definition and only in the United States has it been suggested that rape be included in the definition.

4 For evidence of this trend in Germany, see Note 1. For evidence in other parts of Europe and Britain, see Note 2. For evidence in the United States, see Anti-Defamation League of B'nai B'rith (1989, 1990), Center for Democratic Renewal (n.d.), Clarke (1991), Klanwatch (1991), and U.S. Department of Justice (1989). The U.S. studies show that young American-born black males are the most frequent victims of hate crime (Labaton, 1993; Meddis, 1993) and that neo-Nazi skinheads are responsible for nearly two-thirds of these racial attacks (Hamm, 1993; Herek & Berrill, 1992; Klanwatch, 1991).

5 There is well-established precedent within the terrorism literature for using single case studies for purposes of illustration, as demonstrations of hypotheses and for theory building (e.g., Crenshaw, 1981; Laqueur, 1987; Gibbs, 1989; Wilkinson, 1986).

6 The history of AIDS is based on the work of Mann (1992) and Shilts (1988).

REFERENCES

Anti-Defamation League of B'nai B'rith (1990). "Neo-Nazi Skinheads: A 1990 Status Report." *Terrorism,* 13: 243-275.

_____ (1989). *Skinheads Target the Schools.* New York, NY: ADL.

Arendt, H. (1963). *Eichmann in Jerusalem: A Report on the Banality of Evil.* New York, NY: The Viking Press.

Bauerlein, M. (1992). "The Right Rises in Europe." *Utne Reader,* March/April: 34-38.

Benjamin, D. (1992). "Cracking Down on the Right." *Time,* Dec. 14: 43-45.

Bensinger, G.J. (1991). "Hate Crime: A New/Old Problem." Paper presented at the annual meeting of the American Society of Criminology, San Francisco, November.

Berk, R.A. (1990). "Thinking About Hate-Motivated Crimes." *Journal of Interpersonal Violence,* 5: 334-349.

Bloomington Herald-Times (1992a). "Germans Face Another Night of Ethnic Violence." Aug. 8: A8.

_____ (1992b). "Kohl Vows Crackdown on Neo-Nazis." Aug. 28: A3.

Bowling, B. (1990). "Racist Harassment and the Process of Victimization: Conceptual and Methodological Implications for Crime Surveys." Paper presented at the Realist Criminology Conference, Vancouver, B.C.

Brown, C. (1984). *Black and White Britain: The Third PSI Survey.* London: Heinemann.

Buchanan, P. (1990). "American Women Are Real Victims of Hate Crime." *Terre Haute Tribune-Star,* March 8: A6.

Buckley, W.F. (1992). "Fuel to the German Fire." *National Review,* Dec. 28: 12.

Cartner, H. (1992). "Foreigners Didn't Cause German Violence." *The New York Times,* Sept. 6: A16.

Catterall, T. (1992). "Heil Hitler Slayings Spark Bout of Hysteria." *The Observer,* Nov. 29: A13.

Center for Democratic Renewal (n.d.). *Skinhead Nazis and Youth Information Packet.* Atlanta, GA: CDR.

Chambliss, W.J. (1993). "Foreword." In M.S. Hamm *American Skinheads: The Criminology and Control of Hate Crime.* Westport, CT: Praeger.

_____ (1992). "Call for Papers." Program announcement for the 1993 annual meeting of The Society for the Study of Social Problems.

Chicago Tribune (1992). "Neo-Nazi Bomb Shames German Town." Nov. 24: A1.

Clarke, F.I. (1991). "Hate Violence in the United States." *FBI Law Enforcement Bulletin,* January: 14-17.

Cooper, M.H. (1989). "The Growing Danger of Hate Groups." *Editorial Research Reports,* 18: 262-275.

Coplon, J. (1989). "The Skinhead Reich." *Utne Reader,* May/June: 80-89.

Crenshaw, M. (1981). "The Causes of Terrorism." *Comparative Politics,* 13: 379-399.

Dees, M. (1991). *A Season for Justice: The Life and Times of Civil Rights Lawyer Morris Dees.* New York, NY: Charles Scribner's Sons.

DePalma, A. (1992). "Questions Outweigh Answers in Shooting Spree at College." *The New York Times,* Dec. 28: A1.

Douglas, M.C. (1993). "Auslander Raus! Nazi Raus! An Observation of German Skins and Jugendgagen." *International Journal of Comparative and Applied Criminal Justice* 16: 1-15.

Fisher, M. (1992). "Germany Cracks Down on Neo-Nazis." *Washington Post,* Nov. 28: A1.

Fritsch, J. (1992). "Police Vow New Caution in Labeling Bias Crimes." *The New York Times,* Dec. 22: A11.

Garofalo, J. & S.E. Martin (1991). "The Law Enforcement Response to Bias-Motivated Crimes." In N. Taylor (ed.) *Bias Crime: The Law Enforcement Response.* Chicago, IL: Office of International Criminal Justice.

Gibbs, J.P. (1989). "Conceptualization of Terrorism." *American Sociological Review,* 54: 329-340.

Gordon, P. (1990). *Racial Violence and Harassment.* London: Runnymede Trust.

Gurr, T.R. (1989). "Political Terrorism: Historical Antecedents and Contemporary Trends." In T.R. Gurr (ed.) *Violence in America* (Vol. 2). Newbury Park, CA: Sage.

Haberman, C. (1992). "An Anxious Israel, 2 Germans, a Riveting Tableau." *The New York Times,* Nov. 19: A3.

Hamm, M.S. (1993). *American Skinheads: The Criminology and Control of Hate Crime.* Westport, CT: Praeger.

_____ (1991). "Confronting the Appeal of White Extremism Through Correctional Education." In S. Duguid (ed.) *The 1991 Yearbook of Correctional Education.* Burnaby, B.C.: Simon Fraser University.

Herek, G.M. & K.T. Berrill (1992). *Hate Crimes: Confronting Violence Against Lesbians and Gay Men.* Newbury Park, CA: Sage.

Hiro, D. (1991). *Black British White British: A History of Race Relations in Britain.* London: Grafton Books.

Hunt, S. (1992). "Fascism and the 'Race Issue' in Britain." *Talking Politics,* 5: 23-28.

Jackson, J.O. (1991). "Unity's Shadows." *Time,* July 1: 6-14.

Kelly, J. (1992). "Refugees, Jews Targets of Neo-Nazis." *USA Today,* Nov. 11: A1.

Kinzer, S. (1992a). "Germany Blocks a Big Neo-Nazi Rally Near Berlin." *The New York Times,* Nov. 16: A3.

_____ (1992b). "Youths Adrift in a New Germany Turn to Neo-Nazis." *The New York Times,* Sept. 28: A3.

_____ (1992c). "Neo-Nazi Front Will Fight Its German Banning in Court." *The New York Times,* Nov. 30: A6.

_____ (1992d). "Light Sentences Against Germans Who Killed Foreigner Stir Debate." *The New York Times,* Sept. 16: A4.

_____ (1992e). "Germans Arrest a Neo-Nazi, 19, In Bombing That Killed 3 Turks." *The New York Times,* Dec. 1: A6.

_____ (1992f). "Germany Outlaws A Neo-Nazi Group." *The New York Times,* Nov. 11: A1.

_____ (1992g). "A Look Into the Violent World of a Young Neo-Nazi." *The New York Times,* Dec. 12: A4.

_____ (1992h). "Germans in Accord on a Law to Limit Seekers of Asylum." *The New York Times,* Dec. 8: A1.

Klanwatch (1991). *The Ku Klux Klan: A History of Racism and Violence.* Montgomery, AL: The Southern Poverty Law Center.

Labaton, S. (1993). "Poor Cooperation Deflates FBI Report on Hate Crime." *The New York Times,* Jan. 6: A8.

Lane, C. & K. Breslau (1992). "Germany's Furies." *Newsweek,* Dec. 7: 30-31.

Laqueur, W. (1987). *The Age of Terrorism.* Boston, MA: Little, Brown and Co.

Lewis, F. (1992). "Europe's Champagne Goes Flat." *The New York Times,* Dec. 5: A15.

London Borough of Newham (1986). *The Newham Crime Survey.* London: LBN.

Mann, J.M. (1992). "AIDS—The Second Decade: A Global Perspective." *The Journal of Infectious Diseases,* 165: 245-250.

Marshall, T. (1992). "German Jews' Exodus is Small but Ominous." *Los Angeles Times,* Nov. 28: A4.

Masland, T. (1992). "Muffling the Music of Hate." *Newsweek,* Dec. 14: 53.

Meddis, S.V. (1993). "Race Biggest Factor in Hate Crimes." *USA Today,* Jan. 5: A1.

Meyer, K.E. (1992). "The Ghosts of Weimar." *The New York Times,* Dec. 1: A14.

Miller, S.L. (1992). "Misogyny Masquerading as Ordinary Violence: Counting Hate Crimes Against Women." Paper presented at the annual meeting of the American Society of Criminology. New Orleans, November.

Mücke, T. (1991). "Bericht uber das Project—Miteinander Statt Gegeneiandeer." *Jervental:* 38-47.

Ostrom, V. (1990). "Problems of Cognition as a Challenge to Policy Analysts and Democratic Societies." *Journal of Theoretical Politics*, 2: 243-265.

Padgett, G.L. (1984). "Racially Motivated Violence and Intimidation: Inadequate State Enforcement and Federal Civil Remedies." *Journal of Criminal Law and Criminology,* 26: 591- 625.

Protzman, F. (1992a). "German Attacks Rise As Foreigners Become Scapegoat." *The New York Times,* Nov. 11: A1.

_____ (1992b). "Music of Hate Raises the Volume in Germany." *The New York Times,* Dec. 2: A1.

_____ (1992c). "Germany to Ask Court to Revoke Some Civil Rights of 2 Neo-Nazis." *The New York Times,* Dec. 10: A6.

_____ (1992d). "Germany Moves to Ban a Second Neo-Nazi Party." *The New York Times,* Dec. 11: A9.

Renzetti, C.M. (1993). "Bias Motivated Violence and Hate Crimes Against Women: They Just Don't Count." Paper presented at the annual meeting of the Academy of Criminal Justice Sciences. Kansas City, March.

Ross, J.I. (1992). "Radical Right-Wing Violence in Canada: A Quantitative Analysis." *Terrorism and Political Violence,* 4: 72-101.

Saulsbury, W. & B. Bowling (1991). *The Multi-Agency Approach in Practice: The North Plaistow Racial Harassment Project.* London: Home Office.

Seidel-Pielen, E. (1991). *Krieg im den Stadten.* Berlin: Rotbuch, 34.

Shilts, R. (1988). *And the Band Played On: Politics, People, and the AIDS Epidemic.* New York, NY: Penguin Books.

Sontag, D. (1992). "Across the U.S., Immigrants Find the Land of Resentment." *The New York Times,* Dec. 11: A1.

The Economist (1992). "Germany Looks at Itself, and Winces." Nov. 28: 55-56.

The New York Times (1992). "2 Germans Admit Arson Attack That Killed 3 Turkish Nationals." Dec. 2: A6.

Thornburgh, R. (1990). Address before the Simon Wiesenthal Center. Chicago, March 5.

Toomey, C. (1992). "Women Dreaming of Fourth Reich Swell neo-Nazi Ranks." *The Sunday Times,* Dec. 13: 21.

U.S. Department of Justice (1989). *Terrorism in the United States 1989.* Washington, DC: U.S. Dept. of Justice.

Weiss, J.C. (1991). "Ethnoviolence: Impact and Response in Victims and the Community." In N. Taylor (ed.) *Bias Crime: The Law Enforcement Response.* Chicago, IL: Office of International Criminal Justice.

Whitney, C.R. (1992a). "Germans Emphasize Non-Rioters at Berlin Rally." *The New York Times,* Nov. 10: A6.

_____ (1992b). "350,000 in Germany Protest Violence Against Migrants." *The New York Times,* Nov. 11: A1.

Wilkinson, P. (1986). *Terrorism and the Liberal State.* New York, NY: New York University Press.

Witte, R.B.J. (1992). "State Response to Racist Violence: A Theoretical Framework." Paper presented at the annual meeting of the American Society of Criminology. New Orleans, November.

INDEX

About the Authors

Alexis A. Aronowitz has been living in Berlin, Germany since 1984. She completed her dissertation on integration and delinquency among Turkish guest worker children in Berlin and received her Ph.D. from the State University of New York at Albany in 1988. At that time, she returned to Berlin to become Central Texas College's Law Enforcement Program Manager. In 1991, she completed a research project on juvenile gangs for the Berlin Senate for Youth and Family. Her interests lie in ethnic delinquency and crime.

Richard A. Berk is a Professor at UCLA in the Department of Sociology and in the Interdivisional Program in Statistics. He is also Director of UCLA's Center for the Study of the Environment and Society. He previously taught at Northwestern University, The University of California—Santa Barbara, and The University of California—Berkeley. He recently served as Vice Chairman of the Social Science Research Council's Board of Directors, on a National Academy of Sciences Panel on the Monitoring the Social Consequences of AIDS, and on an NSF Task Force making recommendations on reorganizing the social sciences at the Foundation. He also has been a visiting scholar at the GAO's Program Evaluation and Methodology Division. Dr. Berk has published extensively in a variety of fields, including applied statistics, program evaluation, time use, crime and justice, AIDS, and the environment. He also routinely serves as a consultant to a number of private foundations and federal agencies. Dr. Berk holds a B.A. from Yale University and a Ph.D. in Sociology from Johns Hopkins University.

Tore Björgo is an executive official of The Norwegian Institute of International Affairs. He has recently completed a research project on political violence and terrorism in Scandinavia, financed by the Norwegian Research Council for Applied Social Research. These findings have been published in Björgo's co-edited book with Rob Witte titled *Racist Violence in Europe* (Macmillan 1993).

Benjamin Bowling is of English and Afro-Caribbean origin and grew up in Worcestershire in rural England. He holds a B.A. in psychology from Manchester Metropolitan University and is currently a graduate student at the London School of Economics and Political Science. He is working towards a Ph.D. in Criminology investigating the emergence of racist violence as a social problem in Britain and the development of police, local, and central state policy. He works as a Senior Research Officer in the Home Office Research and Planning Unit in London researching offending and desistance from offending among young people.

Mark S. Hamm is a Professor of Criminology at Indiana State University. A former deputy warden of the Arizona State Prison in Tucson, he has published widely on crime and corrections. His most recent book, *American Skinheads: The Criminology and Control of Hate Crime* (Praeger, 1993), was awarded the Fredric Milton Thrasher Award by the *Gang Journal*. He is currently at work on a book about romantic homicide.

Jeffrey Ian Ross is an Assistant Professor at the University of Lethbridge. He has conducted research, written, and lectured on political violence and policing for over a decade. His articles have appeared in the *Blackwell Encyclopedia of Political Institutions*, the *World Encyclopedia of Peace*, academic journals such as the *Canadian Journal of Political Science Contemporary Sociology, Conflict Quarterly, Comparative Politics, Journal of Peace Research, Low Intensity Conflict and Law Enforcement, Police Studies, Terrorism, Terrorism and Political Violence* and a variety of chapters in academic books, as well as articles in popular magazines in Canada and the United States. In 1986, Ross was the lead expert witness for the Senate of Canada's Special Committee on Terrorism and Public Safety.

Rob Witte is a political scientist at the Criminology Section of the Willem Pompe Institute for Criminal Law, University of Utrecht in The Netherlands. He is completing his doctoral dissertion on state response to racist violence in France, Britain and The Netherlands. He has published a study on the 1990 local elections in The Netherlands with respect to the results of the extreme right parties (*Acta Politica*, 1991). Together with Tore Björgo he has recently published *Racist Violence in Europe* (Macmillan, 1993).